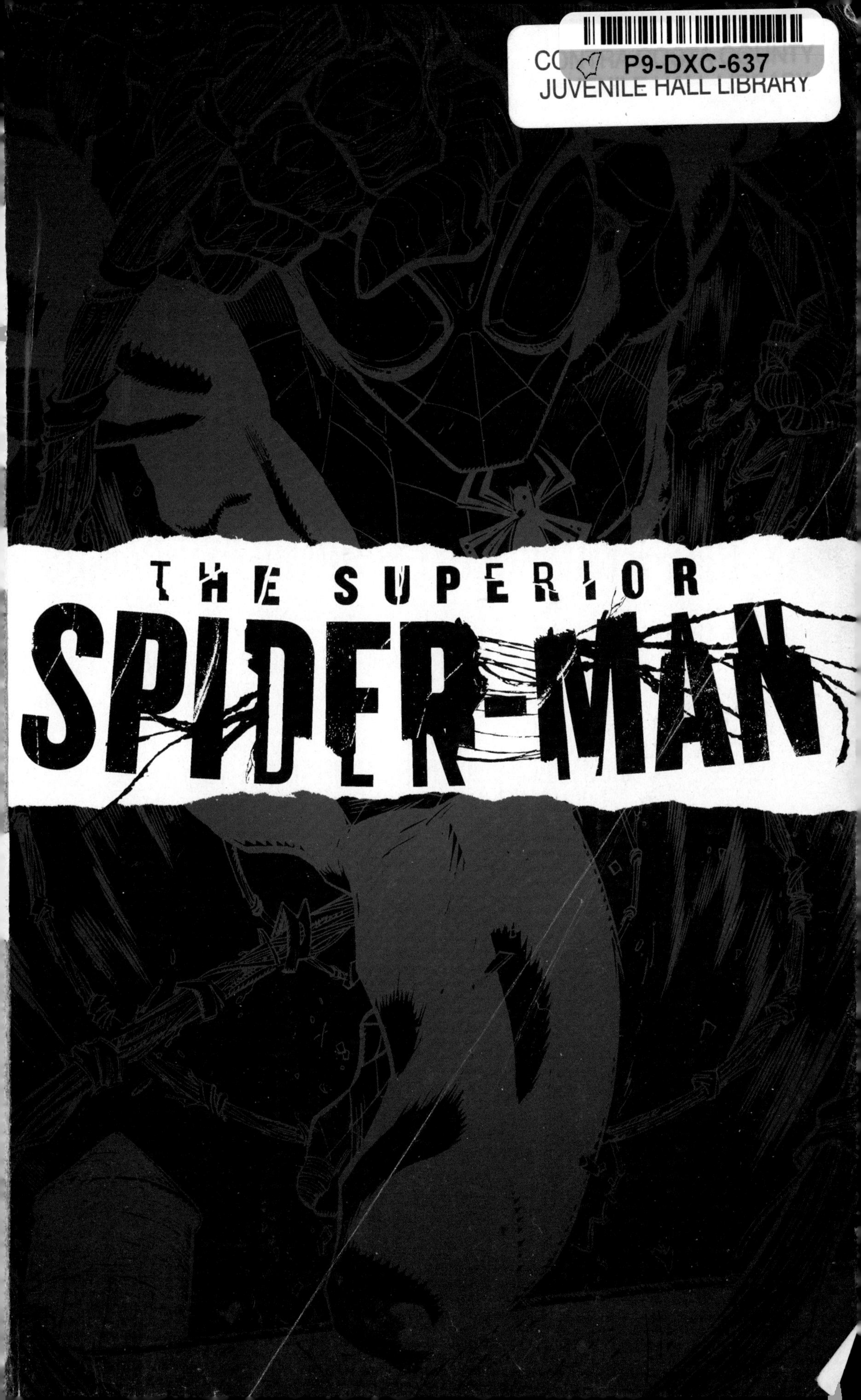
THE SUPERIOR
SPIDER-MAN

THE SUPERIOR SPIDER-MAN
NO ESCAPE

WRITER
DAN SLOTT
WITH **CHRISTOS GAGE** (SCRIPT, #11-13)

PENCILER, #11-13
GIUSEPPE CAMUNCOLI

PENCILER, #14-16
HUMBERTO RAMOS

INKERS, #11-13
JOHN DELL
WITH **TERRY PALLOT**

INKER, #14-16
VICTOR OLAZABA

COLOR ARTISTS
EDGAR DELGADO (#11 & #14-16)
& **ANTONIO FABELA** (#12-13)

COVER ART
GIUSEPPE CAMUNCOLI & EDGAR DELGADO (#11-13)
AND **HUMBERTO RAMOS & EDGAR DELGADO** (#14-16)

LETTERER
VC'S CHRIS ELIOPOULOS

ASSISTANT EDITOR
ELLIE PYLE

EDITOR
STEPHEN WACKER

Collection Editor: **Jennifer Grünwald** • Assistant Editor: **Sarah Brunstad** • Associate Managing Editor: **Alex Starbuck**
Editor, Special Projects: **Mark D. Beazley** • Senior Editor, Special Projects: **Jeff Youngquist**
SVP Print, Sales & Marketing: **David Gabriel** • Book Design: **Jeff Powell**

Editor in Chief: **Axel Alonso** • Chief Creative Officer: **Joe Quesada** • Publisher: **Dan Buckley** • Executive Producer: **Alan Fine**

SUPERIOR SPIDER-MAN VOL. 3: NO ESCAPE. Contains material originally published in magazine form as SUPERIOR SPIDER-MAN #11-16. Second printing 2014. ISBN# 978-0-7851-8472-0. Published by MARVEL WORLDWIDE, INC., a subsidiary of MARVEL ENTERTAINMENT, LLC. OFFICE OF PUBLICATION: 135 West 50th Street, New York, NY 10020. Copyright © 2013 Marvel Characters, Inc. All rights reserved. All characters featured in this issue and the distinctive names and likenesses thereof, and all related indicia are trademarks of Marvel Characters, Inc. No similarity between any of the names, characters, persons, and/or institutions in this magazine with those of any living or dead person or institution is intended, and any such similarity which may exist is purely coincidental. **Printed in Canada.** ALAN FINE, EVP - Office of the President, Marvel Worldwide, Inc. and EVP & CMO Marvel Characters B.V.; DAN BUCKLEY, Publisher & President - Print, Animation & Digital Divisions; JOE QUESADA, Chief Creative Officer; TOM BREVOORT, SVP of Publishing; DAVID BOGART, SVP of Operations & Procurement, Publishing; C.B. CEBULSKI, SVP of Creator & Content Development; DAVID GABRIEL, SVP Print, Sales & Marketing; JIM O'KEEFE, VP of Operations & Logistics; DAN CARR, Executive Director of Publishing Technology; SUSAN CRESPI, Editorial Operations Manager; ALEX MORALES, Publishing Operations Manager; STAN LEE, Chairman Emeritus. For information regarding advertising in Marvel Comics or on Marvel.com, please contact Niza Disla, Director of Marvel Partnerships, at ndisla@marvel.com. For Marvel subscription inquiries, please call 800-217-9158. Manufactured between 5/28/2014 and 6/30/2014 by SOLISCO PRINTERS, SCOTT, QC, CANADA.

1 0 9 8 7 6 5 4 3 2

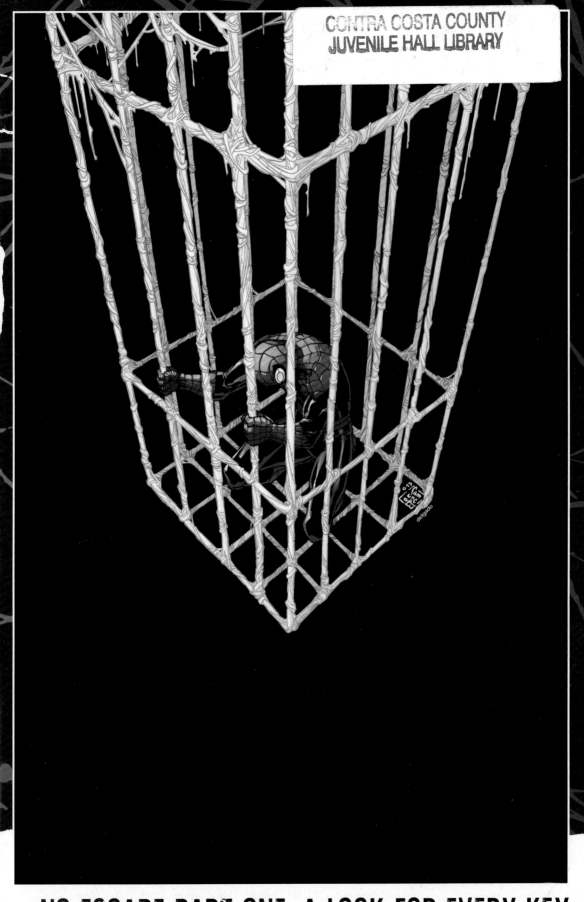

NO ESCAPE PART ONE: A LOCK FOR EVERY KEY

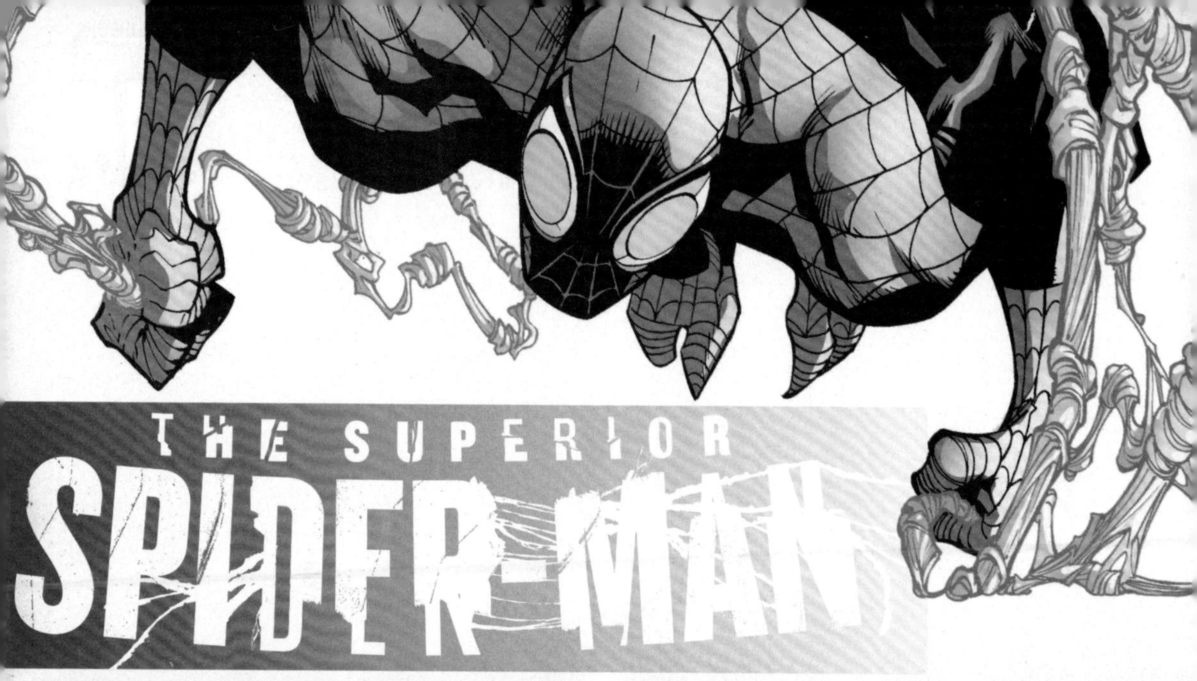

THE SUPERIOR SPIDER-MAN

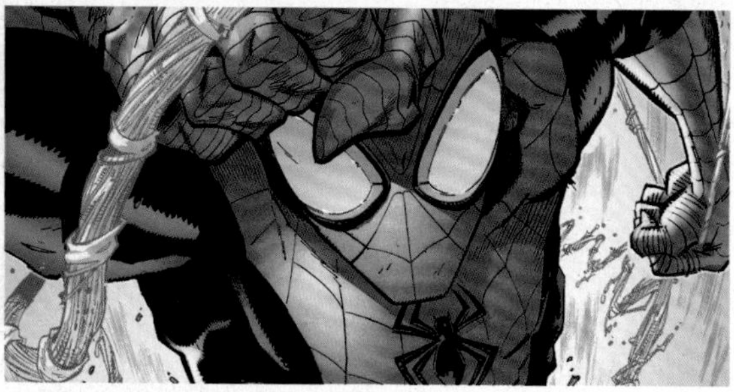

OTTO OCTAVIUS IS A MAN WHO CHEATED DEATH, BUT AT A PRICE. WHEN HE EXCHANGED BODIES WITH **PETER PARKER,** HE GAINED THE AMAZING SKILLS OF SPIDER-MAN — AND ALL OF PETER'S MEMORIES. OTTO FINALLY UNDERSTANDS PETER'S MISSION OF GREAT RESPONSIBILITY.

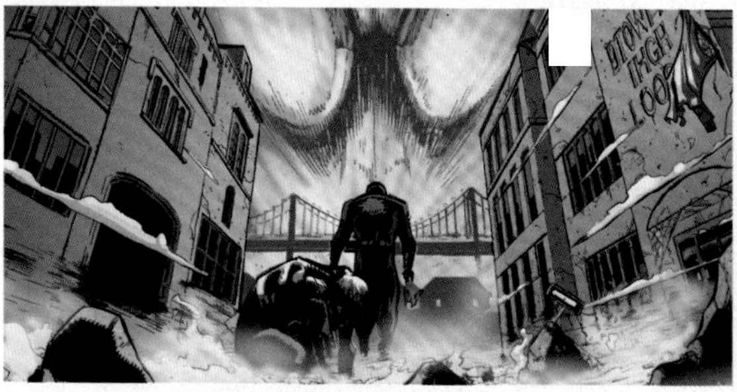

A TINY PIECE OF PETER PARKER REMAINED IN THE SUPERIOR SPIDER-MAN'S BRAIN BUT OTTO BATTLED HIM WITHIN THE REALM OF HIS MIND AND ERADICATED HIM BY ERASING THE LAST OF PETER'S MEMORIES.

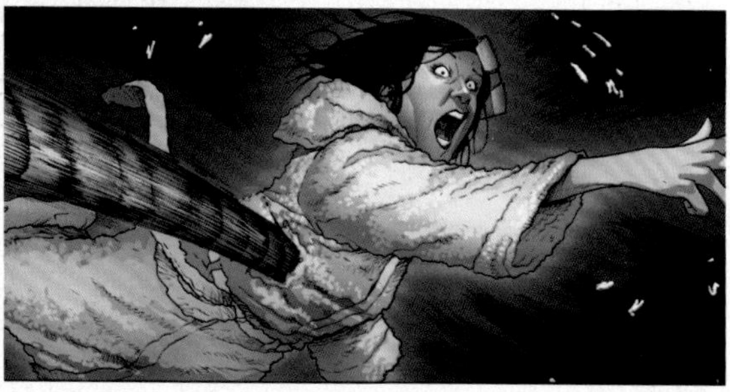

PREVIOUSLY, THE SPIDER-SLAYER **ALISTAIR SMYTHE** KILLED J. JONAH JAMESON'S WIFE, MARLA, WHO DIED SAVING JAMESON'S LIFE.

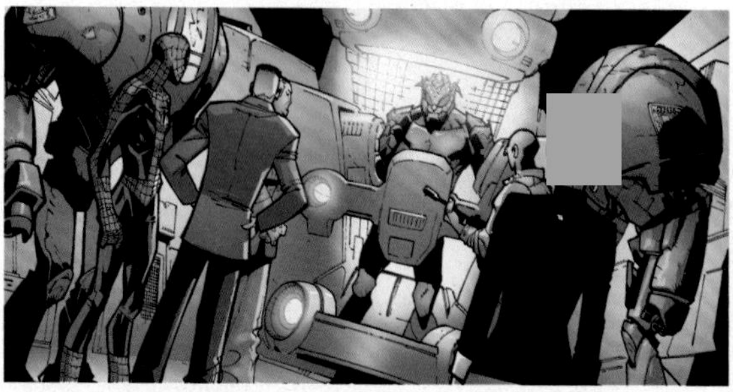

SINCE THEN, **SMYTHE** HAS BEEN IMPRISONED ON THE RAFT, AWAITING THE DAY OF HIS EXECUTION, A DAY JAMESON HAS BEEN LOOKING FORWARD TO.

When you see this: AR, open up the MARVEL AR APP (available on applicable Apple ® iOS or Android TM devices) and use your camera-enabled device to unlock extra-special exclusive features!*

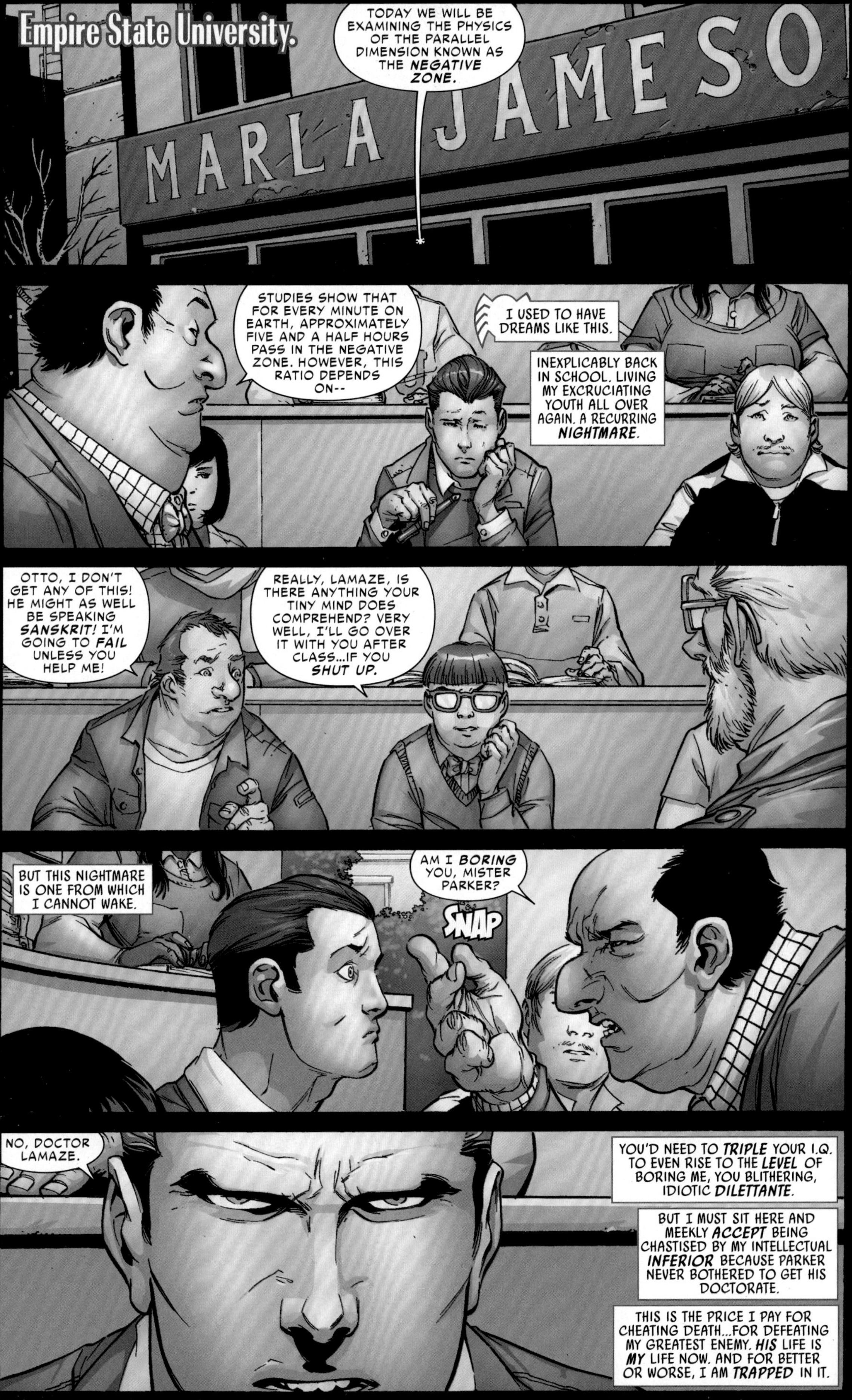

Empire State University.
TODAY WE WILL BE EXAMINING THE PHYSICS OF THE PARALLEL DIMENSION KNOWN AS THE NEGATIVE ZONE.
MARLA JAMESO
STUDIES SHOW THAT FOR EVERY MINUTE ON EARTH, APPROXIMATELY FIVE AND A HALF HOURS PASS IN THE NEGATIVE ZONE. HOWEVER, THIS RATIO DEPENDS ON--
I USED TO HAVE DREAMS LIKE THIS.
INEXPLICABLY BACK IN SCHOOL. LIVING MY EXCRUCIATING YOUTH ALL OVER AGAIN. A RECURRING NIGHTMARE.
OTTO, I DON'T GET ANY OF THIS! HE MIGHT AS WELL BE SPEAKING SANSKRIT! I'M GOING TO FAIL UNLESS YOU HELP ME!
REALLY, LAMAZE, IS THERE ANYTHING YOUR TINY MIND DOES COMPREHEND? VERY WELL, I'LL GO OVER IT WITH YOU AFTER CLASS...IF YOU SHUT UP.
BUT THIS NIGHTMARE IS ONE FROM WHICH I CANNOT WAKE.
AM I BORING YOU, MISTER PARKER?
SNAP
NO, DOCTOR LAMAZE.
YOU'D NEED TO TRIPLE YOUR I.Q. TO EVEN RISE TO THE LEVEL OF BORING ME, YOU BLITHERING, IDIOTIC DILETTANTE.
BUT I MUST SIT HERE AND MEEKLY ACCEPT BEING CHASTISED BY MY INTELLECTUAL INFERIOR BECAUSE PARKER NEVER BOTHERED TO GET HIS DOCTORATE.
THIS IS THE PRICE I PAY FOR CHEATING DEATH...FOR DEFEATING MY GREATEST ENEMY. HIS LIFE IS MY LIFE NOW. AND FOR BETTER OR WORSE, I AM TRAPPED IN IT.

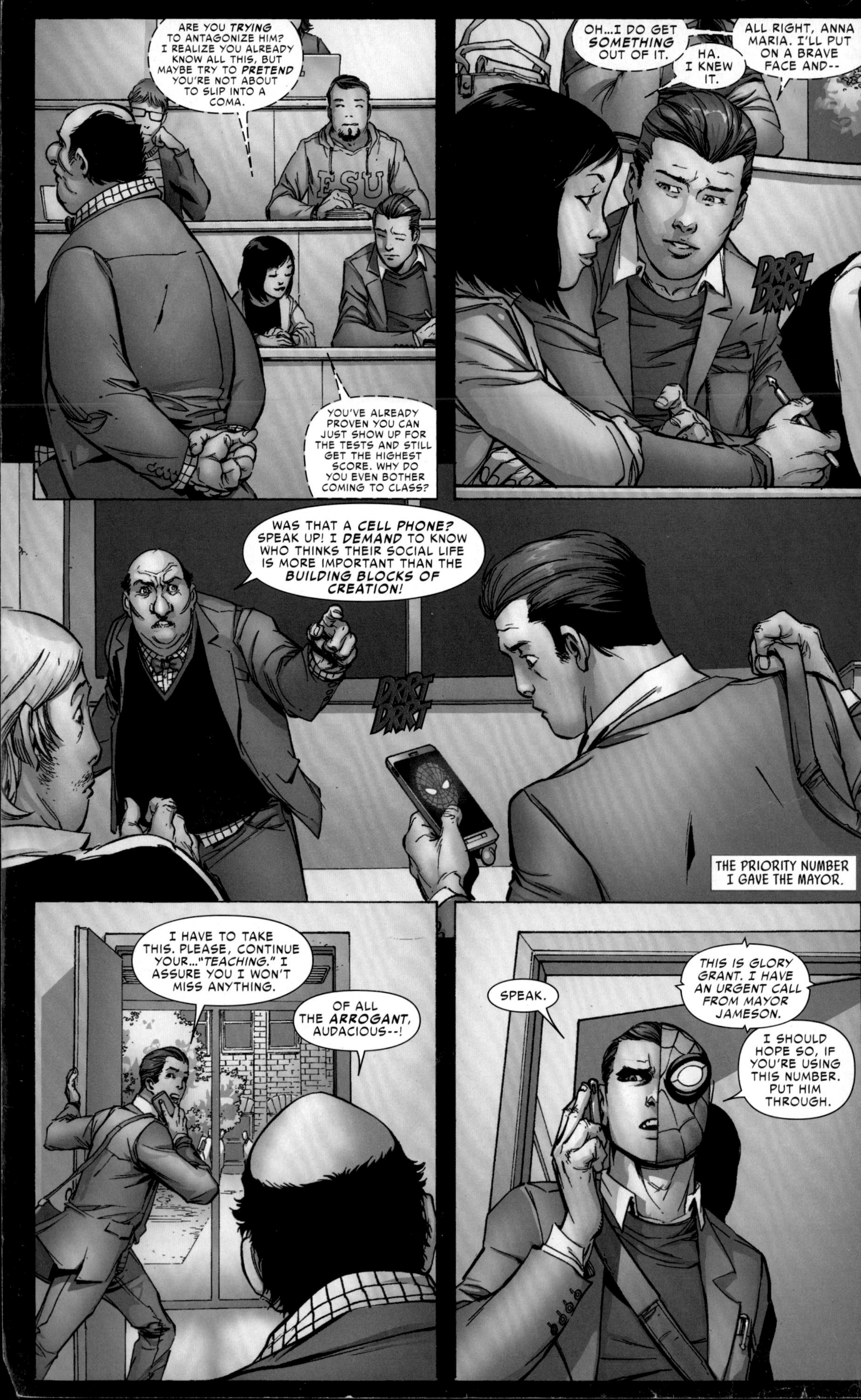
ARE YOU TRYING TO ANTAGONIZE HIM? I REALIZE YOU ALREADY KNOW ALL THIS, BUT MAYBE TRY TO PRETEND YOU'RE NOT ABOUT TO SLIP INTO A COMA.
ESU
YOU'VE ALREADY PROVEN YOU CAN JUST SHOW UP FOR THE TESTS AND STILL GET THE HIGHEST SCORE. WHY DO YOU EVEN BOTHER COMING TO CLASS?
OH...I DO GET SOMETHING OUT OF IT.
HA. I KNEW IT.
ALL RIGHT, ANNA MARIA. I'LL PUT ON A BRAVE FACE AND--
DRRT DRRT
WAS THAT A CELL PHONE? SPEAK UP! I DEMAND TO KNOW WHO THINKS THEIR SOCIAL LIFE IS MORE IMPORTANT THAN THE BUILDING BLOCKS OF CREATION!
DRRT DRRT
THE PRIORITY NUMBER I GAVE THE MAYOR.
I HAVE TO TAKE THIS. PLEASE, CONTINUE YOUR..."TEACHING." I ASSURE YOU I WON'T MISS ANYTHING.
OF ALL THE ARROGANT, AUDACIOUS--!
SPEAK.
THIS IS GLORY GRANT. I HAVE AN URGENT CALL FROM MAYOR JAMESON.
I SHOULD HOPE SO, IF YOU'RE USING THIS NUMBER. PUT HIM THROUGH.

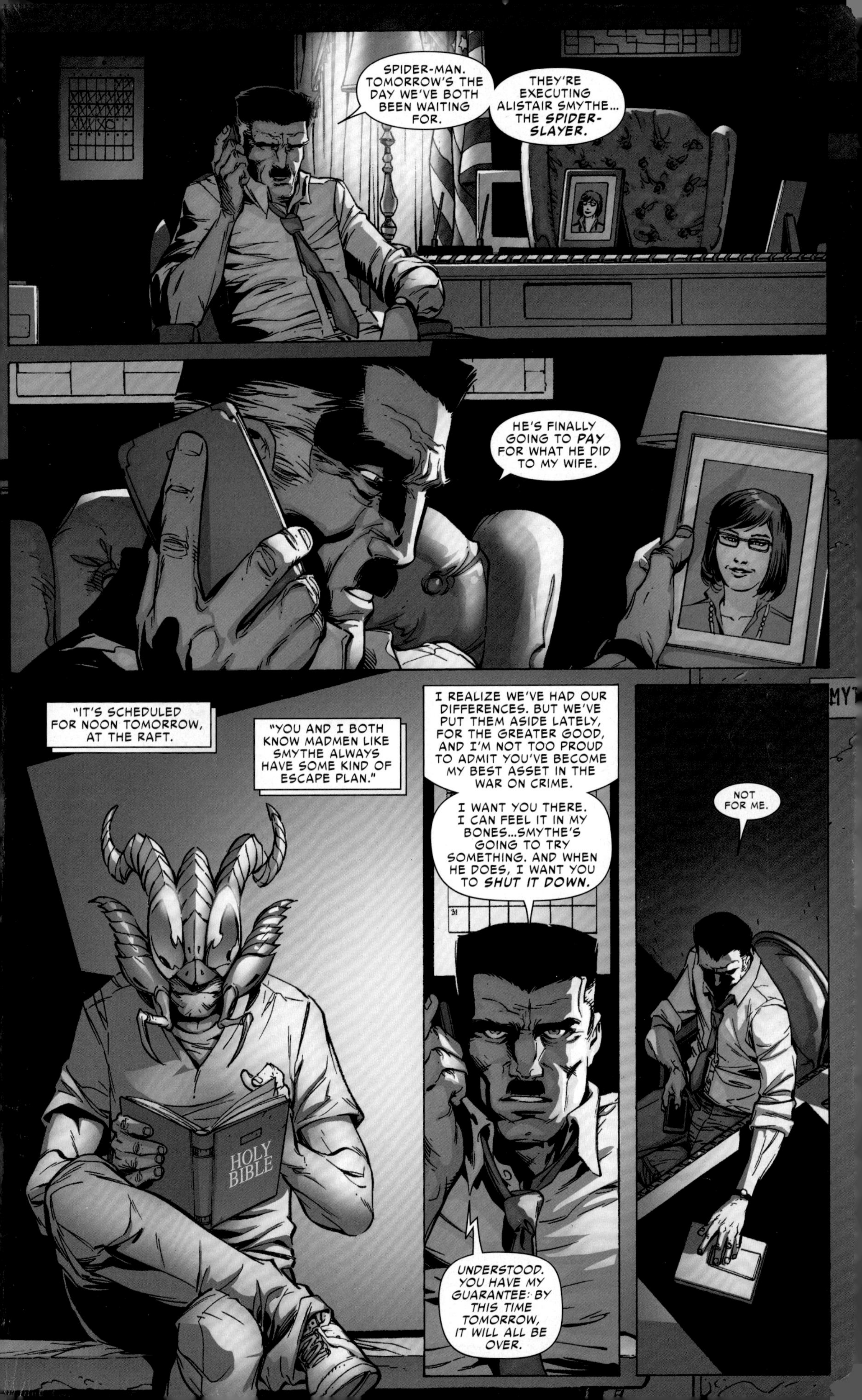
SPIDER-MAN. TOMORROW'S THE DAY WE'VE BOTH BEEN WAITING FOR.
THEY'RE EXECUTING ALISTAIR SMYTHE... THE SPIDER-SLAYER.
HE'S FINALLY GOING TO PAY FOR WHAT HE DID TO MY WIFE.
"IT'S SCHEDULED FOR NOON TOMORROW, AT THE RAFT.
"YOU AND I BOTH KNOW MADMEN LIKE SMYTHE ALWAYS HAVE SOME KIND OF ESCAPE PLAN."
HOLY BIBLE
I REALIZE WE'VE HAD OUR DIFFERENCES. BUT WE'VE PUT THEM ASIDE LATELY, FOR THE GREATER GOOD, AND I'M NOT TOO PROUD TO ADMIT YOU'VE BECOME MY BEST ASSET IN THE WAR ON CRIME.
I WANT YOU THERE. I CAN FEEL IT IN MY BONES...SMYTHE'S GOING TO TRY SOMETHING. AND WHEN HE DOES, I WANT YOU TO SHUT IT DOWN.
UNDERSTOOD. YOU HAVE MY GUARANTEE: BY THIS TIME TOMORROW, IT WILL ALL BE OVER.
NOT FOR ME.

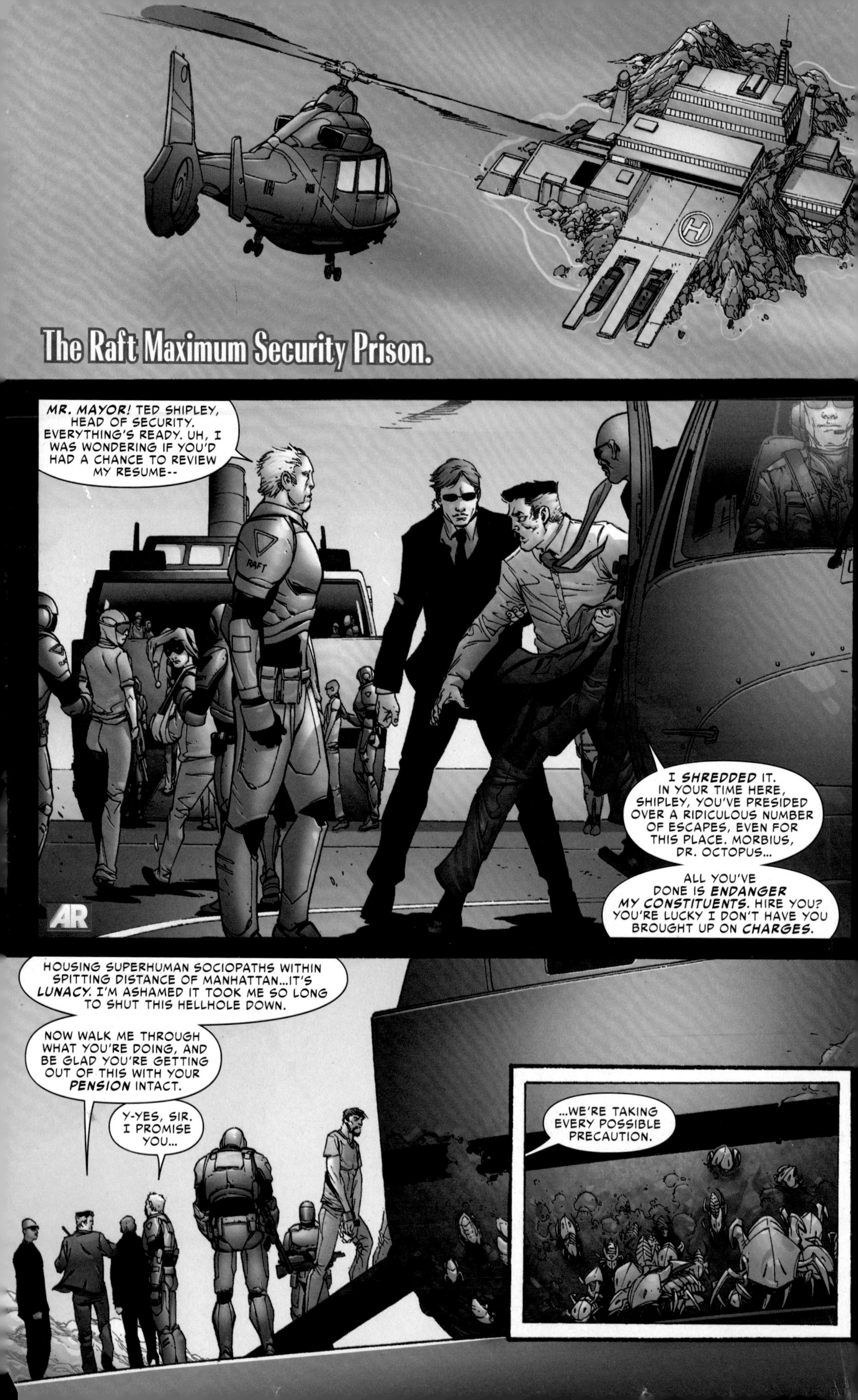
The Raft Maximum Security Prison.
MR. MAYOR! TED SHIPLEY, HEAD OF SECURITY. EVERYTHING'S READY. UH, I WAS WONDERING IF YOU'D HAD A CHANCE TO REVIEW MY RESUME--
RAFT
I SHREDDED IT. IN YOUR TIME HERE, SHIPLEY, YOU'VE PRESIDED OVER A RIDICULOUS NUMBER OF ESCAPES, EVEN FOR THIS PLACE. MORBIUS, DR. OCTOPUS...
ALL YOU'VE DONE IS ENDANGER MY CONSTITUENTS. HIRE YOU? YOU'RE LUCKY I DON'T HAVE YOU BROUGHT UP ON CHARGES.
HOUSING SUPERHUMAN SOCIOPATHS WITHIN SPITTING DISTANCE OF MANHATTAN...IT'S LUNACY. I'M ASHAMED IT TOOK ME SO LONG TO SHUT THIS HELLHOLE DOWN.
NOW WALK ME THROUGH WHAT YOU'RE DOING, AND BE GLAD YOU'RE GETTING OUT OF THIS WITH YOUR PENSION INTACT.
Y-YES, SIR. I PROMISE YOU...
...WE'RE TAKING EVERY POSSIBLE PRECAUTION.

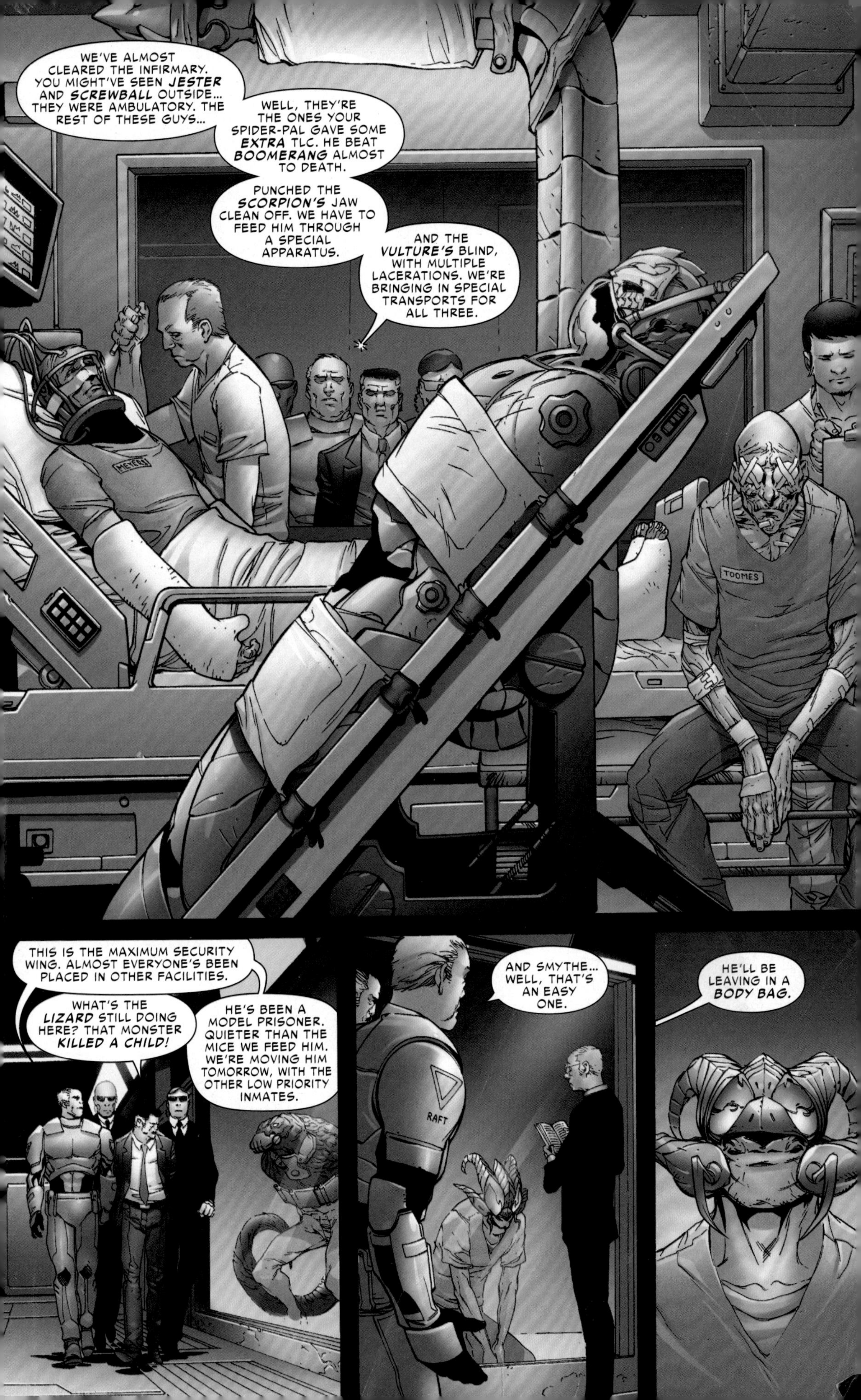
WE'VE ALMOST CLEARED THE INFIRMARY. YOU MIGHT'VE SEEN JESTER AND SCREWBALL OUTSIDE... THEY WERE AMBULATORY. THE REST OF THESE GUYS...
WELL, THEY'RE THE ONES YOUR SPIDER-PAL GAVE SOME EXTRA TLC. HE BEAT BOOMERANG ALMOST TO DEATH.
PUNCHED THE SCORPION'S JAW CLEAN OFF. WE HAVE TO FEED HIM THROUGH A SPECIAL APPARATUS.
AND THE VULTURE'S BLIND, WITH MULTIPLE LACERATIONS. WE'RE BRINGING IN SPECIAL TRANSPORTS FOR ALL THREE.
MEYERS
TOOMES
THIS IS THE MAXIMUM SECURITY WING. ALMOST EVERYONE'S BEEN PLACED IN OTHER FACILITIES.
WHAT'S THE LIZARD STILL DOING HERE? THAT MONSTER KILLED A CHILD!
HE'S BEEN A MODEL PRISONER. QUIETER THAN THE MICE WE FEED HIM. WE'RE MOVING HIM TOMORROW, WITH THE OTHER LOW PRIORITY INMATES.
AND SMYTHE... WELL, THAT'S AN EASY ONE.
RAFT
HE'LL BE LEAVING IN A BODY BAG.

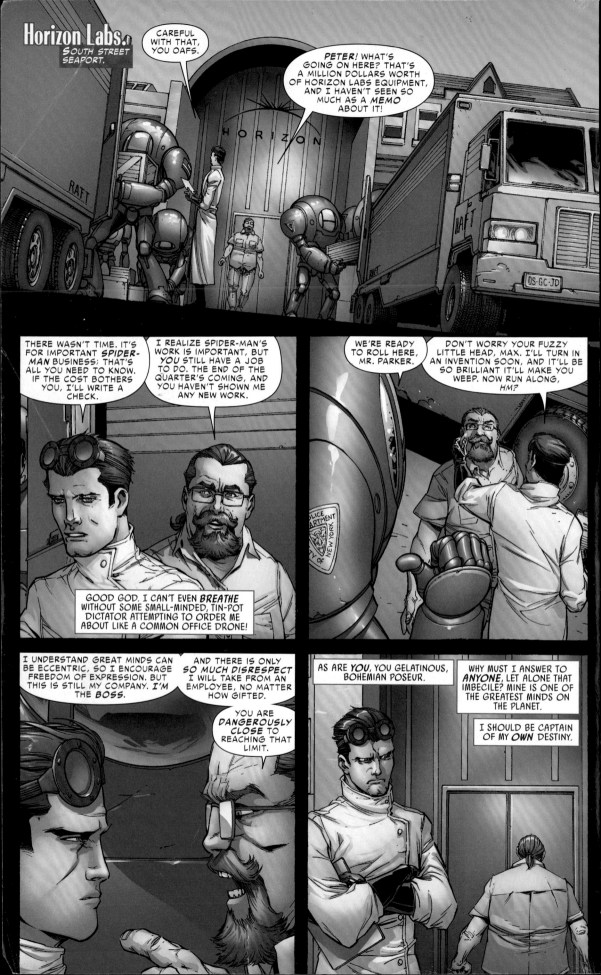

Horizon Labs.
SOUTH STREET SEAPORT.

CAREFUL WITH THAT, YOU OAFS.

PETER! WHAT'S GOING ON HERE? THAT'S A MILLION DOLLARS WORTH OF HORIZON LABS EQUIPMENT, AND I HAVEN'T SEEN SO MUCH AS A MEMO ABOUT IT!

THERE WASN'T TIME. IT'S FOR IMPORTANT SPIDER-MAN BUSINESS; THAT'S ALL YOU NEED TO KNOW. IF THE COST BOTHERS YOU, I'LL WRITE A CHECK.

I REALIZE SPIDER-MAN'S WORK IS IMPORTANT, BUT YOU STILL HAVE A JOB TO DO. THE END OF THE QUARTER'S COMING, AND YOU HAVEN'T SHOWN ME ANY NEW WORK.

WE'RE READY TO ROLL HERE, MR. PARKER.

DON'T WORRY YOUR FUZZY LITTLE HEAD, MAX. I'LL TURN IN AN INVENTION SOON, AND IT'LL BE SO BRILLIANT IT'LL MAKE YOU WEEP. NOW RUN ALONG, HM?

GOOD GOD. I CAN'T EVEN BREATHE WITHOUT SOME SMALL-MINDED, TIN-POT DICTATOR ATTEMPTING TO ORDER ME ABOUT LIKE A COMMON OFFICE DRONE!

I UNDERSTAND GREAT MINDS CAN BE ECCENTRIC, SO I ENCOURAGE FREEDOM OF EXPRESSION. BUT THIS IS STILL MY COMPANY. I'M THE BOSS.

AND THERE IS ONLY SO MUCH DISRESPECT I WILL TAKE FROM AN EMPLOYEE, NO MATTER HOW GIFTED.

YOU ARE DANGEROUSLY CLOSE TO REACHING THAT LIMIT.

AS ARE YOU, YOU GELATINOUS, BOHEMIAN POSEUR.

WHY MUST I ANSWER TO ANYONE, LET ALONE THAT IMBECILE? MINE IS ONE OF THE GREATEST MINDS ON THE PLANET.

I SHOULD BE CAPTAIN OF MY OWN DESTINY.

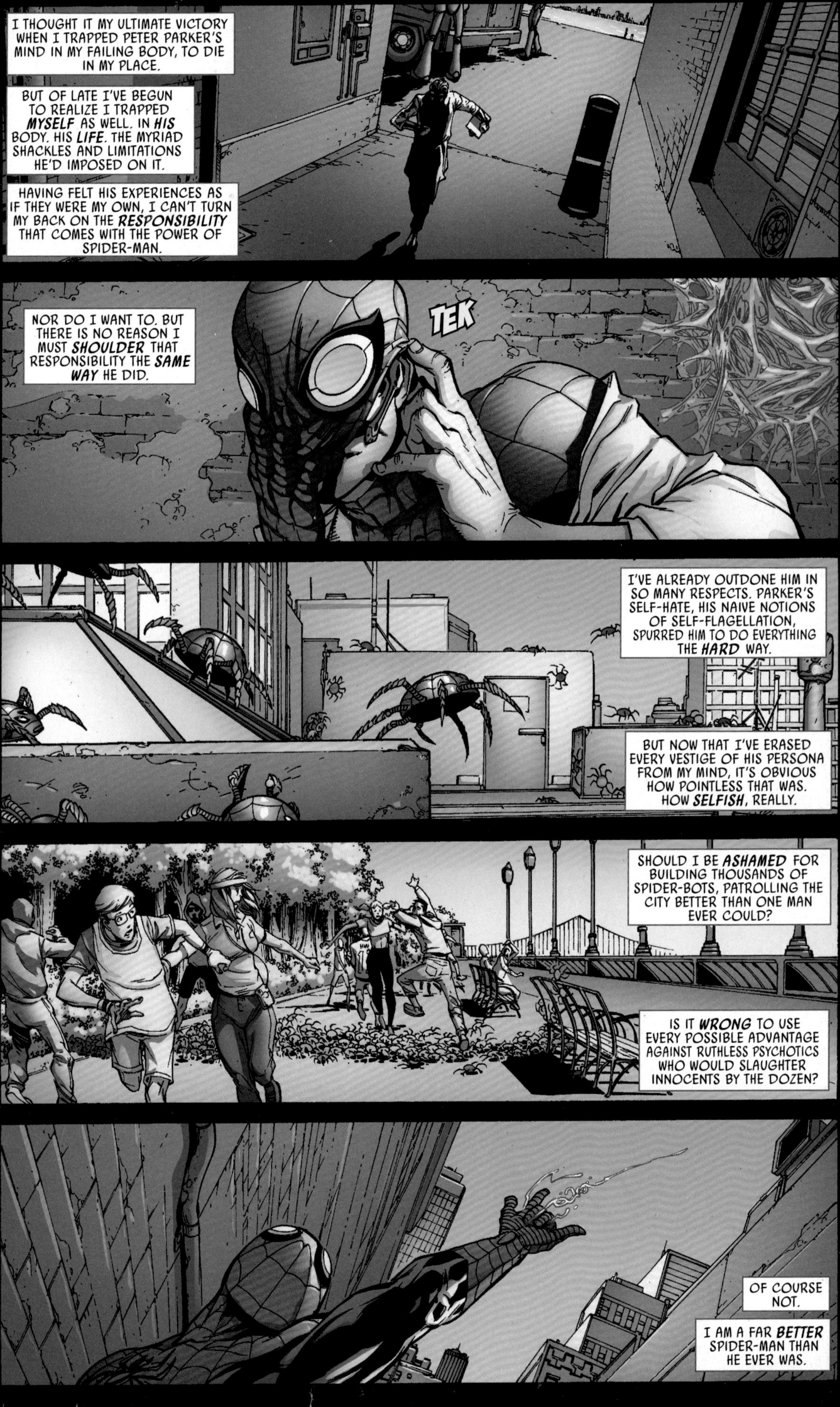
I THOUGHT IT MY ULTIMATE VICTORY WHEN I TRAPPED PETER PARKER'S MIND IN MY FAILING BODY, TO DIE IN MY PLACE.
BUT OF LATE I'VE BEGUN TO REALIZE I TRAPPED MYSELF AS WELL. IN HIS BODY. HIS LIFE. THE MYRIAD SHACKLES AND LIMITATIONS HE'D IMPOSED ON IT.
HAVING FELT HIS EXPERIENCES AS IF THEY WERE MY OWN, I CAN'T TURN MY BACK ON THE RESPONSIBILITY THAT COMES WITH THE POWER OF SPIDER-MAN.
NOR DO I WANT TO. BUT THERE IS NO REASON I MUST SHOULDER THAT RESPONSIBILITY THE SAME WAY HE DID.
TEK
I'VE ALREADY OUTDONE HIM IN SO MANY RESPECTS. PARKER'S SELF-HATE, HIS NAIVE NOTIONS OF SELF-FLAGELLATION, SPURRED HIM TO DO EVERYTHING THE HARD WAY.
BUT NOW THAT I'VE ERASED EVERY VESTIGE OF HIS PERSONA FROM MY MIND, IT'S OBVIOUS HOW POINTLESS THAT WAS. HOW SELFISH, REALLY.
SHOULD I BE ASHAMED FOR BUILDING THOUSANDS OF SPIDER-BOTS, PATROLLING THE CITY BETTER THAN ONE MAN EVER COULD?
IS IT WRONG TO USE EVERY POSSIBLE ADVANTAGE AGAINST RUTHLESS PSYCHOTICS WHO WOULD SLAUGHTER INNOCENTS BY THE DOZEN?
OF COURSE NOT.
I AM A FAR BETTER SPIDER-MAN THAN HE EVER WAS.

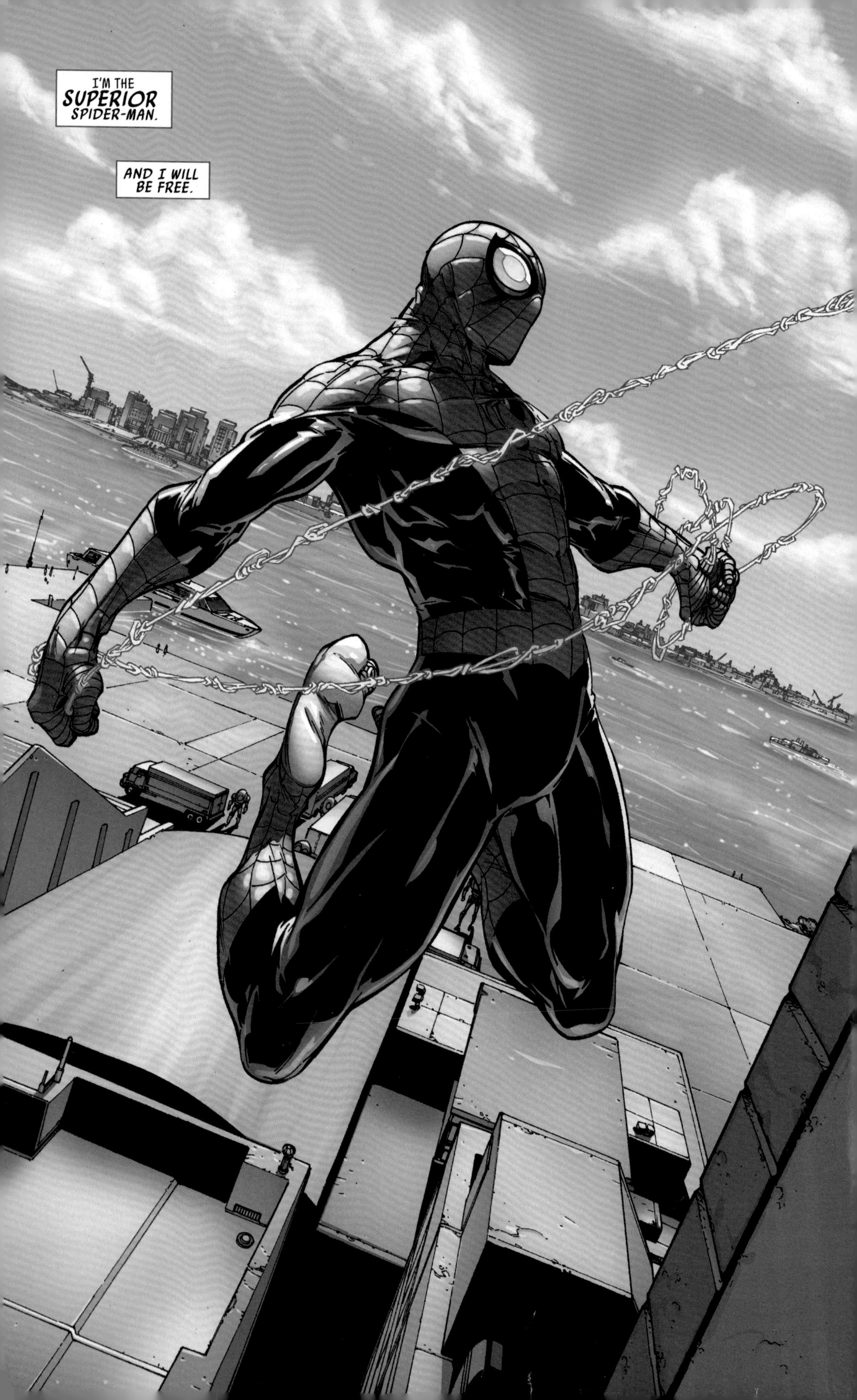
I'M THE SUPERIOR SPIDER-MAN.
AND I WILL BE FREE.

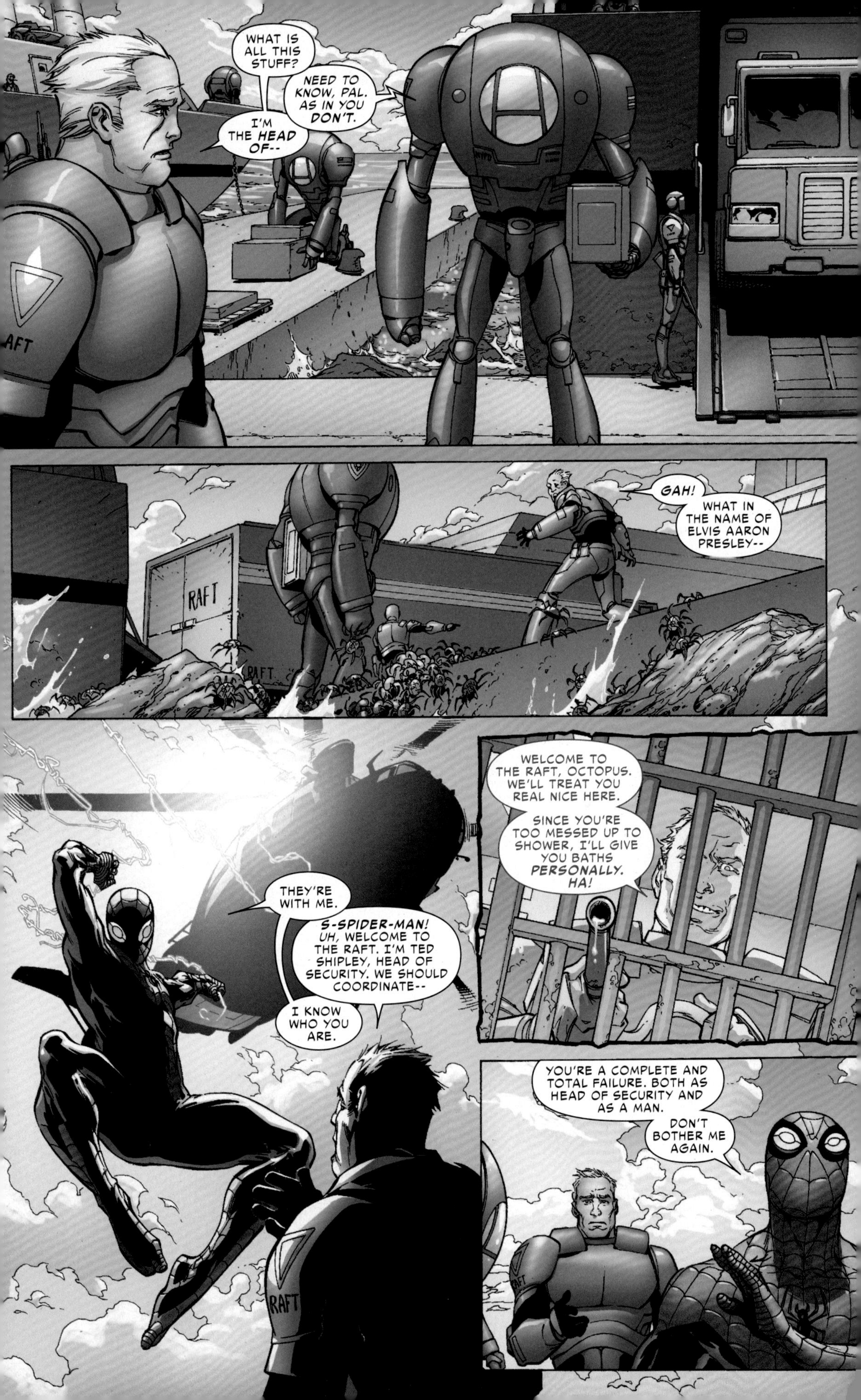
WHAT IS ALL THIS STUFF?
NEED TO KNOW, PAL. AS IN YOU *DON'T*.
I'M THE *HEAD* OF--
RAFT
GAH!
WHAT IN THE NAME OF ELVIS AARON PRESLEY--
RAFT
RAFT
THEY'RE WITH ME.
S-SPIDER-MAN! UH, WELCOME TO THE RAFT. I'M TED SHIPLEY, HEAD OF SECURITY. WE SHOULD COORDINATE--
I KNOW WHO YOU ARE.
RAFT
WELCOME TO THE RAFT, OCTOPUS. WE'LL TREAT YOU REAL NICE HERE.
SINCE YOU'RE TOO MESSED UP TO SHOWER, I'LL GIVE YOU BATHS *PERSONALLY*. *HA!*
YOU'RE A COMPLETE AND TOTAL FAILURE. BOTH AS HEAD OF SECURITY AND AS A MAN.
DON'T BOTHER ME AGAIN.

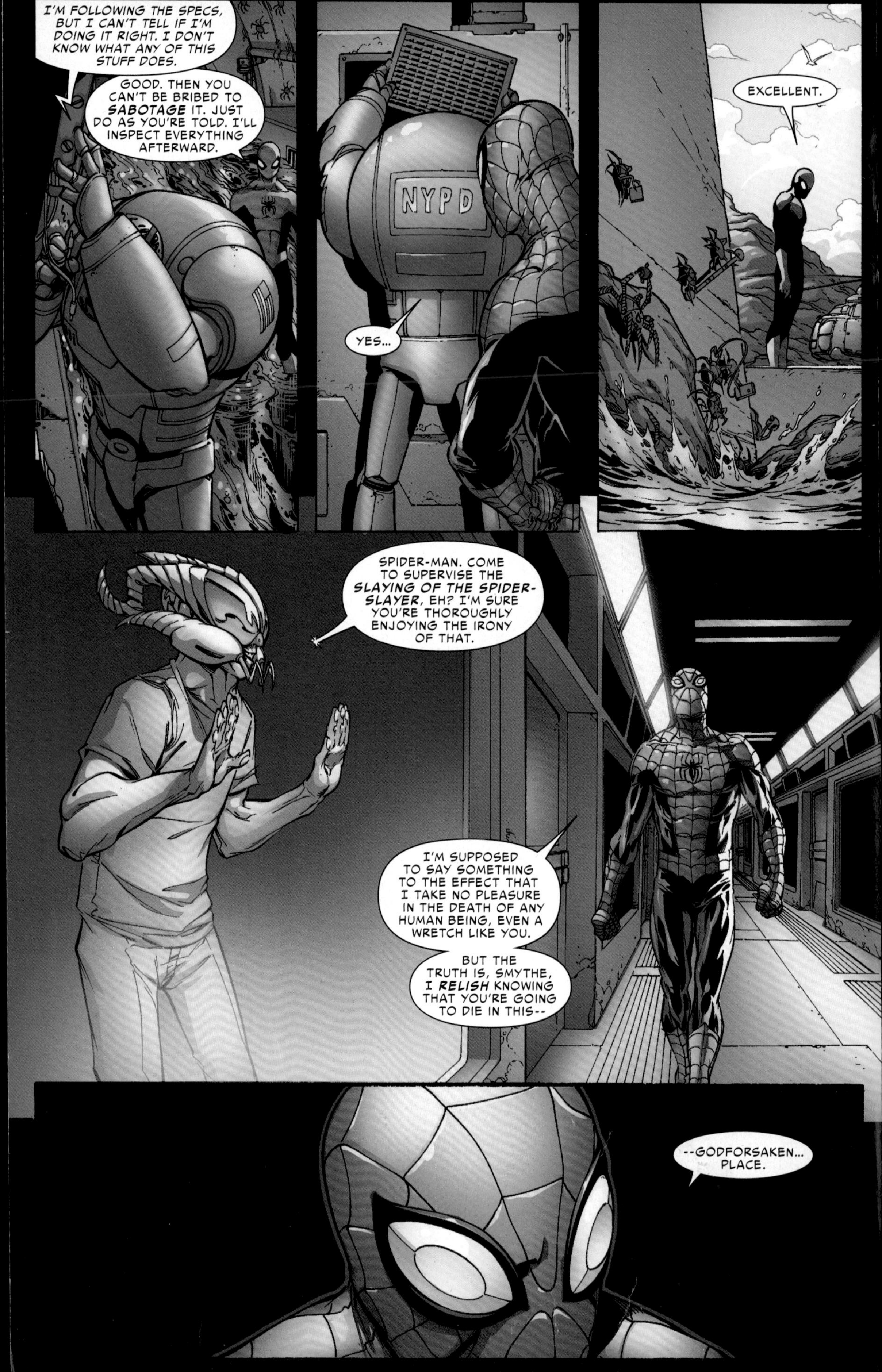
I'M FOLLOWING THE SPECS, BUT I CAN'T TELL IF I'M DOING IT RIGHT. I DON'T KNOW WHAT ANY OF THIS STUFF DOES.
GOOD. THEN YOU CAN'T BE BRIBED TO SABOTAGE IT. JUST DO AS YOU'RE TOLD. I'LL INSPECT EVERYTHING AFTERWARD.
NYPD
YES...
EXCELLENT.
SPIDER-MAN. COME TO SUPERVISE THE SLAYING OF THE SPIDER-SLAYER, EH? I'M SURE YOU'RE THOROUGHLY ENJOYING THE IRONY OF THAT.
I'M SUPPOSED TO SAY SOMETHING TO THE EFFECT THAT I TAKE NO PLEASURE IN THE DEATH OF ANY HUMAN BEING, EVEN A WRETCH LIKE YOU.
BUT THE TRUTH IS, SMYTHE, I RELISH KNOWING THAT YOU'RE GOING TO DIE IN THIS--
--GODFORSAKEN... PLACE.

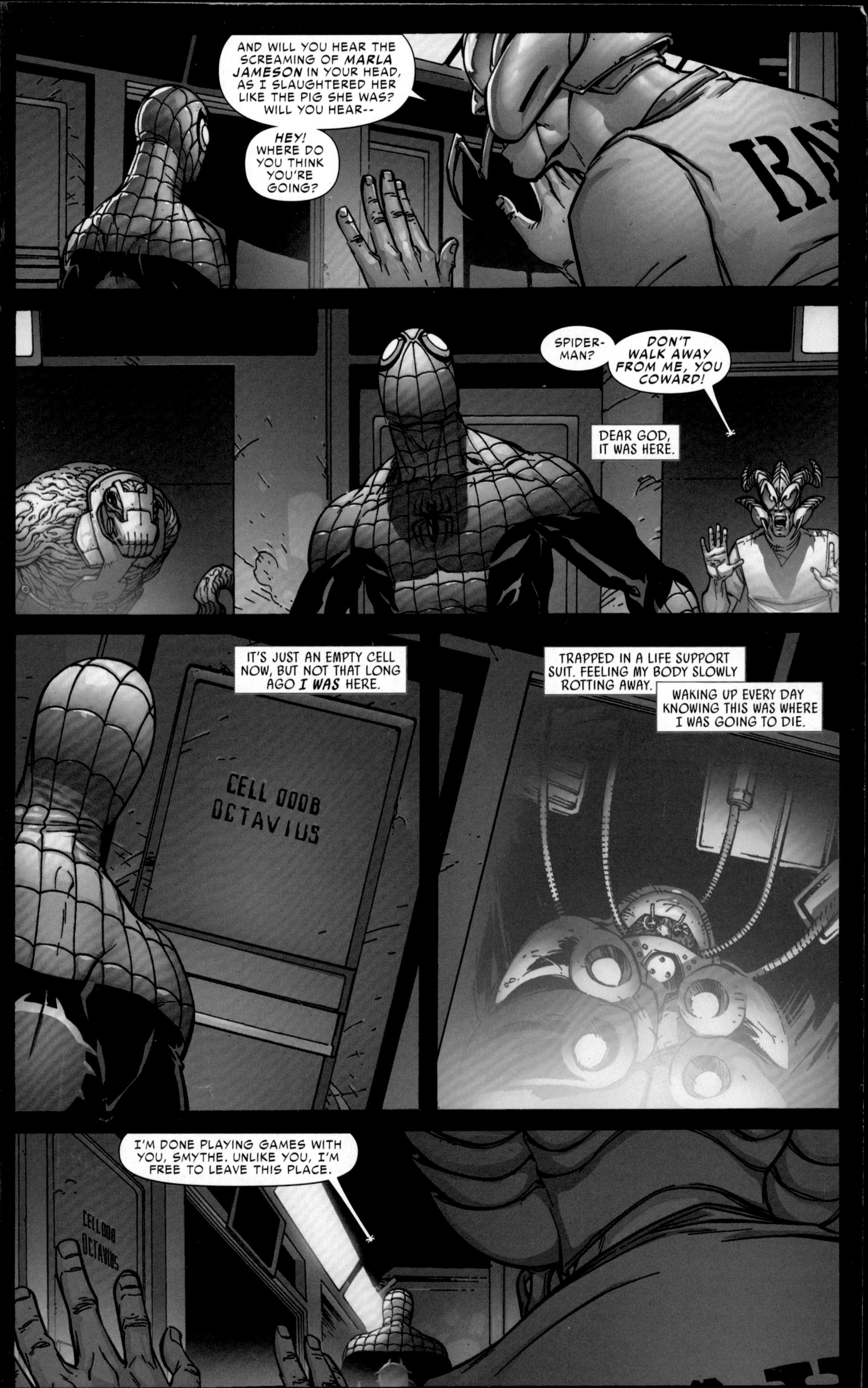
AND WILL YOU HEAR THE SCREAMING OF MARLA JAMESON IN YOUR HEAD, AS I SLAUGHTERED HER LIKE THE PIG SHE WAS? WILL YOU HEAR--
HEY! WHERE DO YOU THINK YOU'RE GOING?
SPIDER-MAN?
DON'T WALK AWAY FROM ME, YOU COWARD!
DEAR GOD, IT WAS HERE.
IT'S JUST AN EMPTY CELL NOW, BUT NOT THAT LONG AGO I WAS HERE.
CELL 000B OCTAVIUS
TRAPPED IN A LIFE SUPPORT SUIT. FEELING MY BODY SLOWLY ROTTING AWAY.
WAKING UP EVERY DAY KNOWING THIS WAS WHERE I WAS GOING TO DIE.
I'M DONE PLAYING GAMES WITH YOU, SMYTHE. UNLIKE YOU, I'M FREE TO LEAVE THIS PLACE.

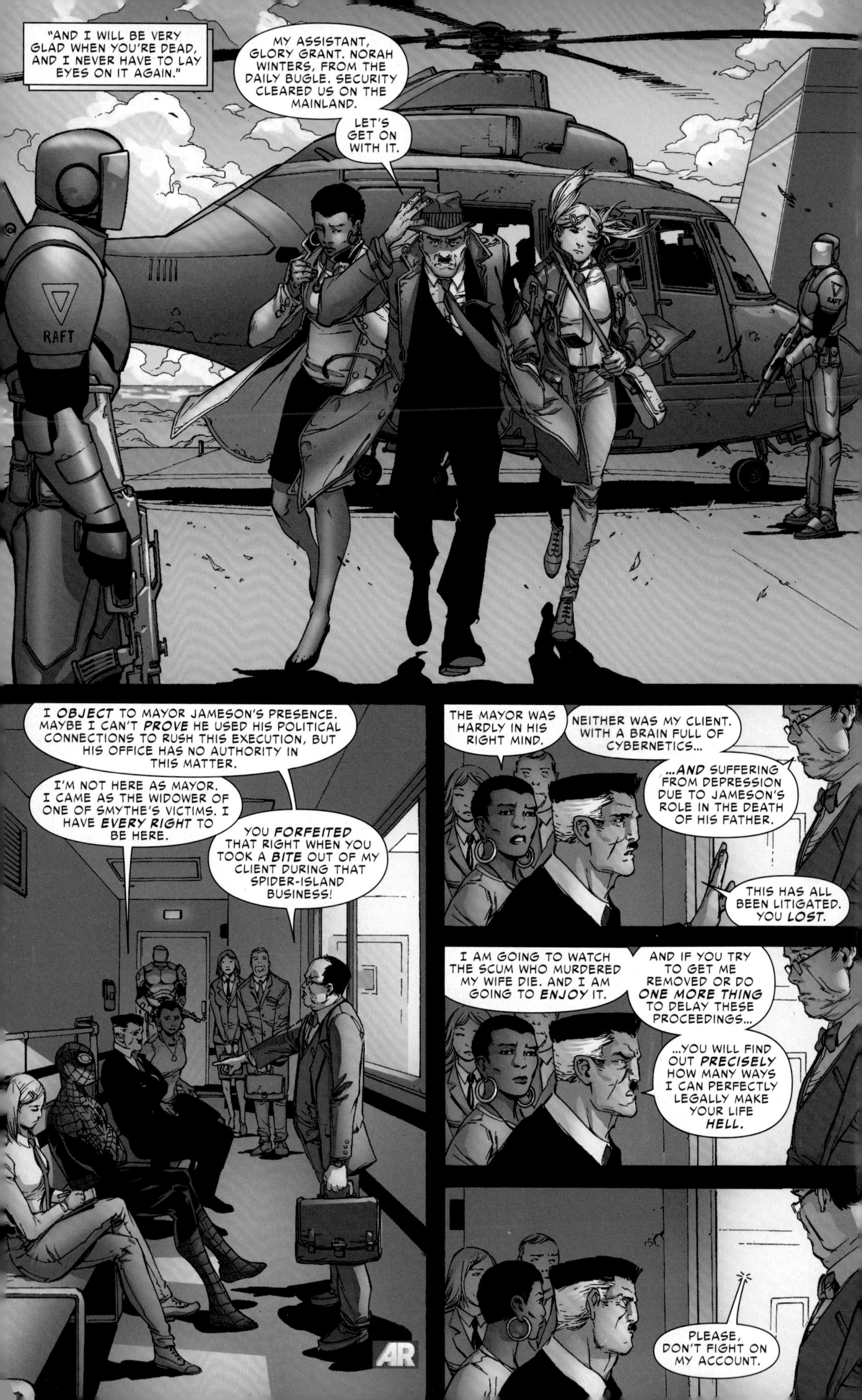
"AND I WILL BE VERY GLAD WHEN YOU'RE DEAD, AND I NEVER HAVE TO LAY EYES ON IT AGAIN."
MY ASSISTANT, GLORY GRANT. NORAH WINTERS, FROM THE DAILY BUGLE. SECURITY CLEARED US ON THE MAINLAND.
LET'S GET ON WITH IT.
RAFT
RAFT
I OBJECT TO MAYOR JAMESON'S PRESENCE. MAYBE I CAN'T PROVE HE USED HIS POLITICAL CONNECTIONS TO RUSH THIS EXECUTION, BUT HIS OFFICE HAS NO AUTHORITY IN THIS MATTER.
I'M NOT HERE AS MAYOR. I CAME AS THE WIDOWER OF ONE OF SMYTHE'S VICTIMS. I HAVE EVERY RIGHT TO BE HERE.
YOU FORFEITED THAT RIGHT WHEN YOU TOOK A BITE OUT OF MY CLIENT DURING THAT SPIDER-ISLAND BUSINESS!
THE MAYOR WAS HARDLY IN HIS RIGHT MIND.
NEITHER WAS MY CLIENT. WITH A BRAIN FULL OF CYBERNETICS...
...AND SUFFERING FROM DEPRESSION DUE TO JAMESON'S ROLE IN THE DEATH OF HIS FATHER.
THIS HAS ALL BEEN LITIGATED. YOU LOST.
I AM GOING TO WATCH THE SCUM WHO MURDERED MY WIFE DIE. AND I AM GOING TO ENJOY IT.
AND IF YOU TRY TO GET ME REMOVED OR DO ONE MORE THING TO DELAY THESE PROCEEDINGS...
...YOU WILL FIND OUT PRECISELY HOW MANY WAYS I CAN PERFECTLY LEGALLY MAKE YOUR LIFE HELL.
PLEASE, DON'T FIGHT ON MY ACCOUNT.

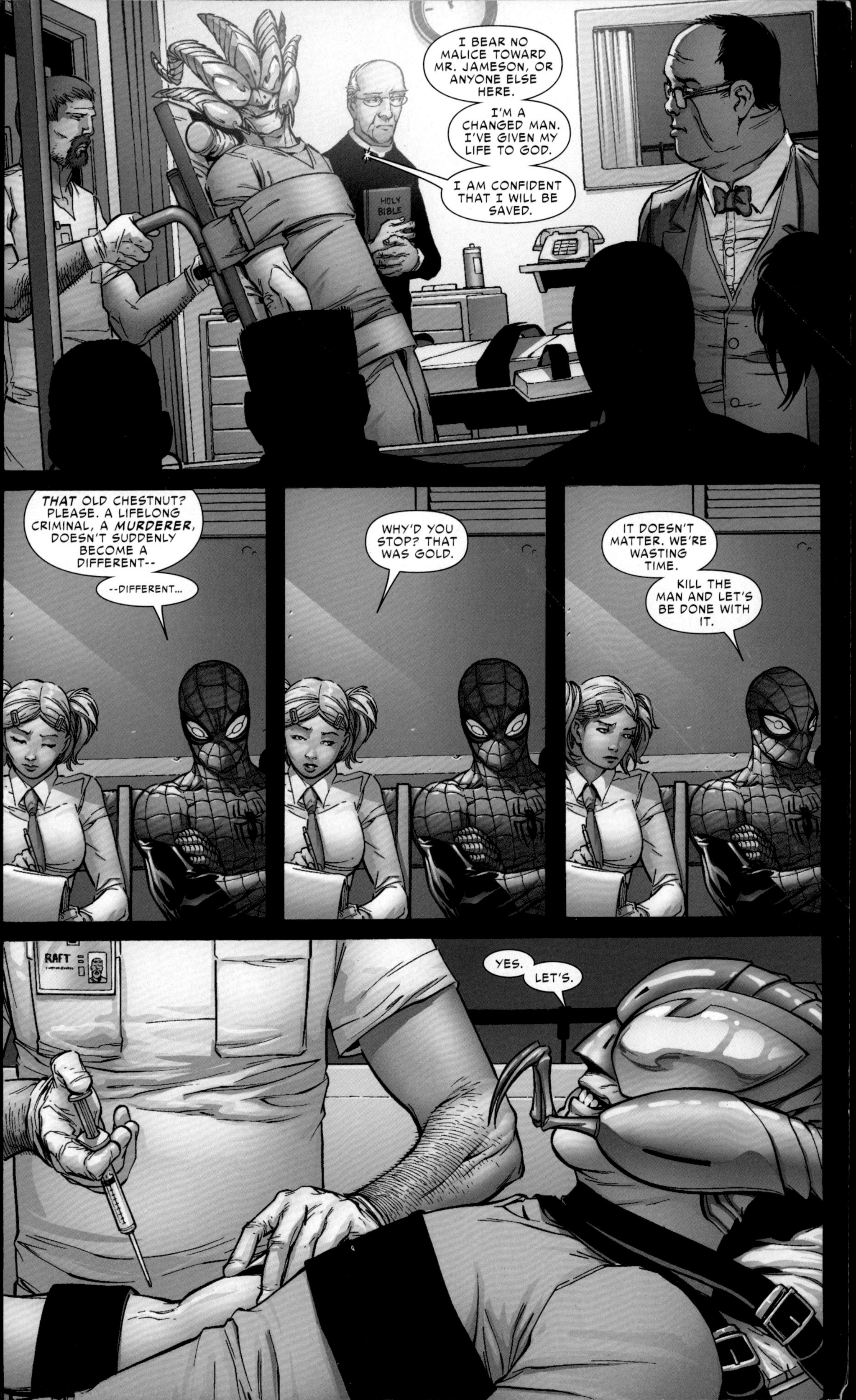
I BEAR NO MALICE TOWARD MR. JAMESON, OR ANYONE ELSE HERE.
I'M A CHANGED MAN. I'VE GIVEN MY LIFE TO GOD.
I AM CONFIDENT THAT I WILL BE SAVED.
HOLY BIBLE
THAT OLD CHESTNUT? PLEASE. A LIFELONG CRIMINAL, A MURDERER, DOESN'T SUDDENLY BECOME A DIFFERENT--
--DIFFERENT...
WHY'D YOU STOP? THAT WAS GOLD.
IT DOESN'T MATTER. WE'RE WASTING TIME.
KILL THE MAN AND LET'S BE DONE WITH IT.
RAFT
YES.
LET'S.

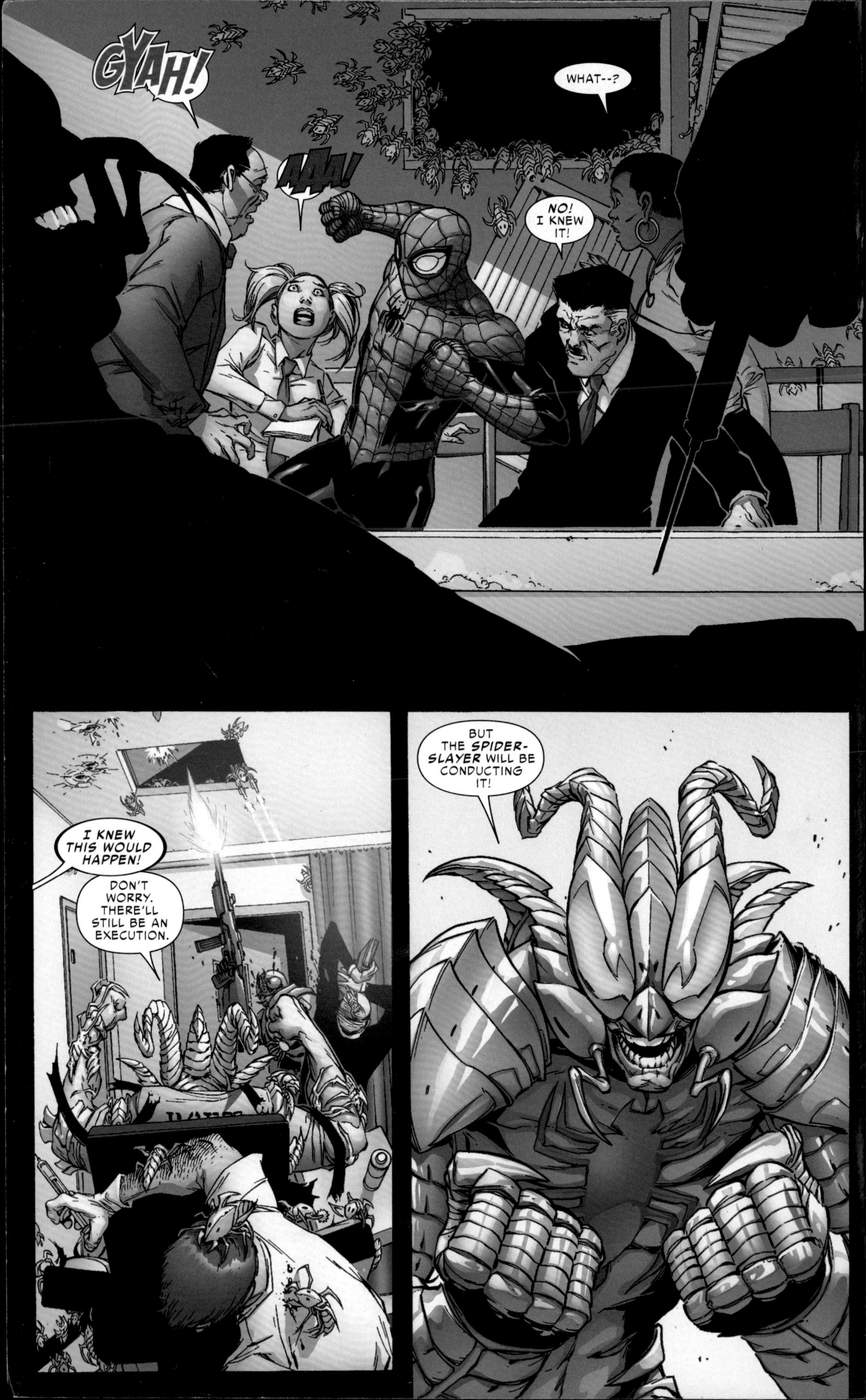
GYAH!
AAAA!
WHAT--?
NO! I KNEW IT!
I KNEW THIS WOULD HAPPEN!
DON'T WORRY. THERE'LL STILL BE AN EXECUTION.
BUT THE SPIDER-SLAYER WILL BE CONDUCTING IT!

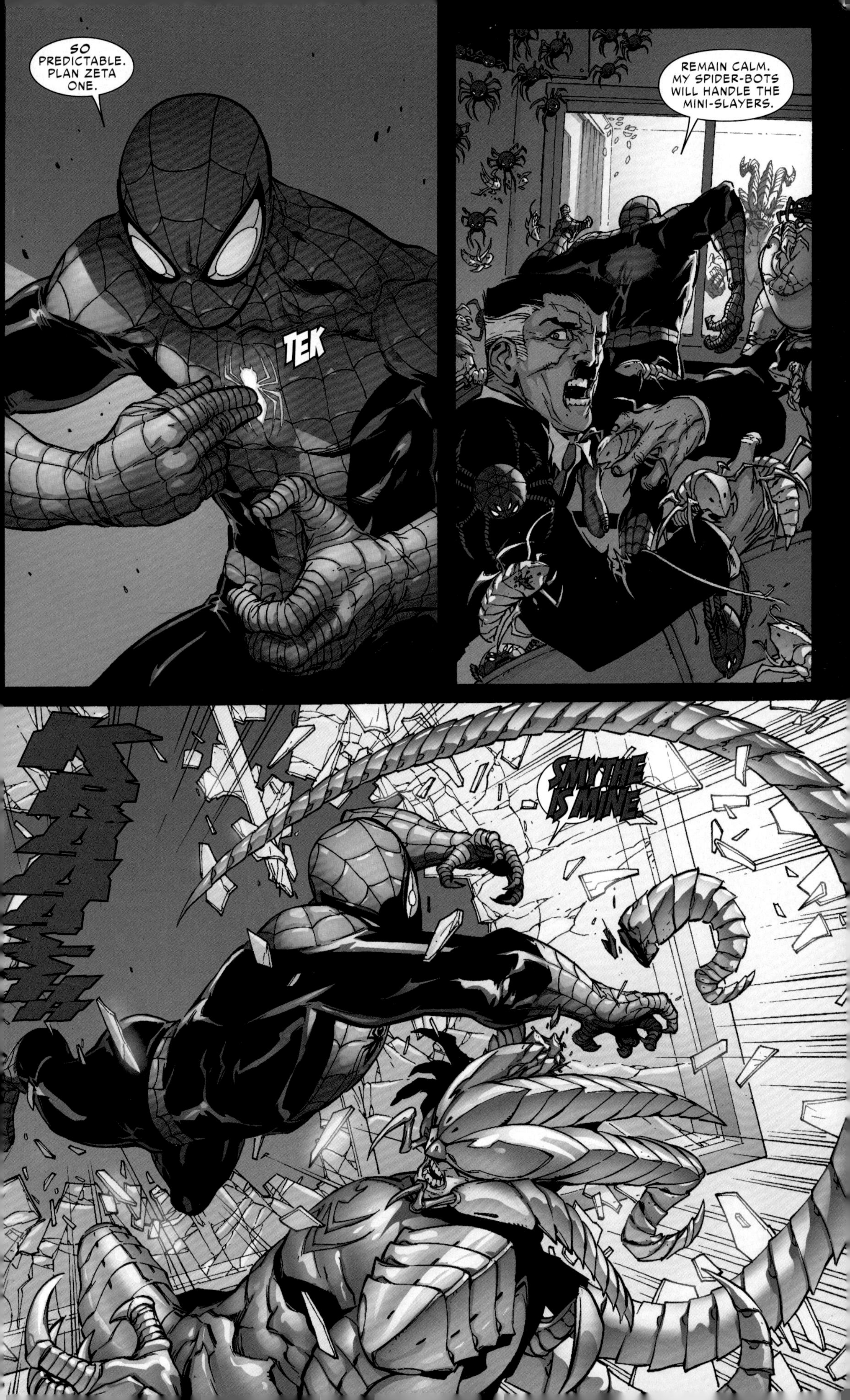
SO PREDICTABLE. PLAN ZETA ONE.
TEK
REMAIN CALM. MY SPIDER-BOTS WILL HANDLE THE MINI-SLAYERS.
SMYTHE IS MINE.

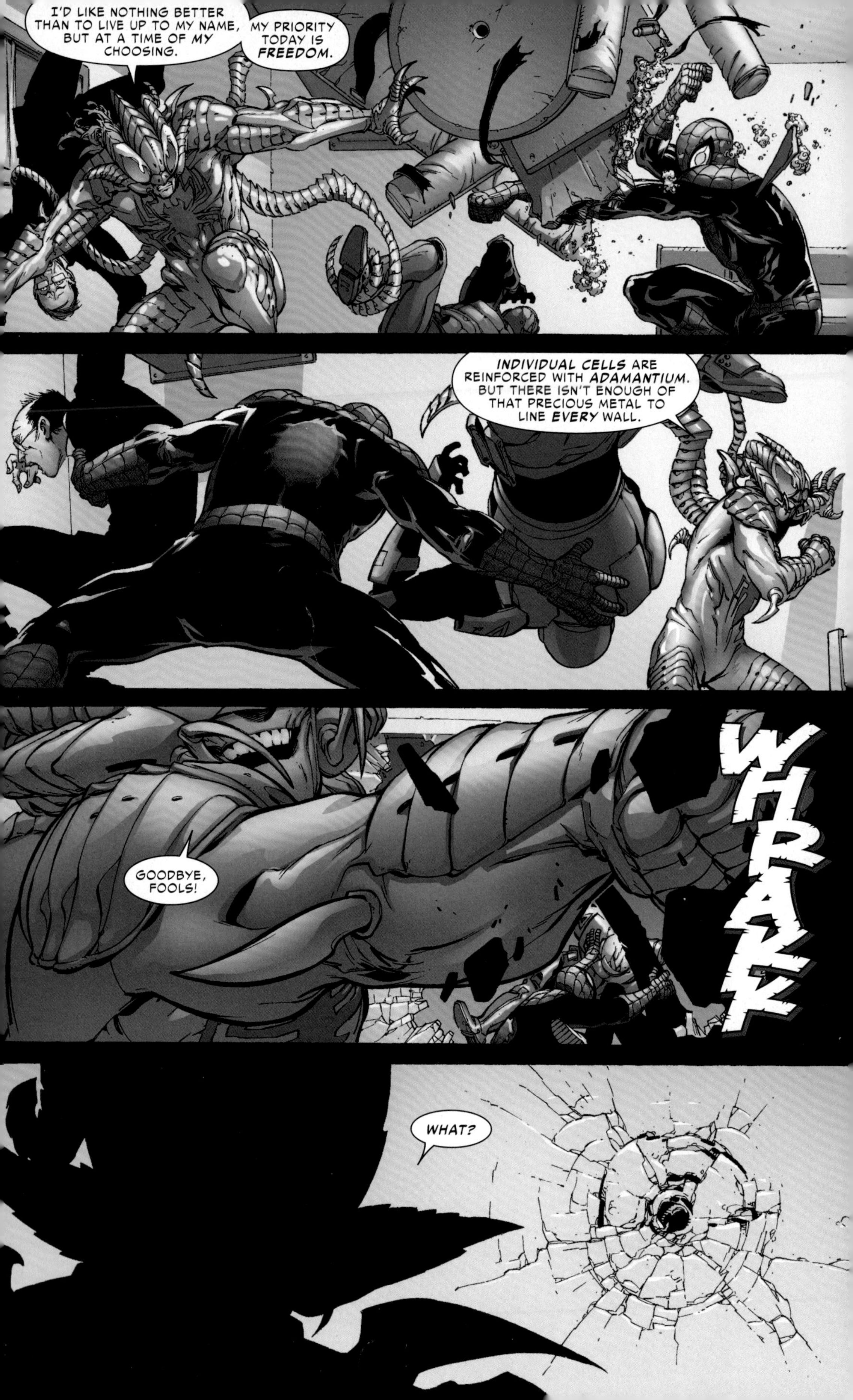
I'D LIKE NOTHING BETTER THAN TO LIVE UP TO MY NAME, BUT AT A TIME OF MY CHOOSING.
MY PRIORITY TODAY IS FREEDOM.
INDIVIDUAL CELLS ARE REINFORCED WITH ADAMANTIUM. BUT THERE ISN'T ENOUGH OF THAT PRECIOUS METAL TO LINE EVERY WALL.
GOODBYE, FOOLS!
WHRAKK
WHAT?

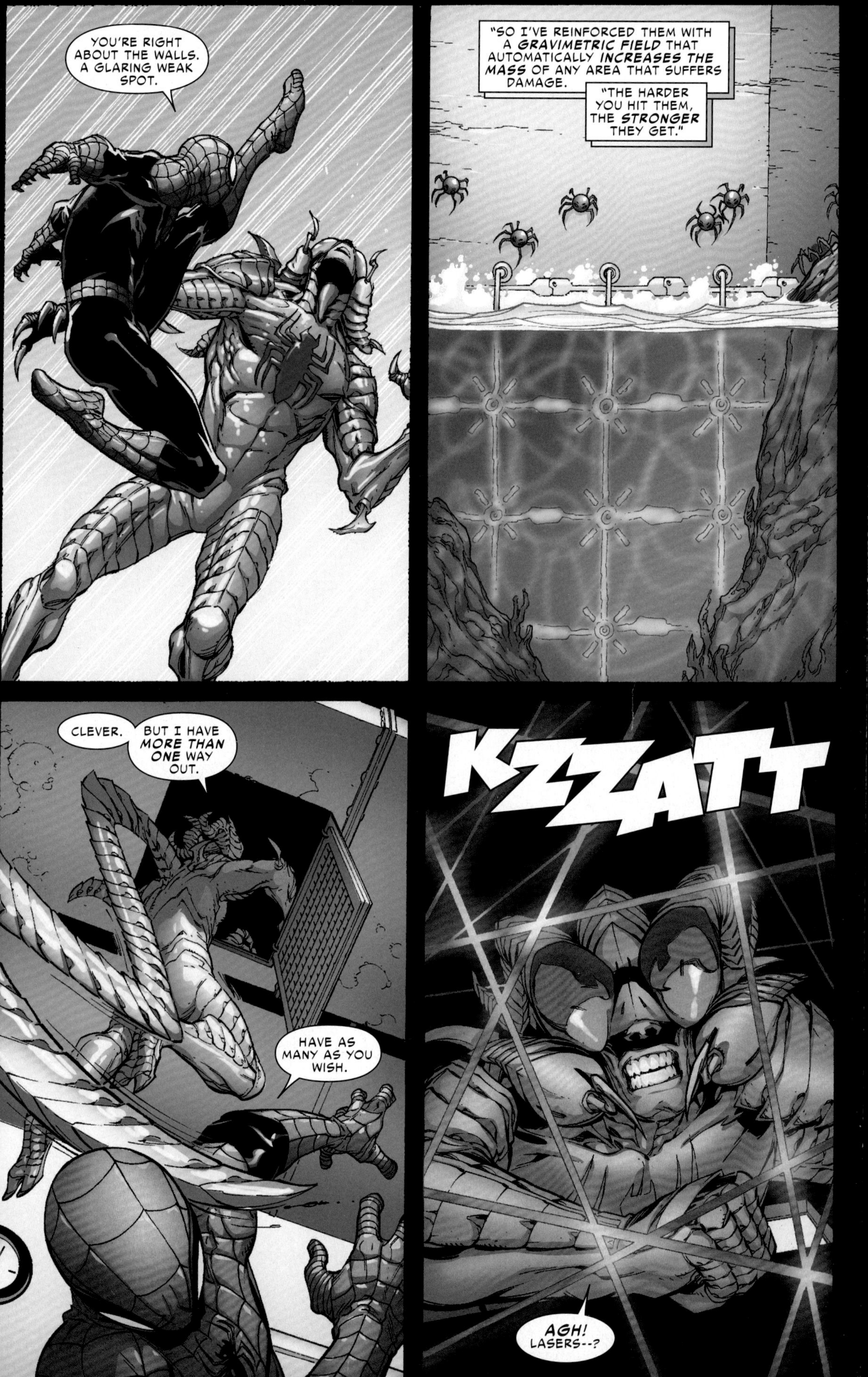
YOU'RE RIGHT ABOUT THE WALLS. A GLARING WEAK SPOT.
"SO I'VE REINFORCED THEM WITH A GRAVIMETRIC FIELD THAT AUTOMATICALLY INCREASES THE MASS OF ANY AREA THAT SUFFERS DAMAGE.
"THE HARDER YOU HIT THEM, THE STRONGER THEY GET."
CLEVER.
BUT I HAVE MORE THAN ONE WAY OUT.
HAVE AS MANY AS YOU WISH.
KZZATT
AGH! LASERS--?

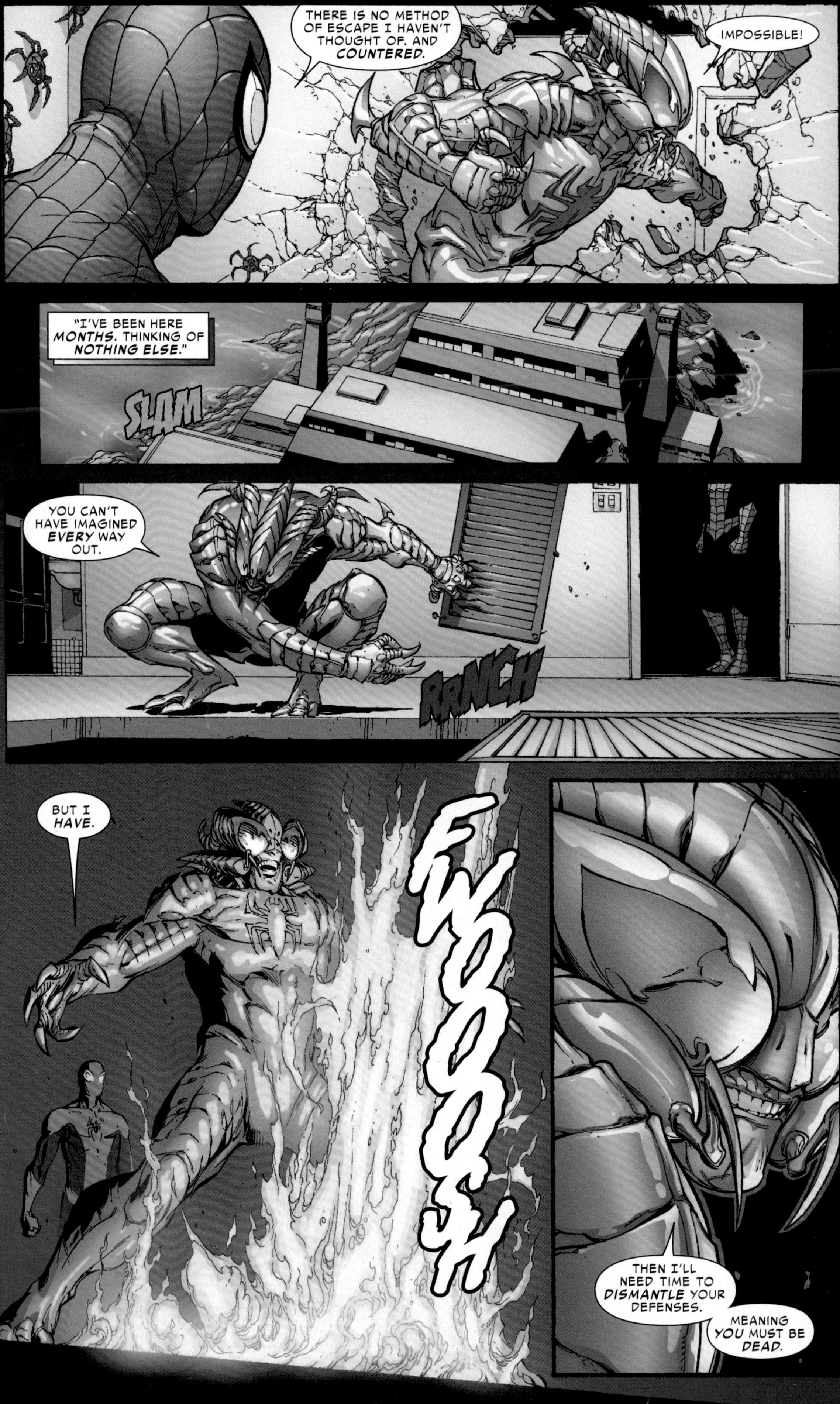
THERE IS NO METHOD OF ESCAPE I HAVEN'T THOUGHT OF. AND COUNTERED.
IMPOSSIBLE!
"I'VE BEEN HERE MONTHS. THINKING OF NOTHING ELSE."
SLAM
YOU CAN'T HAVE IMAGINED EVERY WAY OUT.
RRNCH
BUT I HAVE.
FWOOSH
THEN I'LL NEED TIME TO DISMANTLE YOUR DEFENSES.
MEANING YOU MUST BE DEAD.

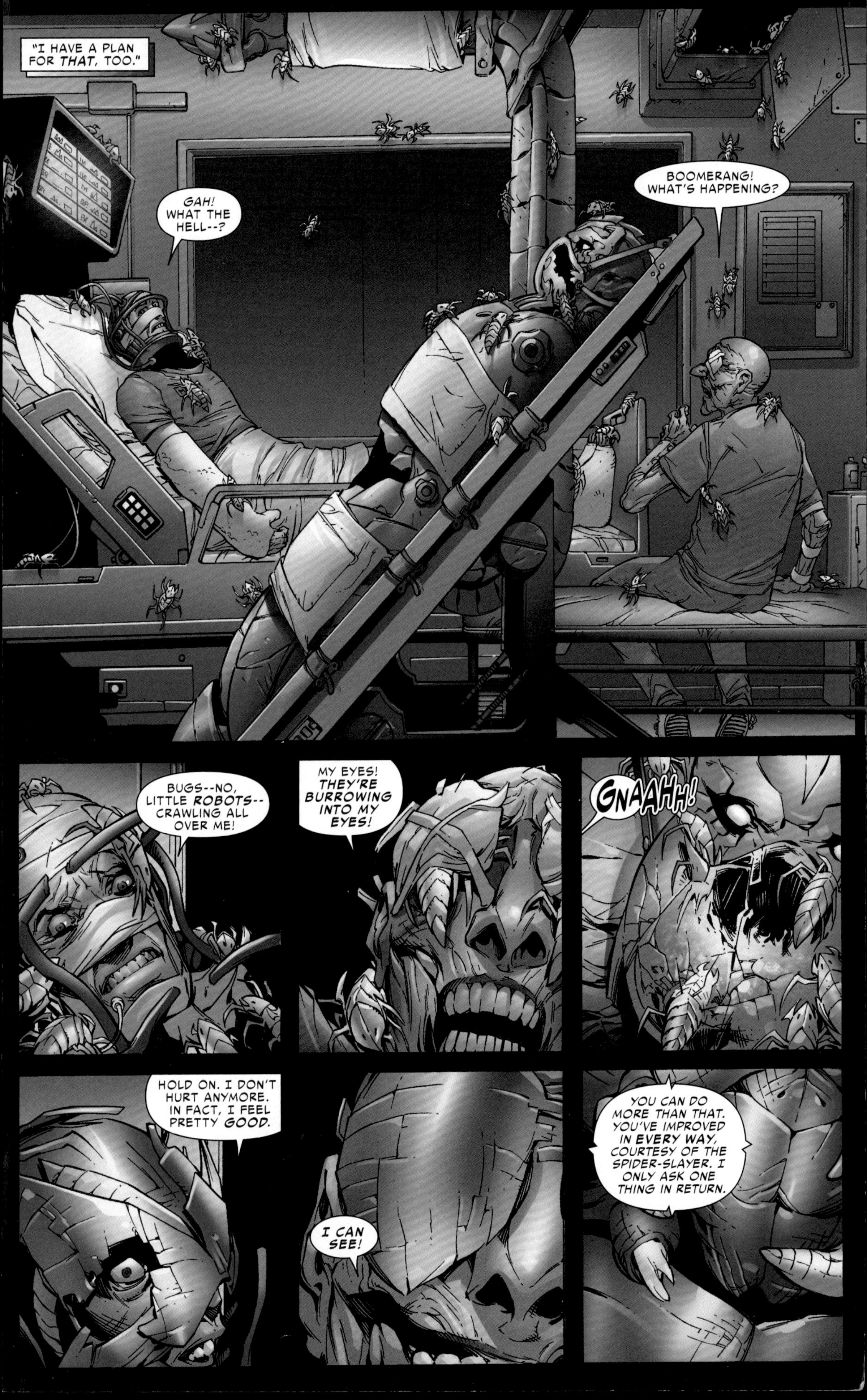
"I HAVE A PLAN FOR THAT, TOO."
GAH! WHAT THE HELL--?
BOOMERANG! WHAT'S HAPPENING?
BUGS--NO, LITTLE ROBOTS--CRAWLING ALL OVER ME!
MY EYES! THEY'RE BURROWING INTO MY EYES!
GNAAHH!
HOLD ON. I DON'T HURT ANYMORE. IN FACT, I FEEL PRETTY GOOD.
I CAN SEE!
YOU CAN DO MORE THAN THAT. YOU'VE IMPROVED IN EVERY WAY, COURTESY OF THE SPIDER-SLAYER. I ONLY ASK ONE THING IN RETURN.

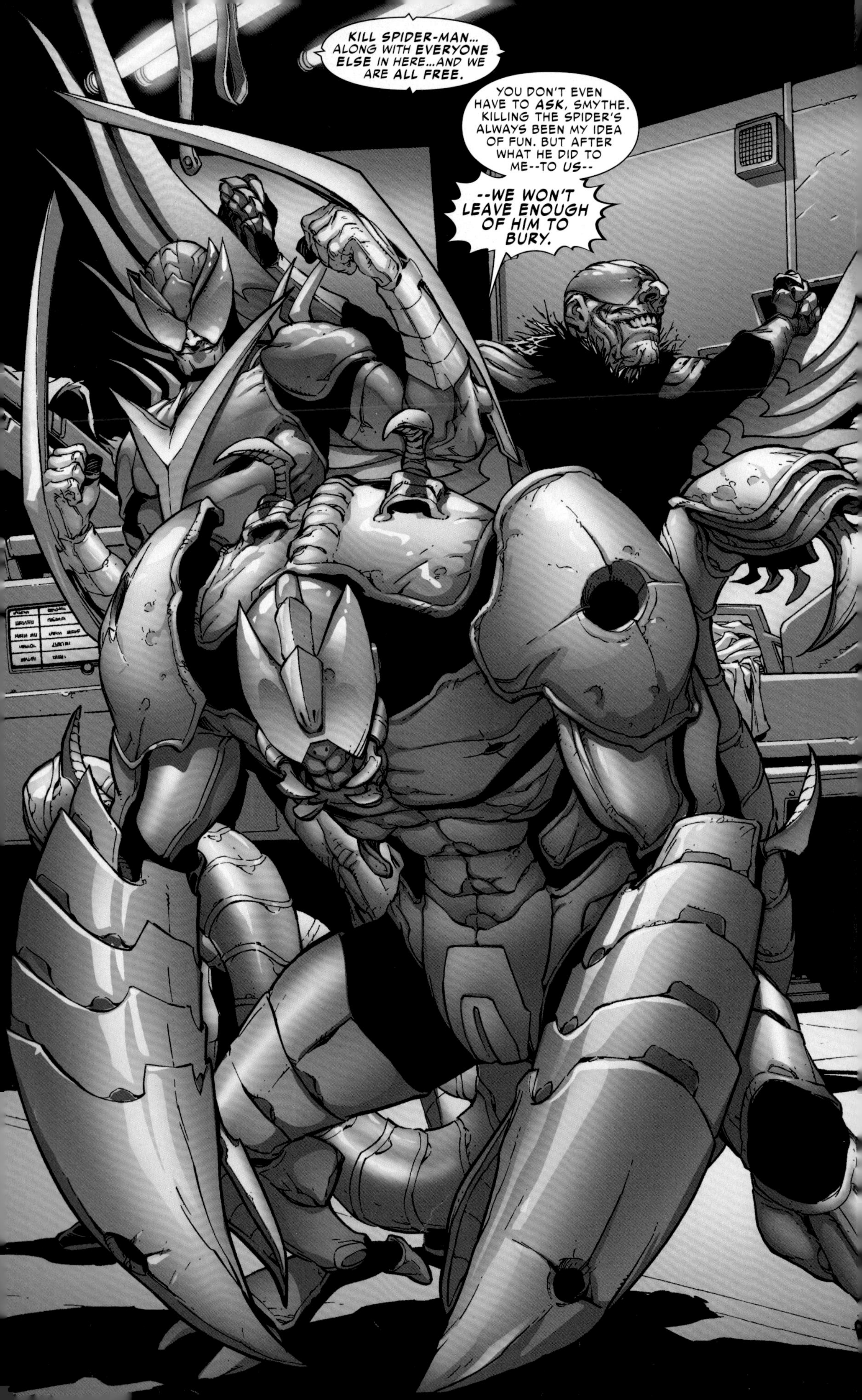
KILL SPIDER-MAN... ALONG WITH EVERYONE ELSE IN HERE...AND WE ARE ALL FREE.
YOU DON'T EVEN HAVE TO ASK, SMYTHE. KILLING THE SPIDER'S ALWAYS BEEN MY IDEA OF FUN. BUT AFTER WHAT HE DID TO ME--TO US--
--WE WON'T LEAVE ENOUGH OF HIM TO BURY.

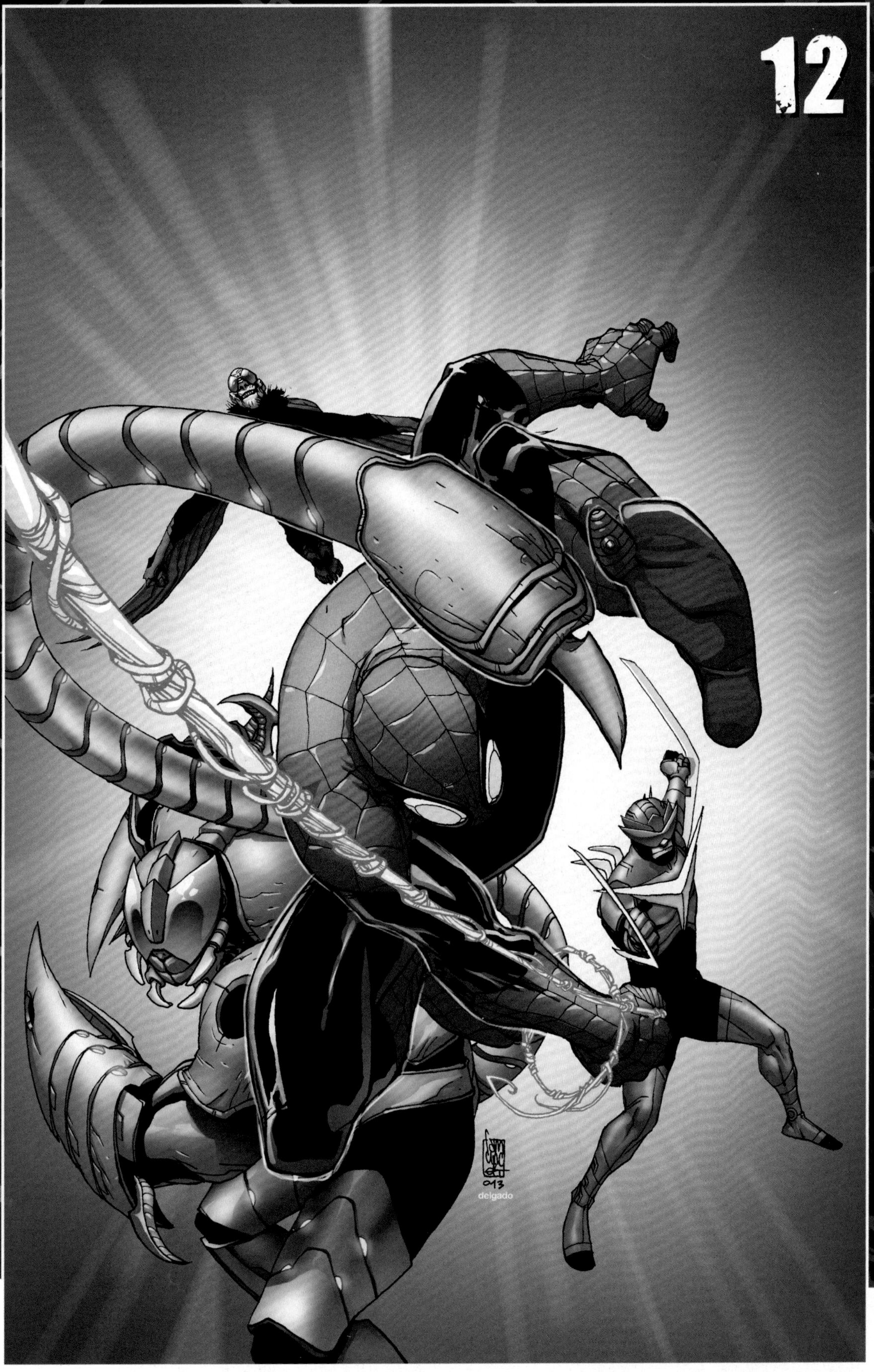
12
delgado

NO ESCAPE PART TWO: LOCKDOWN

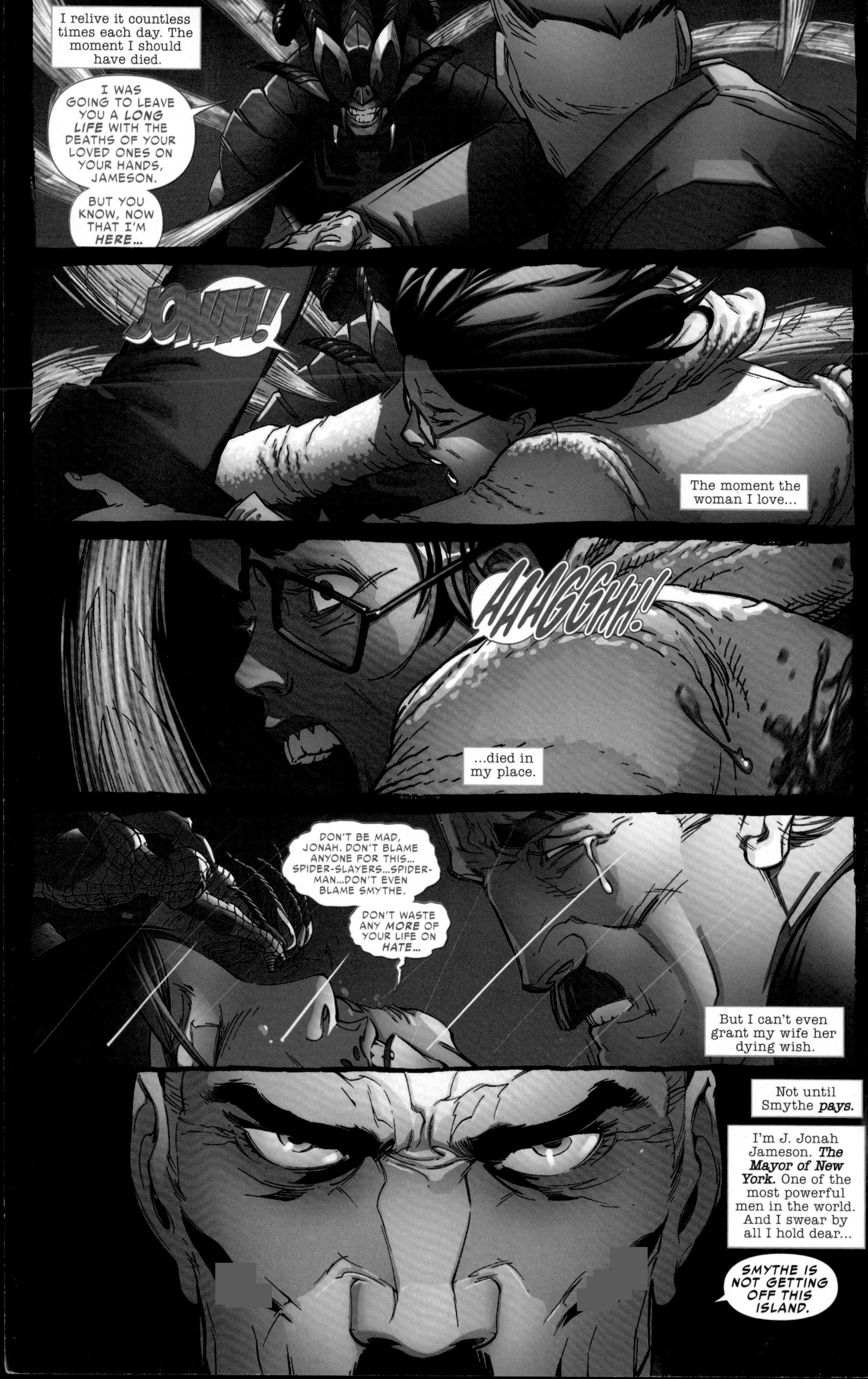
I relive it countless times each day. The moment I should have died.
I WAS GOING TO LEAVE YOU A LONG LIFE WITH THE DEATHS OF YOUR LOVED ONES ON YOUR HANDS, JAMESON.
BUT YOU KNOW, NOW THAT I'M HERE...
JONAH!
The moment the woman I love...
AAAGGHH!
...died in my place.
DON'T BE MAD, JONAH. DON'T BLAME ANYONE FOR THIS... SPIDER-SLAYERS...SPIDER-MAN...DON'T EVEN BLAME SMYTHE.
DON'T WASTE ANY MORE OF YOUR LIFE ON HATE...
But I can't even grant my wife her dying wish.
Not until Smythe pays.
I'm J. Jonah Jameson. The Mayor of New York. One of the most powerful men in the world. And I swear by all I hold dear...
SMYTHE IS NOT GETTING OFF THIS ISLAND.

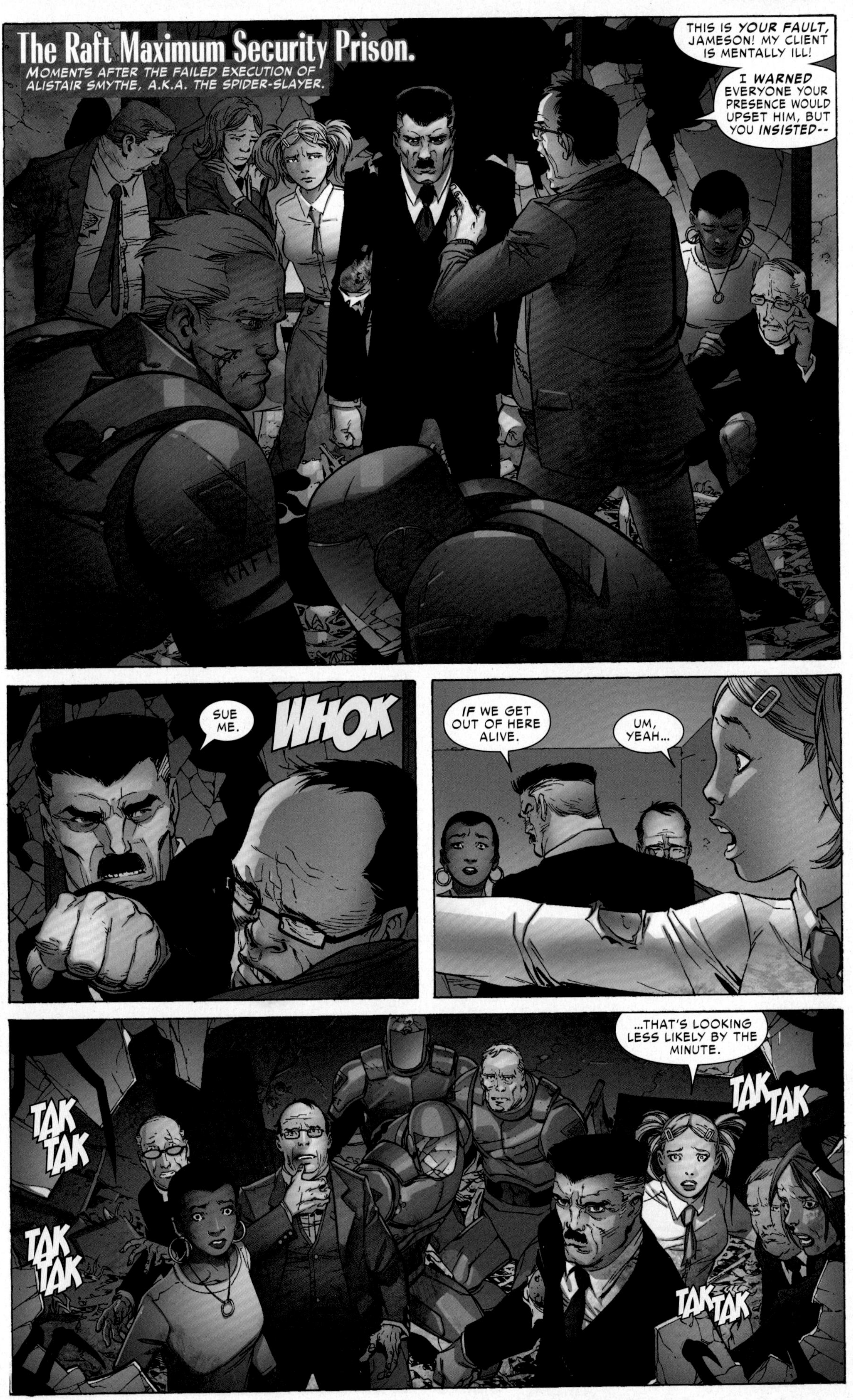
The Raft Maximum Security Prison.
MOMENTS AFTER THE FAILED EXECUTION OF ALISTAIR SMYTHE, A.K.A. THE SPIDER-SLAYER.
THIS IS YOUR FAULT, JAMESON! MY CLIENT IS MENTALLY ILL!
I WARNED EVERYONE YOUR PRESENCE WOULD UPSET HIM, BUT YOU INSISTED--
SUE ME.
WHOK
IF WE GET OUT OF HERE ALIVE.
UM, YEAH...
...THAT'S LOOKING LESS LIKELY BY THE MINUTE.
TAK TAK
TAK TAK
TAK TAK
TAK TAK

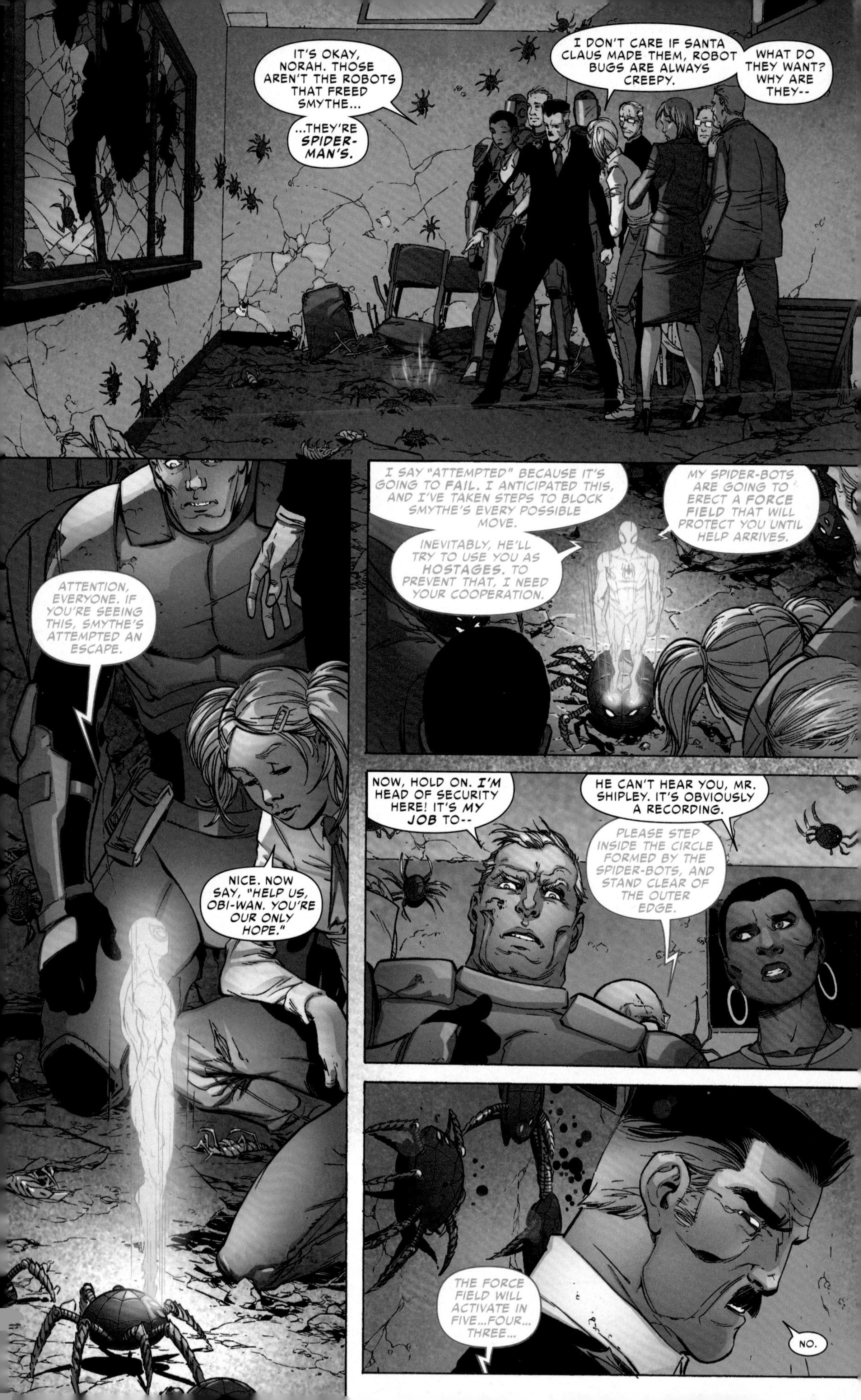
IT'S OKAY, NORAH. THOSE AREN'T THE ROBOTS THAT FREED SMYTHE...
...THEY'RE SPIDER-MAN'S.
I DON'T CARE IF SANTA CLAUS MADE THEM, ROBOT BUGS ARE ALWAYS CREEPY.
WHAT DO THEY WANT? WHY ARE THEY--
ATTENTION, EVERYONE. IF YOU'RE SEEING THIS, SMYTHE'S ATTEMPTED AN ESCAPE.
NICE. NOW SAY, "HELP US, OBI-WAN. YOU'RE OUR ONLY HOPE."
I SAY "ATTEMPTED" BECAUSE IT'S GOING TO FAIL. I ANTICIPATED THIS, AND I'VE TAKEN STEPS TO BLOCK SMYTHE'S EVERY POSSIBLE MOVE.
INEVITABLY, HE'LL TRY TO USE YOU AS HOSTAGES. TO PREVENT THAT, I NEED YOUR COOPERATION.
MY SPIDER-BOTS ARE GOING TO ERECT A FORCE FIELD THAT WILL PROTECT YOU UNTIL HELP ARRIVES.
NOW, HOLD ON. I'M HEAD OF SECURITY HERE! IT'S MY JOB TO--
HE CAN'T HEAR YOU, MR. SHIPLEY. IT'S OBVIOUSLY A RECORDING.
PLEASE STEP INSIDE THE CIRCLE FORMED BY THE SPIDER-BOTS, AND STAND CLEAR OF THE OUTER EDGE.
THE FORCE FIELD WILL ACTIVATE IN FIVE...FOUR... THREE...
NO.

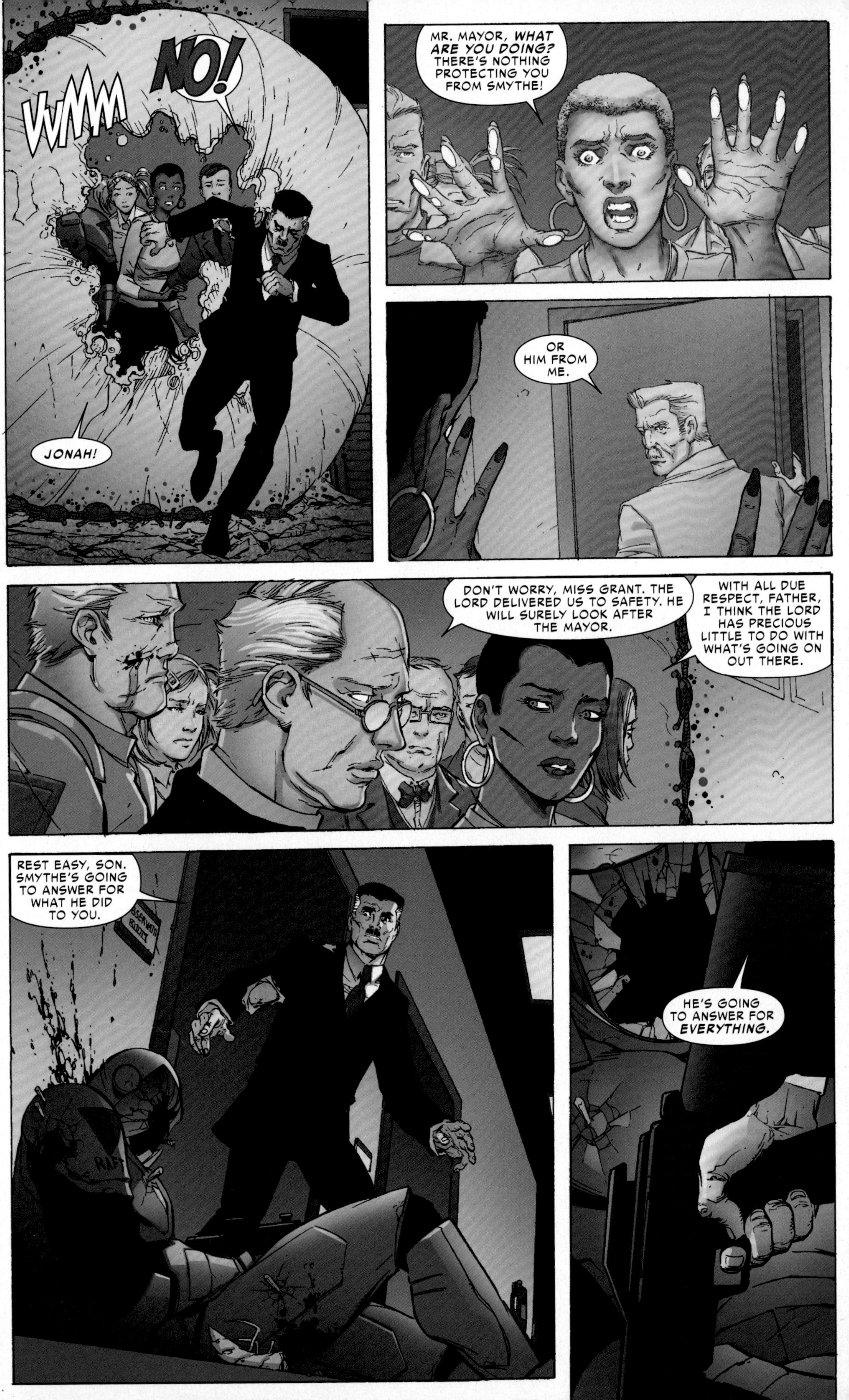
VVMM
NO!
JONAH!
MR. MAYOR, WHAT ARE YOU DOING? THERE'S NOTHING PROTECTING YOU FROM SMYTHE!
OR HIM FROM ME.
DON'T WORRY, MISS GRANT. THE LORD DELIVERED US TO SAFETY. HE WILL SURELY LOOK AFTER THE MAYOR.
WITH ALL DUE RESPECT, FATHER, I THINK THE LORD HAS PRECIOUS LITTLE TO DO WITH WHAT'S GOING ON OUT THERE.
REST EASY, SON. SMYTHE'S GOING TO ANSWER FOR WHAT HE DID TO YOU.
HE'S GOING TO ANSWER FOR EVERYTHING.

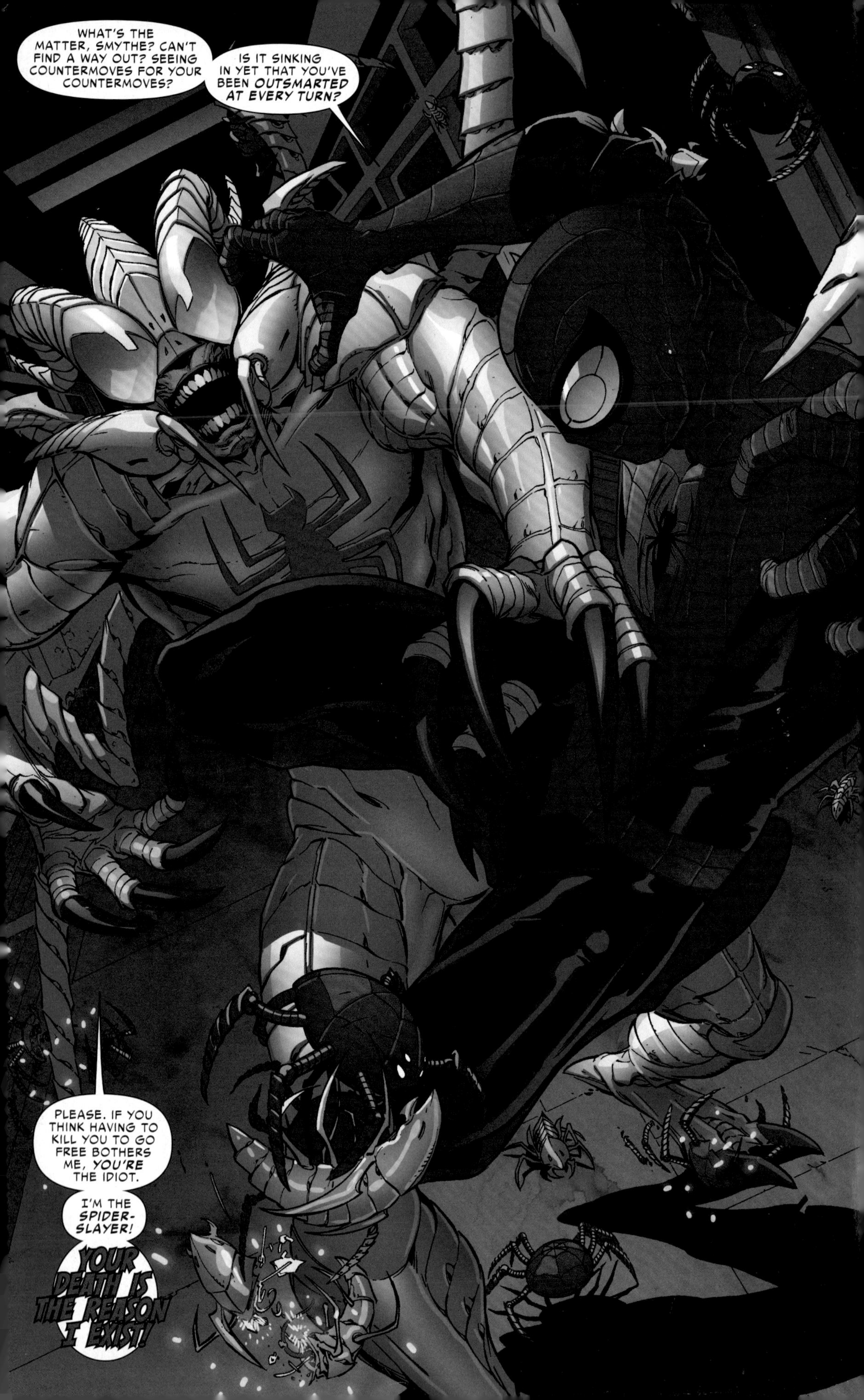
WHAT'S THE MATTER, SMYTHE? CAN'T FIND A WAY OUT? SEEING COUNTERMOVES FOR YOUR COUNTERMOVES?
IS IT SINKING IN YET THAT YOU'VE BEEN *OUTSMARTED AT EVERY TURN?*
PLEASE. IF YOU THINK HAVING TO KILL YOU TO GO FREE BOTHERS ME, *YOU'RE* THE IDIOT.
I'M THE *SPIDER-SLAYER!*
YOUR DEATH IS THE REASON I EXIST!

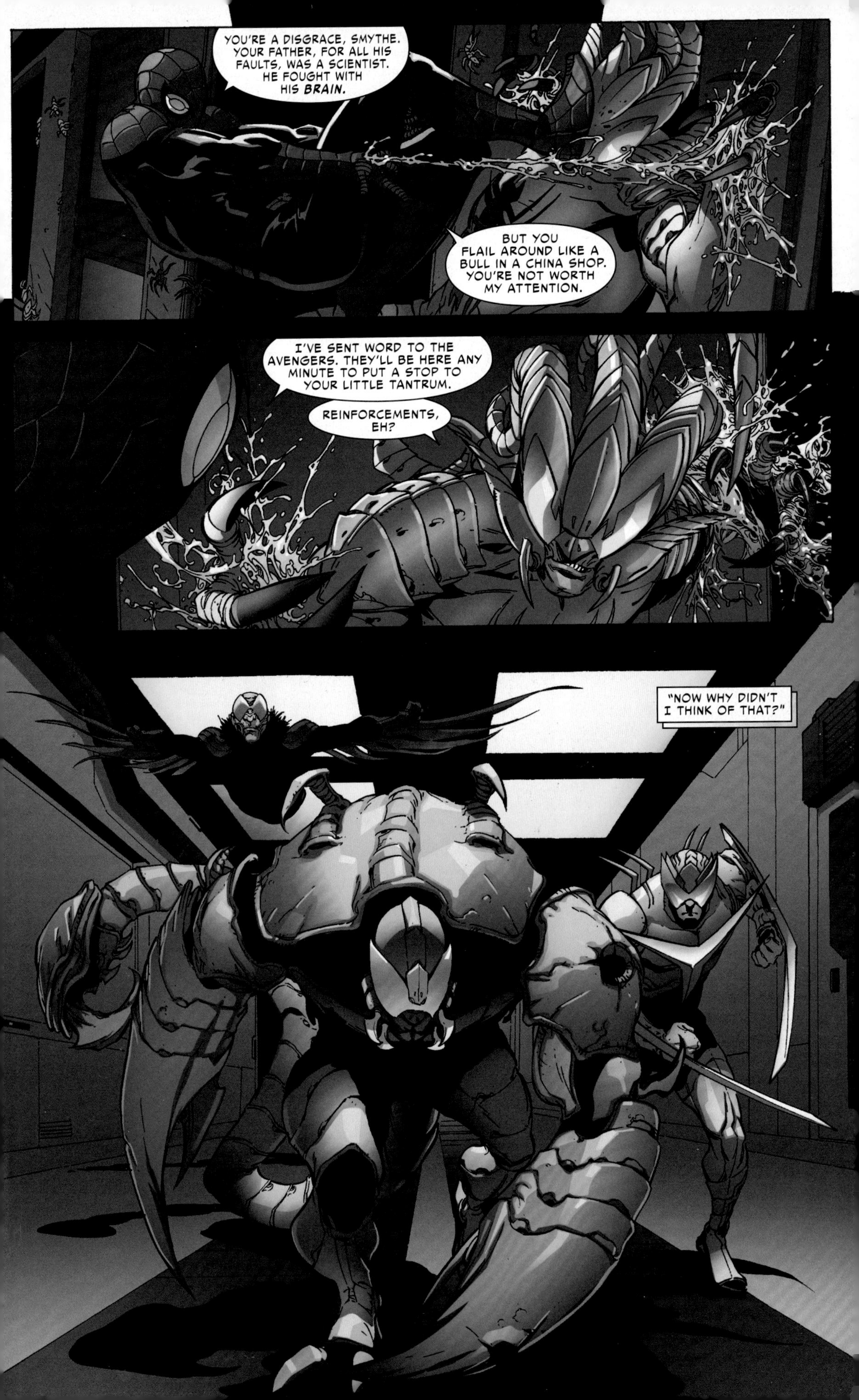
YOU'RE A DISGRACE, SMYTHE. YOUR FATHER, FOR ALL HIS FAULTS, WAS A SCIENTIST. HE FOUGHT WITH HIS *BRAIN*.
BUT YOU FLAIL AROUND LIKE A BULL IN A CHINA SHOP. YOU'RE NOT WORTH MY ATTENTION.
I'VE SENT WORD TO THE AVENGERS. THEY'LL BE HERE ANY MINUTE TO PUT A STOP TO YOUR LITTLE TANTRUM.
REINFORCEMENTS, EH?
"NOW WHY DIDN'T I THINK OF THAT?"

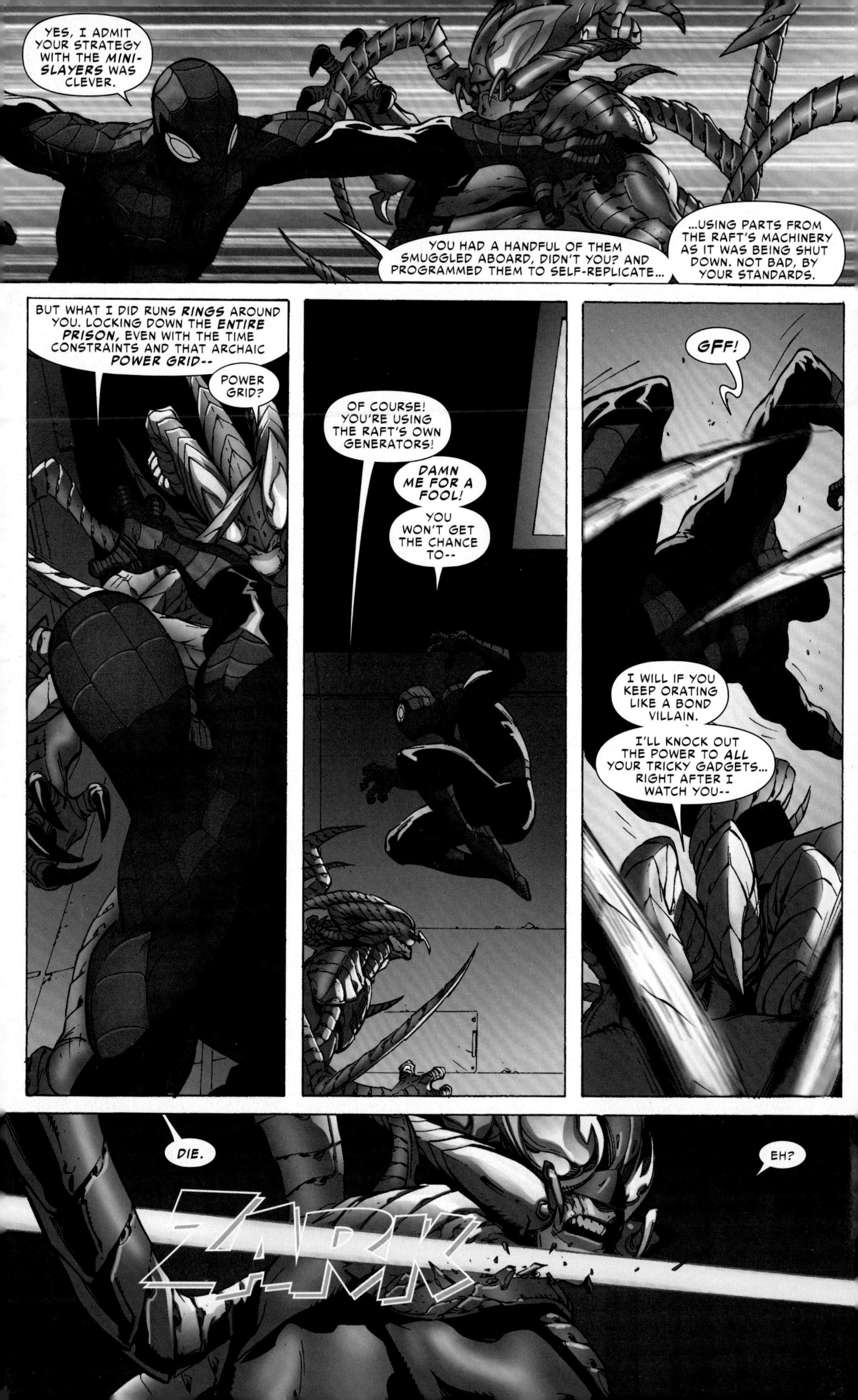

YES, I ADMIT YOUR STRATEGY WITH THE MINI-SLAYERS WAS CLEVER.
YOU HAD A HANDFUL OF THEM SMUGGLED ABOARD, DIDN'T YOU? AND PROGRAMMED THEM TO SELF-REPLICATE...
...USING PARTS FROM THE RAFT'S MACHINERY AS IT WAS BEING SHUT DOWN. NOT BAD, BY YOUR STANDARDS.
BUT WHAT I DID RUNS RINGS AROUND YOU. LOCKING DOWN THE ENTIRE PRISON, EVEN WITH THE TIME CONSTRAINTS AND THAT ARCHAIC POWER GRID--
POWER GRID?
OF COURSE! YOU'RE USING THE RAFT'S OWN GENERATORS!
DAMN ME FOR A FOOL!
YOU WON'T GET THE CHANCE TO--
GFF!
I WILL IF YOU KEEP ORATING LIKE A BOND VILLAIN.
I'LL KNOCK OUT THE POWER TO ALL YOUR TRICKY GADGETS... RIGHT AFTER I WATCH YOU--
DIE.
EH?
ZARK

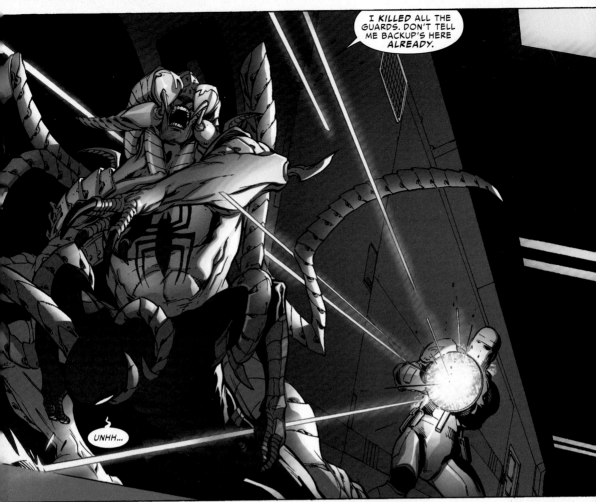

I KILLED ALL THE GUARDS. DON'T TELL ME BACKUP'S HERE ALREADY.

UNHH...

IT'S YOUR LUCKY DAY, SPIDER-MAN.

I'D RATHER GET OUT THAN EVEN.

UP, YOU MALINGERER! HE'S GETTING AWAY!

WHAT'S WRONG WITH YOU? YOU LED WITH YOUR JAW LIKE SOME KIND OF AMATEUR!

WHY SHOULD I... TAKE ORDERS FROM YOU...WHEN YOU CLEARLY IGNORED MINE...

...JAMESON!

I CAN'T PROTECT YOU AND FIGHT SMYTHE.

I DON'T NEED OR WANT YOUR PROTECTION.

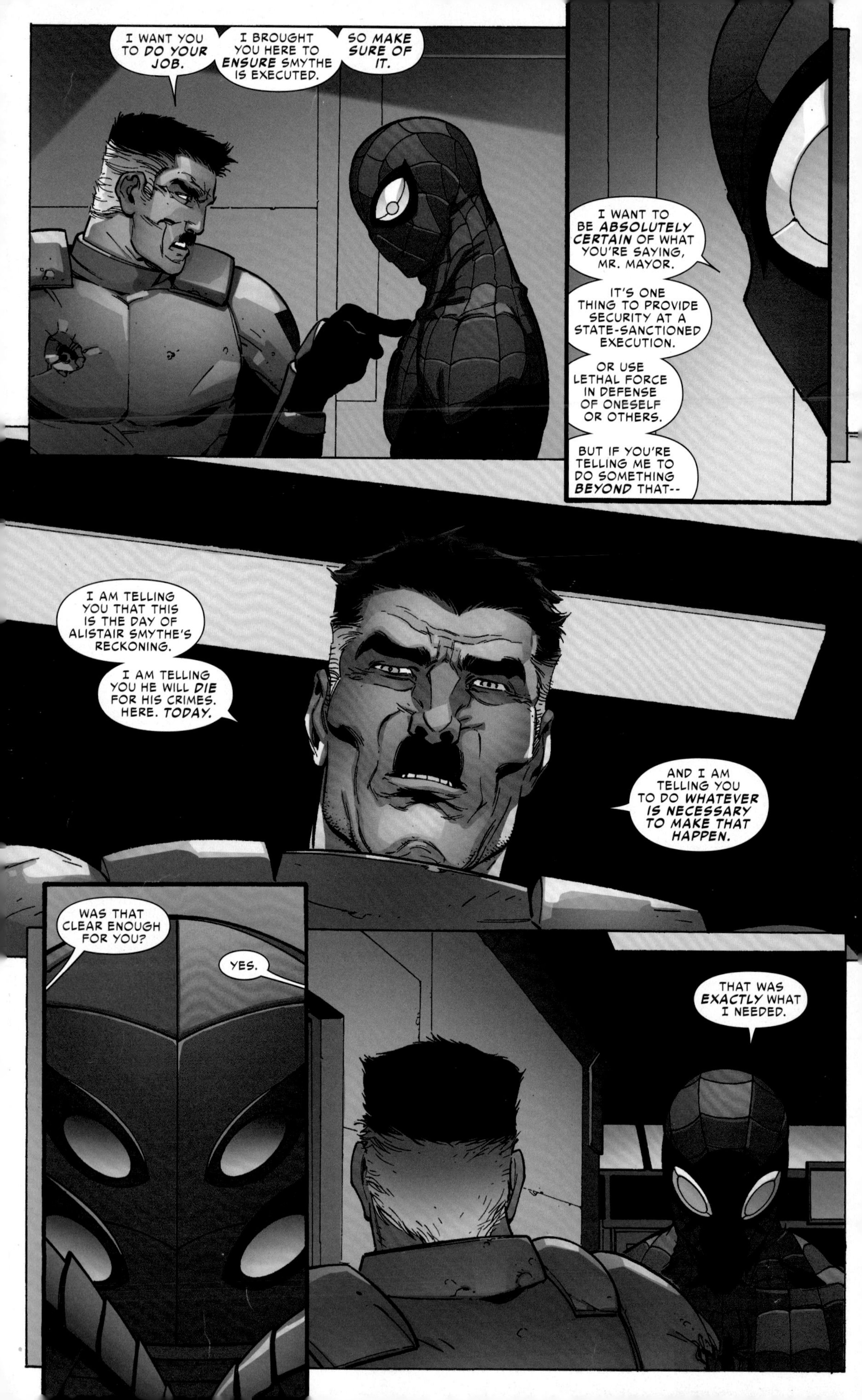
I WANT YOU TO DO YOUR JOB.
I BROUGHT YOU HERE TO ENSURE SMYTHE IS EXECUTED.
SO MAKE SURE OF IT.
I WANT TO BE ABSOLUTELY CERTAIN OF WHAT YOU'RE SAYING, MR. MAYOR.
IT'S ONE THING TO PROVIDE SECURITY AT A STATE-SANCTIONED EXECUTION.
OR USE LETHAL FORCE IN DEFENSE OF ONESELF OR OTHERS.
BUT IF YOU'RE TELLING ME TO DO SOMETHING BEYOND THAT--
I AM TELLING YOU THAT THIS IS THE DAY OF ALISTAIR SMYTHE'S RECKONING.
I AM TELLING YOU HE WILL DIE FOR HIS CRIMES. HERE. TODAY.
AND I AM TELLING YOU TO DO WHATEVER IS NECESSARY TO MAKE THAT HAPPEN.
WAS THAT CLEAR ENOUGH FOR YOU?
YES.
THAT WAS EXACTLY WHAT I NEEDED.

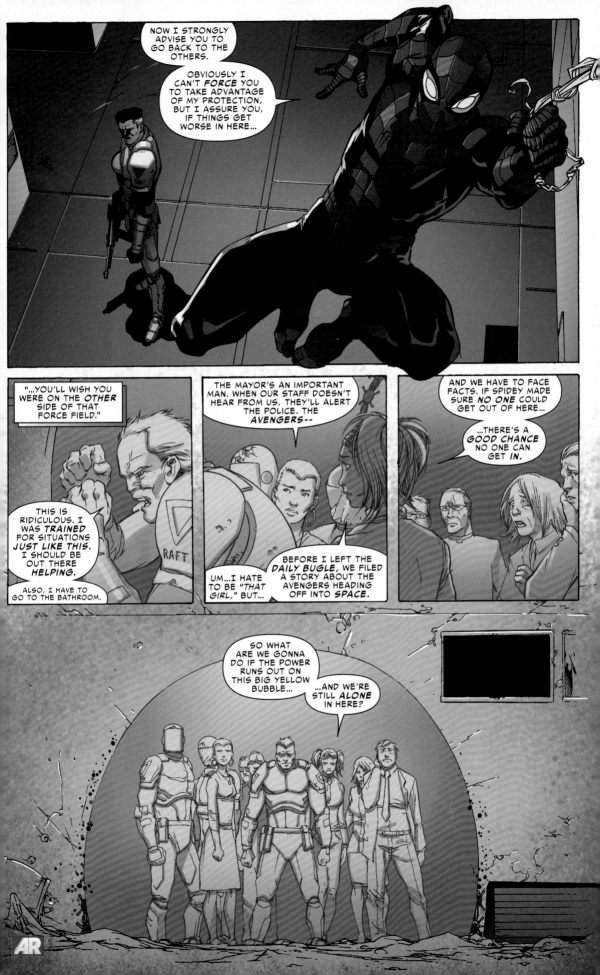

NOW I STRONGLY ADVISE YOU TO GO BACK TO THE OTHERS.

OBVIOUSLY I CAN'T *FORCE* YOU TO TAKE ADVANTAGE OF MY PROTECTION, BUT I ASSURE YOU, IF THINGS GET WORSE IN HERE...

"...YOU'LL WISH YOU WERE ON THE *OTHER* SIDE OF THAT FORCE FIELD."

THIS IS RIDICULOUS. I WAS *TRAINED* FOR SITUATIONS *JUST LIKE THIS.* I SHOULD BE OUT THERE *HELPING.*

ALSO, I HAVE TO GO TO THE BATHROOM.

THE MAYOR'S AN IMPORTANT MAN. WHEN OUR STAFF DOESN'T HEAR FROM US, THEY'LL ALERT THE POLICE. THE *AVENGERS*--

UM...I HATE TO BE "*THAT GIRL,*" BUT...

BEFORE I LEFT THE *DAILY BUGLE,* WE FILED A STORY ABOUT THE AVENGERS HEADING OFF INTO *SPACE.*

AND WE HAVE TO FACE FACTS. IF SPIDEY MADE SURE *NO ONE* COULD GET OUT OF HERE...

...THERE'S A *GOOD CHANCE* NO ONE CAN GET *IN.*

SO WHAT ARE WE GONNA DO IF THE POWER RUNS OUT ON THIS BIG YELLOW BUBBLE...

...AND WE'RE STILL *ALONE* IN HERE?

AR

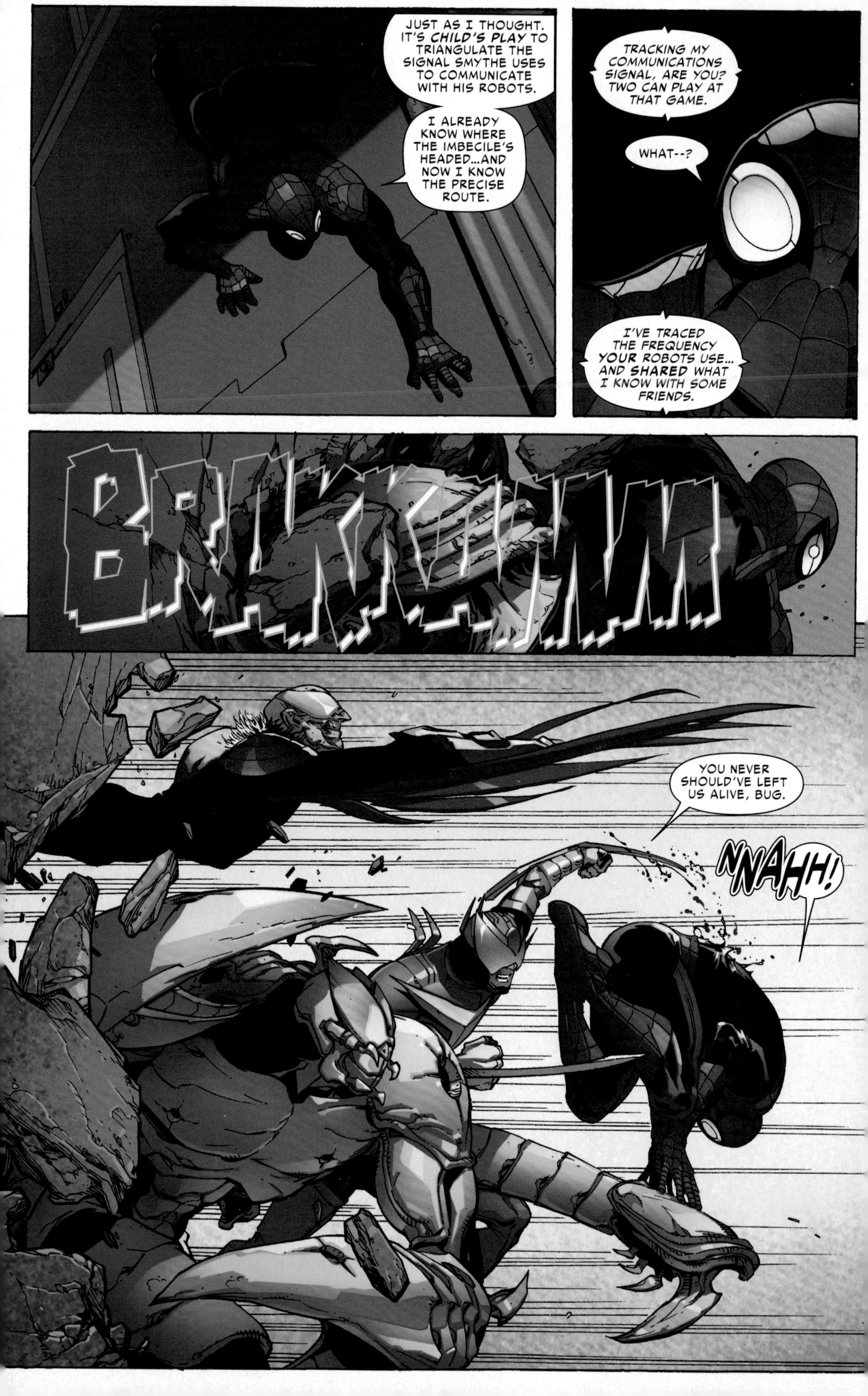
JUST AS I THOUGHT. IT'S CHILD'S PLAY TO TRIANGULATE THE SIGNAL SMYTHE USES TO COMMUNICATE WITH HIS ROBOTS.
I ALREADY KNOW WHERE THE IMBECILE'S HEADED...AND NOW I KNOW THE PRECISE ROUTE.
TRACKING MY COMMUNICATIONS SIGNAL, ARE YOU? TWO CAN PLAY AT THAT GAME.
WHAT--?
I'VE TRACED THE FREQUENCY YOUR ROBOTS USE... AND SHARED WHAT I KNOW WITH SOME FRIENDS.
YOU NEVER SHOULD'VE LEFT US ALIVE, BUG.
NNAHH!

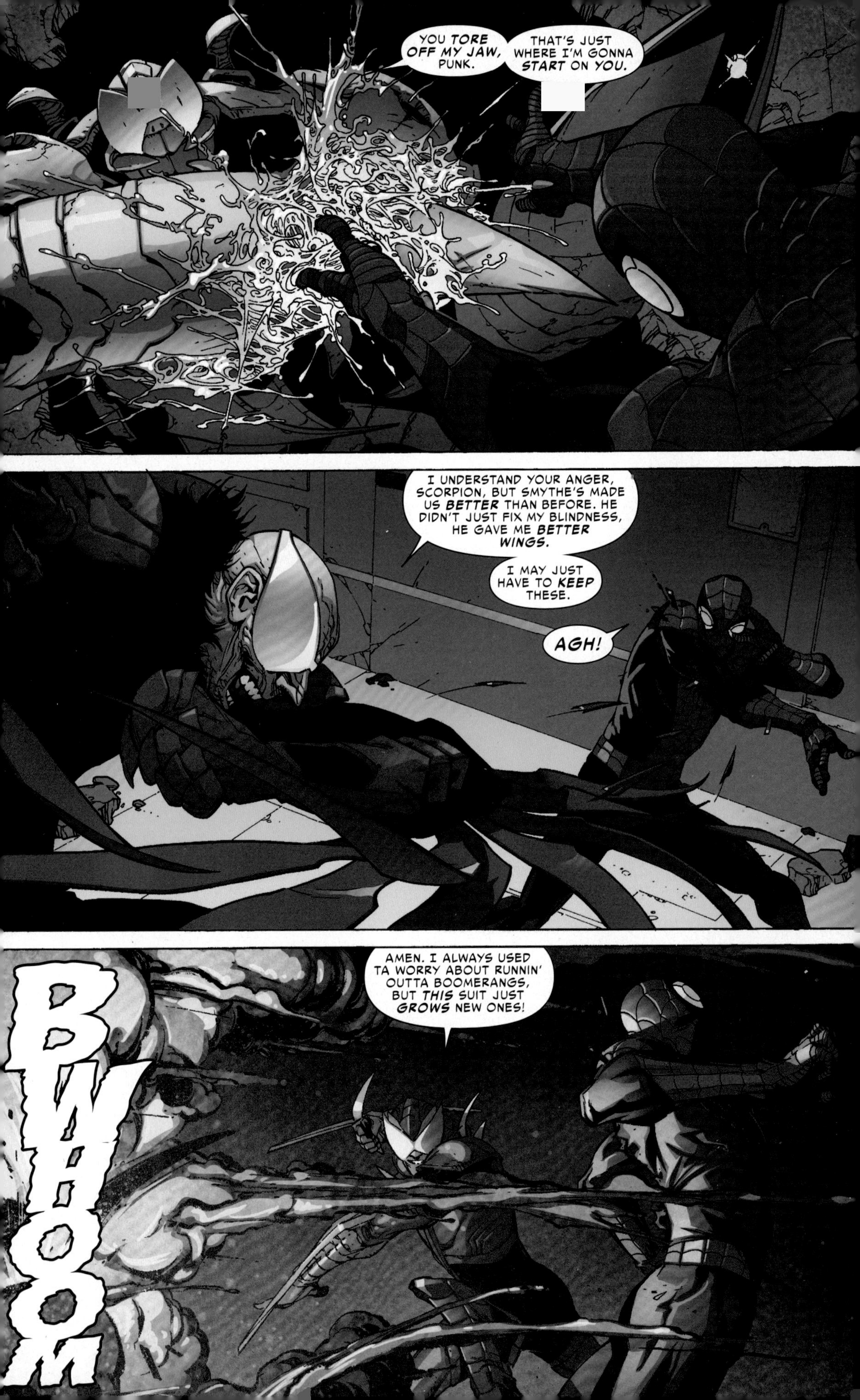

YOU TORE OFF MY JAW, PUNK.
THAT'S JUST WHERE I'M GONNA START ON YOU.
I UNDERSTAND YOUR ANGER, SCORPION, BUT SMYTHE'S MADE US BETTER THAN BEFORE. HE DIDN'T JUST FIX MY BLINDNESS, HE GAVE ME BETTER WINGS.
I MAY JUST HAVE TO KEEP THESE.
AGH!
BWHOOM
AMEN. I ALWAYS USED TA WORRY ABOUT RUNNIN' OUTTA BOOMERANGS, BUT THIS SUIT JUST GROWS NEW ONES!

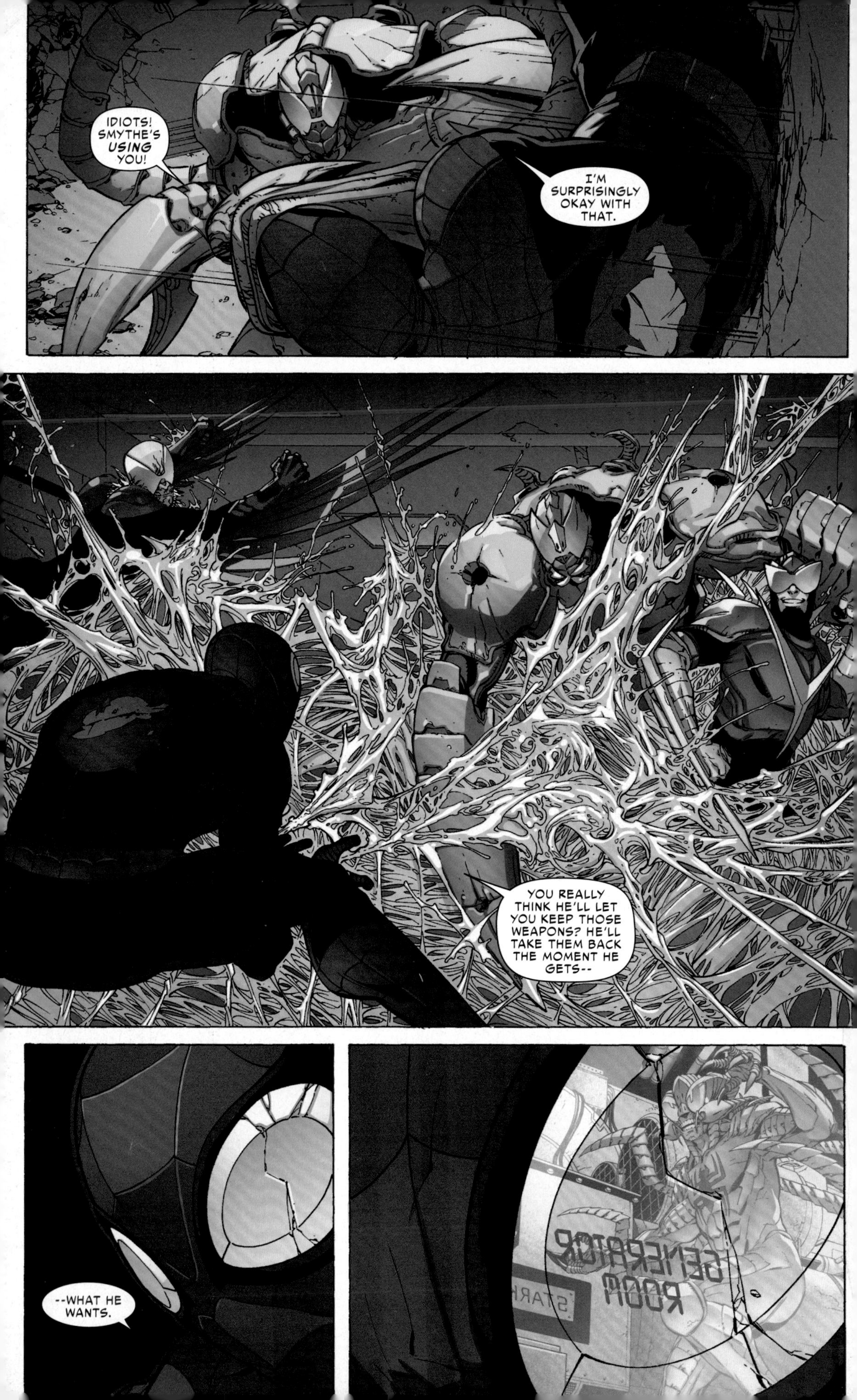
IDIOTS! SMYTHE'S *USING* YOU!
I'M SURPRISINGLY OKAY WITH THAT.
YOU REALLY THINK HE'LL LET YOU KEEP THOSE WEAPONS? HE'LL TAKE THEM BACK THE MOMENT HE GETS--
--WHAT HE WANTS.
GENERATOR ROOM
STARK

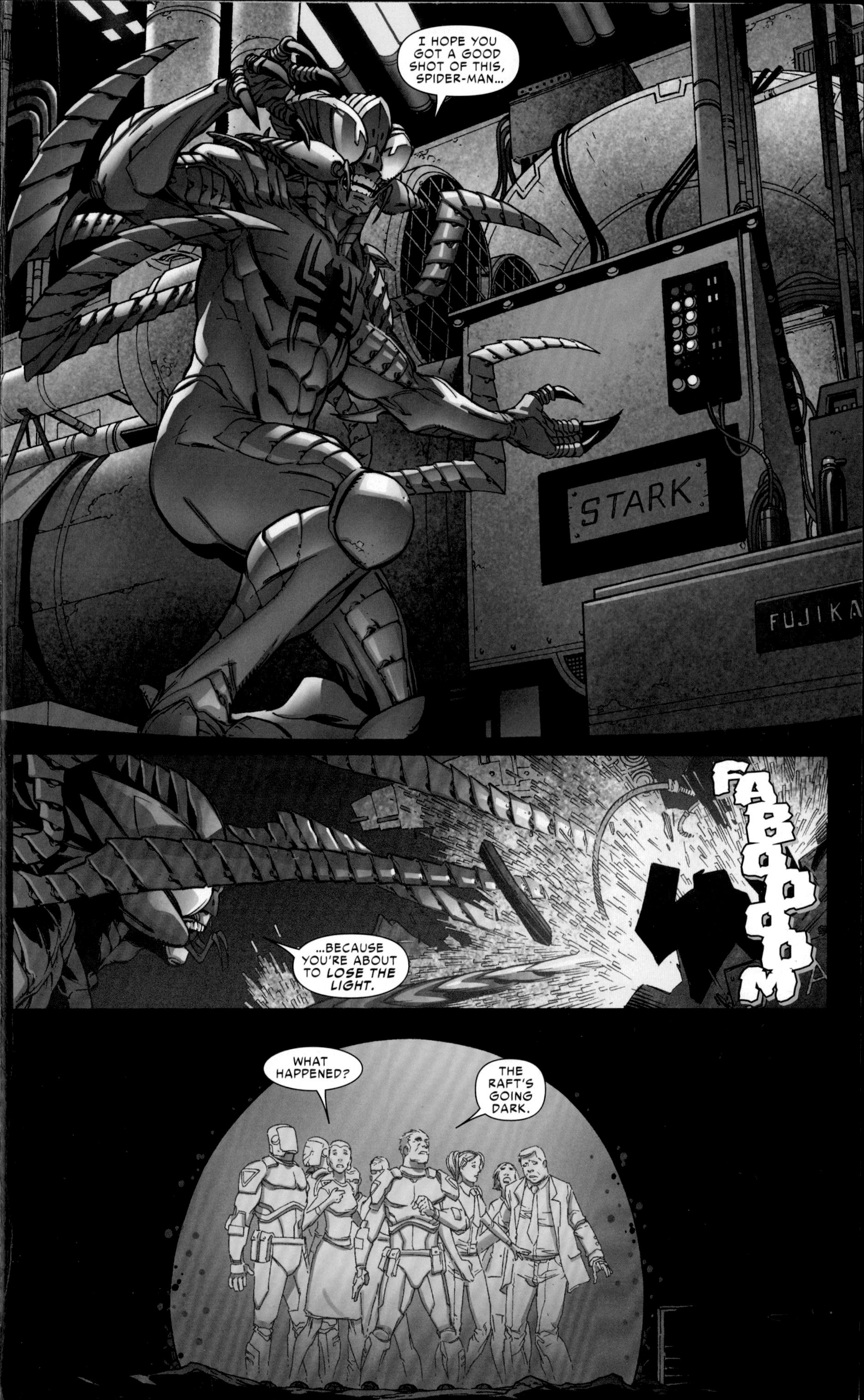

I HOPE YOU GOT A GOOD SHOT OF THIS, SPIDER-MAN...
STARK
FUJIKA
FABOOOM
...BECAUSE YOU'RE ABOUT TO LOSE THE LIGHT.
WHAT HAPPENED?
THE RAFT'S GOING DARK.

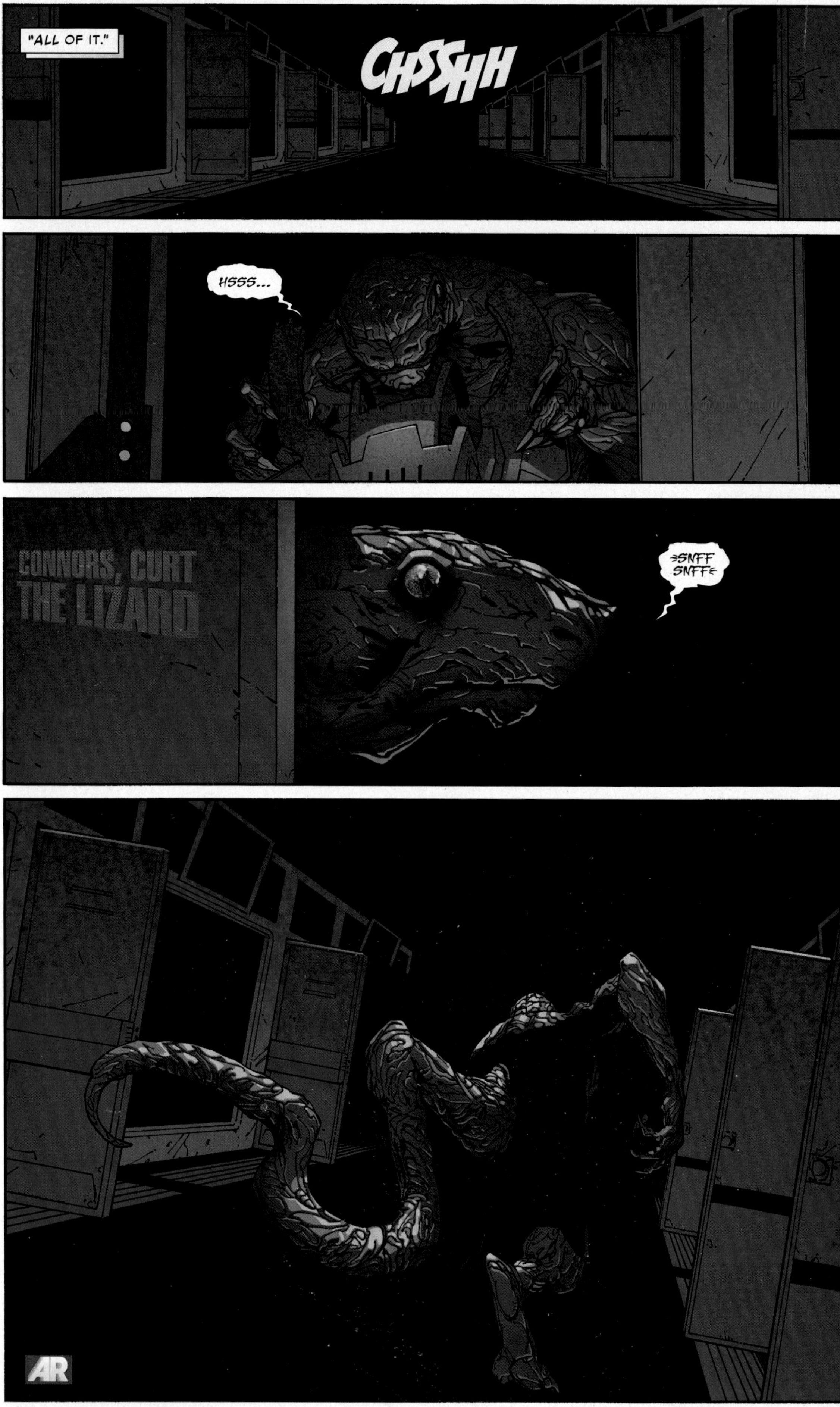
"ALL OF IT."
CHSSHH
HSSS...
CONNORS, CURT
THE LIZARD
SNFF SNFF
AR

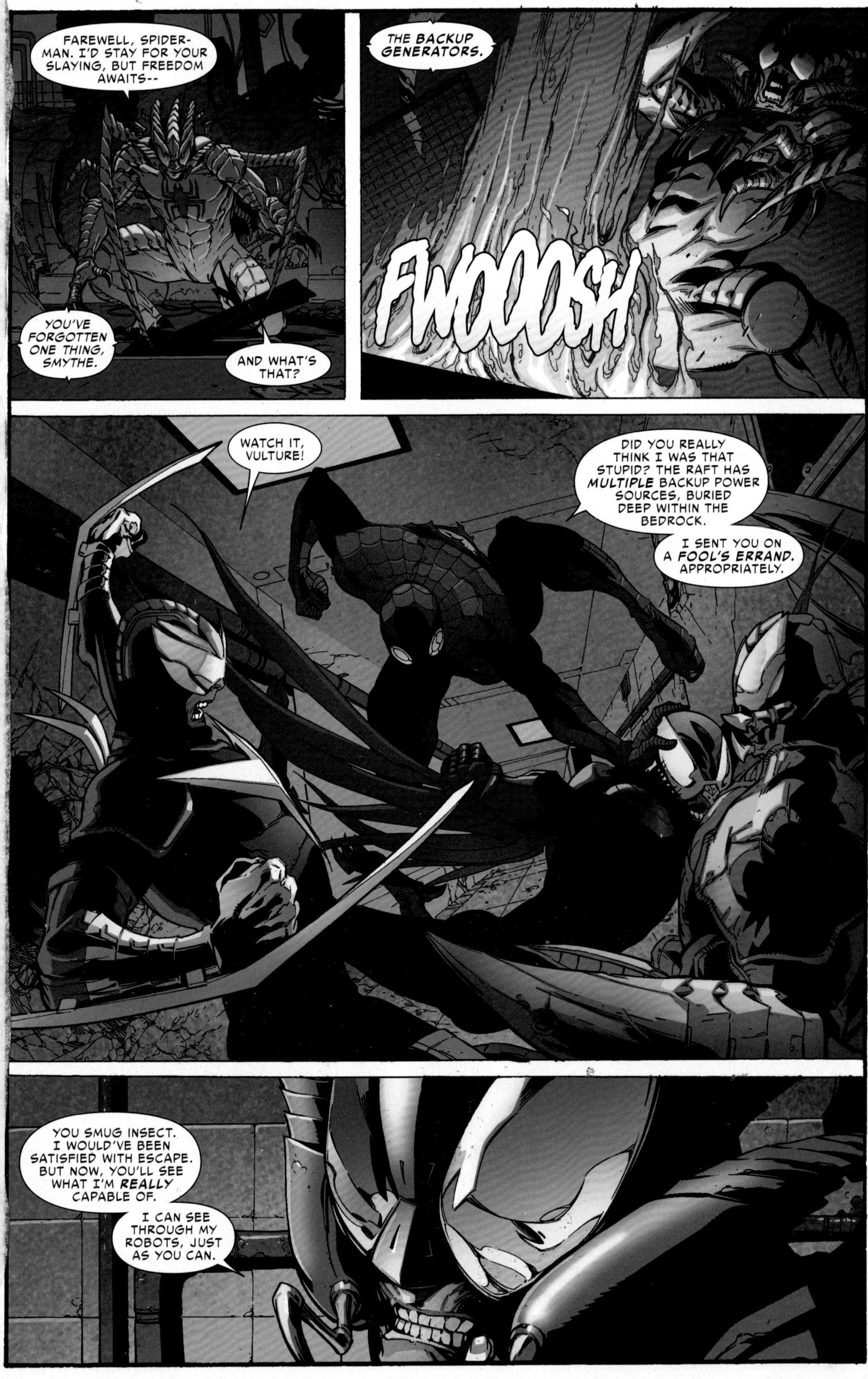

FAREWELL, SPIDER-MAN. I'D STAY FOR YOUR SLAYING, BUT FREEDOM AWAITS--
YOU'VE FORGOTTEN ONE THING, SMYTHE.
AND WHAT'S THAT?
THE BACKUP GENERATORS.
FWOOOSH
WATCH IT, VULTURE!
DID YOU REALLY THINK I WAS THAT STUPID? THE RAFT HAS MULTIPLE BACKUP POWER SOURCES, BURIED DEEP WITHIN THE BEDROCK.
I SENT YOU ON A FOOL'S ERRAND. APPROPRIATELY.
YOU SMUG INSECT. I WOULD'VE BEEN SATISFIED WITH ESCAPE. BUT NOW, YOU'LL SEE WHAT I'M REALLY CAPABLE OF.
I CAN SEE THROUGH MY ROBOTS, JUST AS YOU CAN.

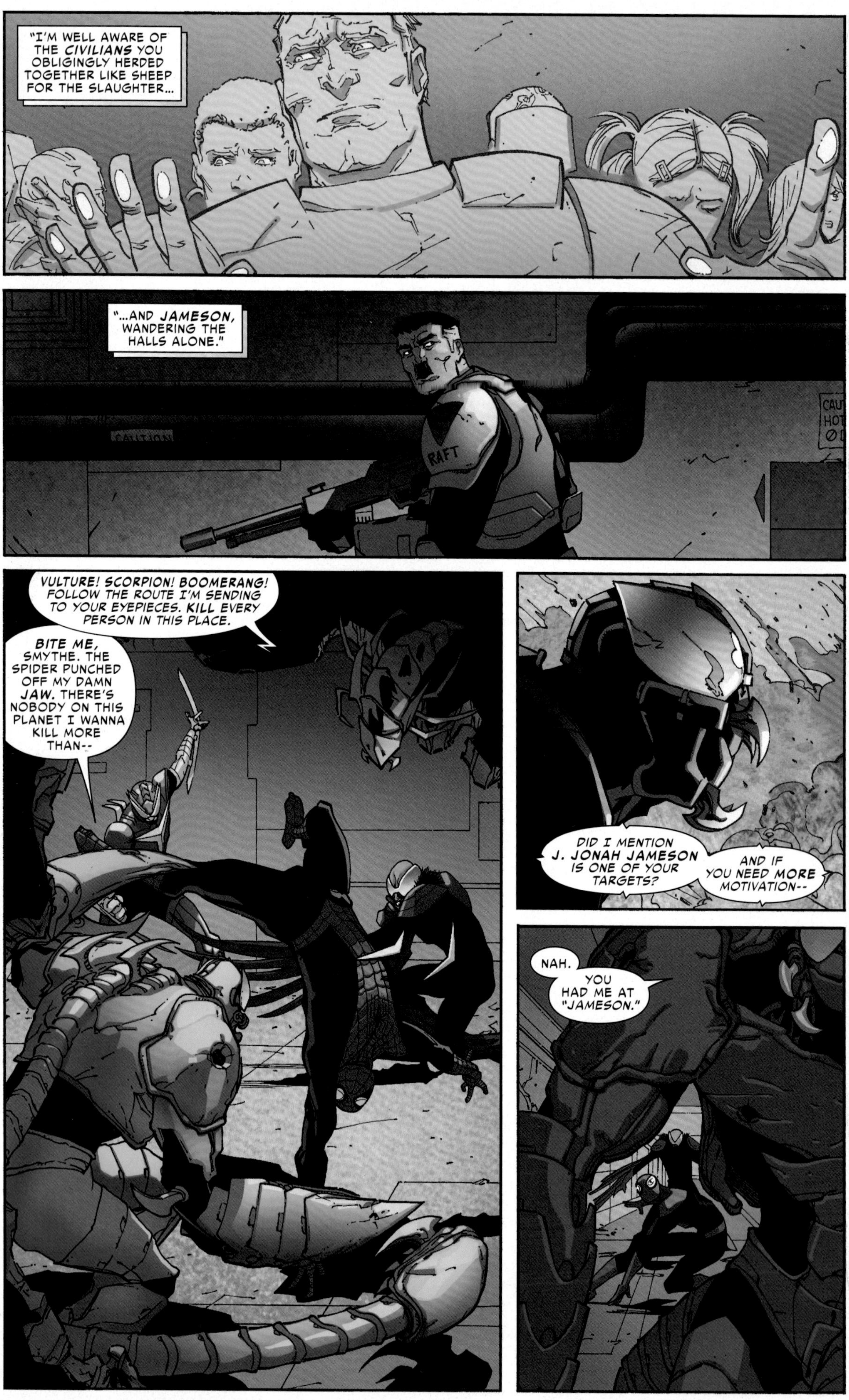
"I'M WELL AWARE OF THE CIVILIANS YOU OBLIGINGLY HERDED TOGETHER LIKE SHEEP FOR THE SLAUGHTER...
"...AND JAMESON, WANDERING THE HALLS ALONE."
RAFT
VULTURE! SCORPION! BOOMERANG! FOLLOW THE ROUTE I'M SENDING TO YOUR EYEPIECES. KILL EVERY PERSON IN THIS PLACE.
BITE ME, SMYTHE. THE SPIDER PUNCHED OFF MY DAMN JAW. THERE'S NOBODY ON THIS PLANET I WANNA KILL MORE THAN--
DID I MENTION J. JONAH JAMESON IS ONE OF YOUR TARGETS?
AND IF YOU NEED MORE MOTIVATION--
NAH.
YOU HAD ME AT "JAMESON."

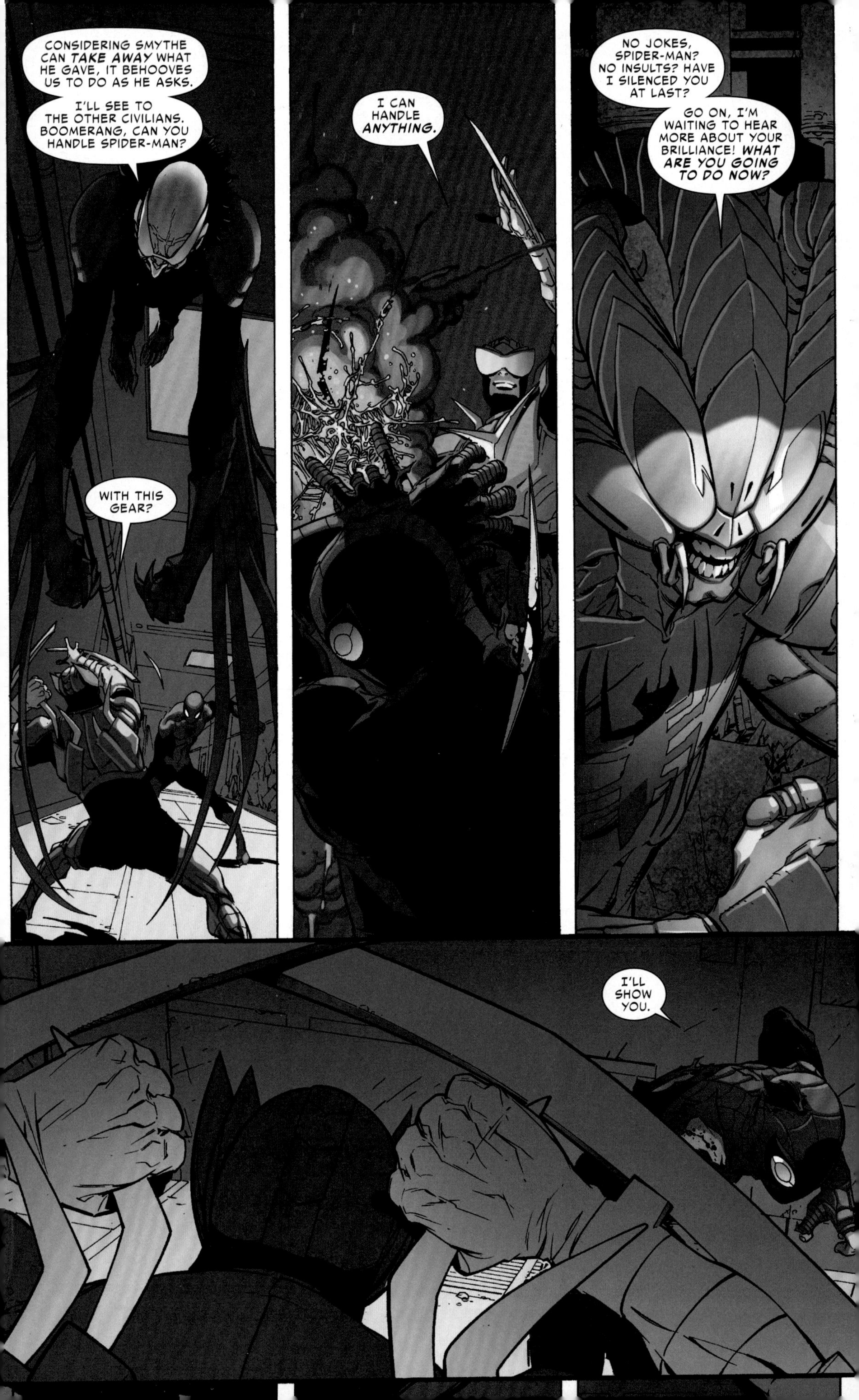
CONSIDERING SMYTHE CAN TAKE AWAY WHAT HE GAVE, IT BEHOOVES US TO DO AS HE ASKS.
I'LL SEE TO THE OTHER CIVILIANS. BOOMERANG, CAN YOU HANDLE SPIDER-MAN?
WITH THIS GEAR?
I CAN HANDLE ANYTHING.
NO JOKES, SPIDER-MAN? NO INSULTS? HAVE I SILENCED YOU AT LAST?
GO ON, I'M WAITING TO HEAR MORE ABOUT YOUR BRILLIANCE! WHAT ARE YOU GOING TO DO NOW?
I'LL SHOW YOU.

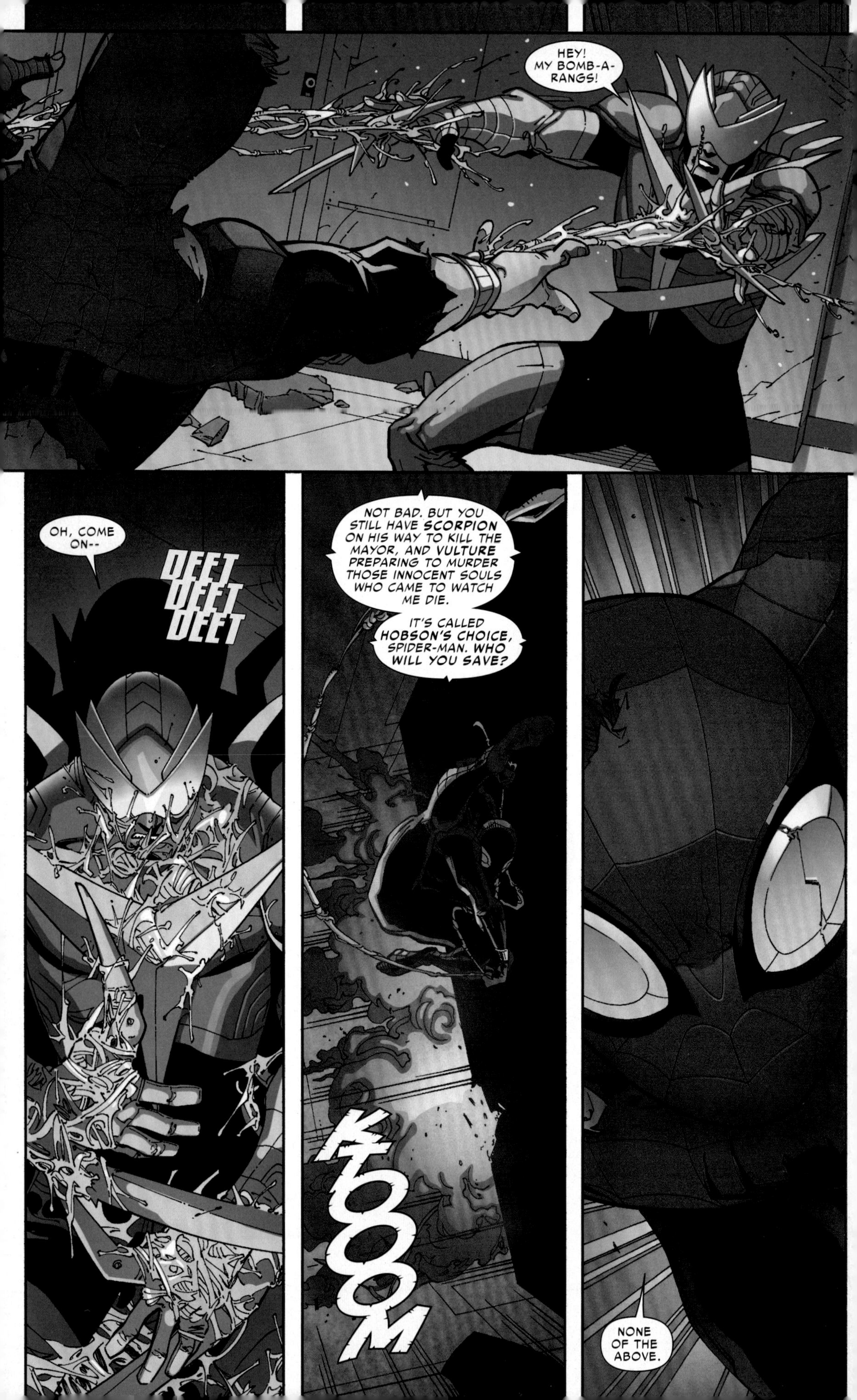
HEY! MY BOMB-A-RANGS!
OH, COME ON--
DEET DEET DEET
NOT BAD. BUT YOU STILL HAVE SCORPION ON HIS WAY TO KILL THE MAYOR, AND VULTURE PREPARING TO MURDER THOSE INNOCENT SOULS WHO CAME TO WATCH ME DIE.
IT'S CALLED HOBSON'S CHOICE, SPIDER-MAN. WHO WILL YOU SAVE?
KTOOOM
NONE OF THE ABOVE.

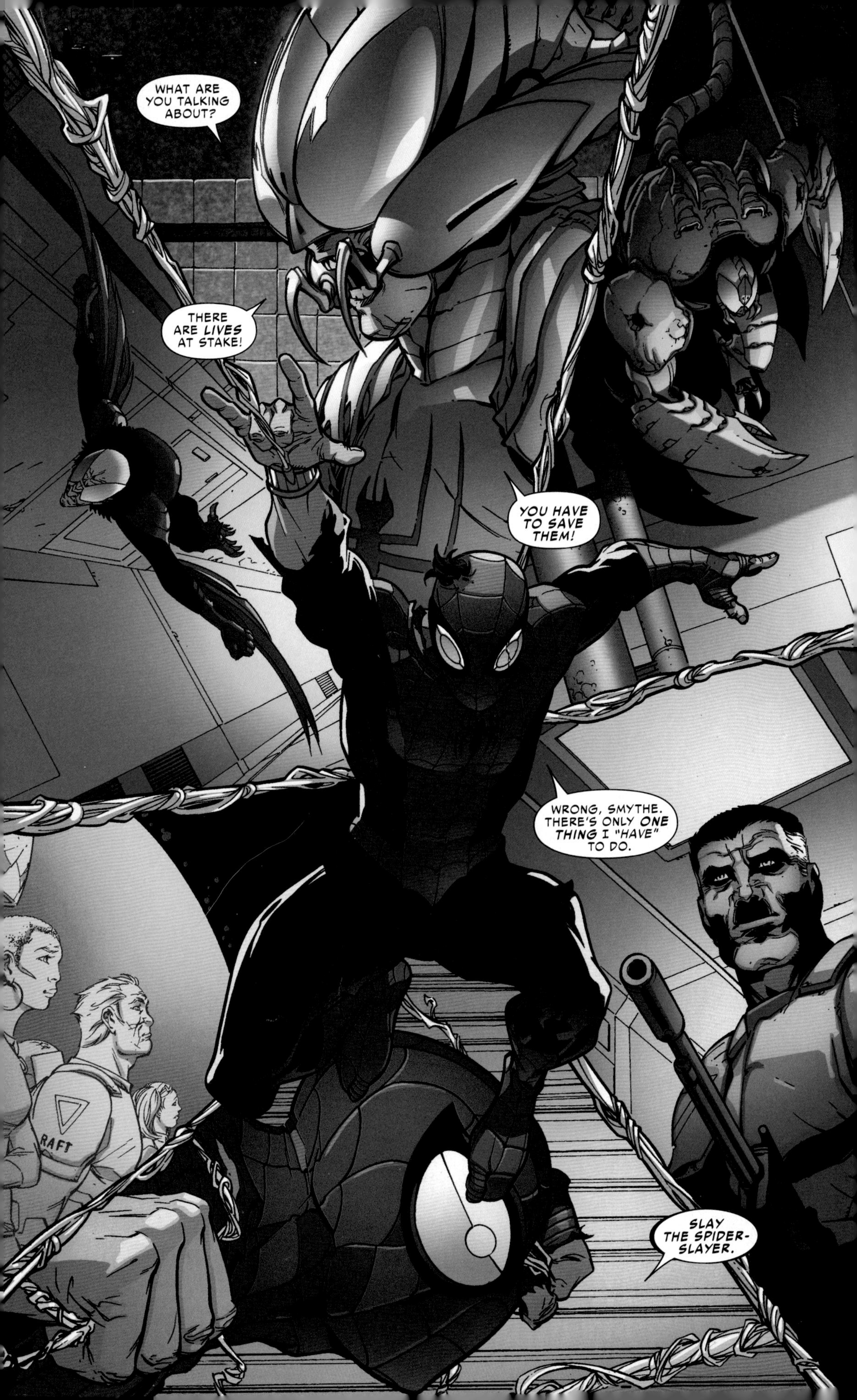
WHAT ARE YOU TALKING ABOUT?
THERE ARE *LIVES* AT STAKE!
YOU HAVE TO SAVE THEM!
WRONG, SMYTHE. THERE'S ONLY *ONE THING* I "HAVE" TO DO.
SLAY THE SPIDER-SLAYER.
RAFT

13

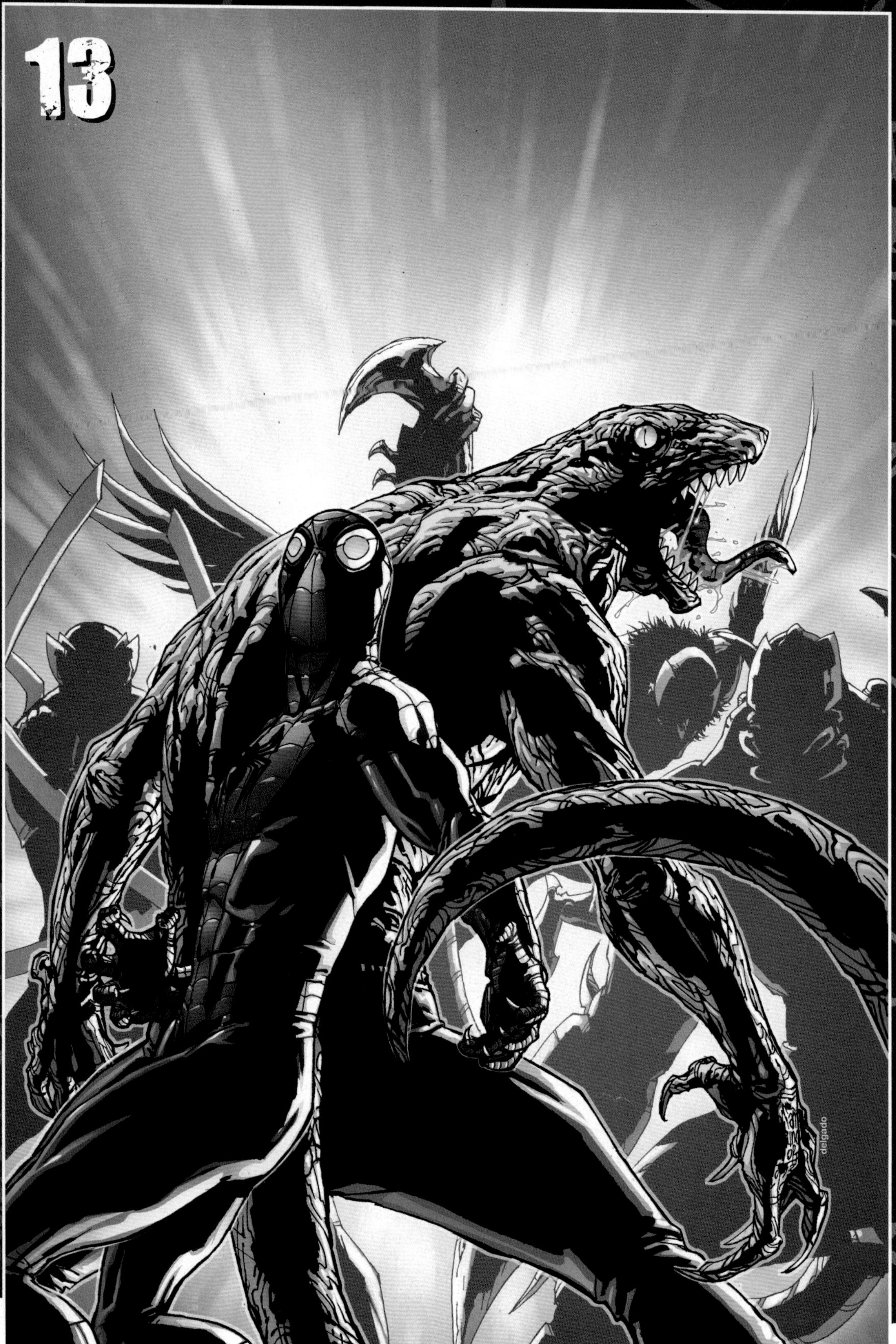
delgado

NO ESCAPE PART THREE: THE SLAYERS & THE SLAIN

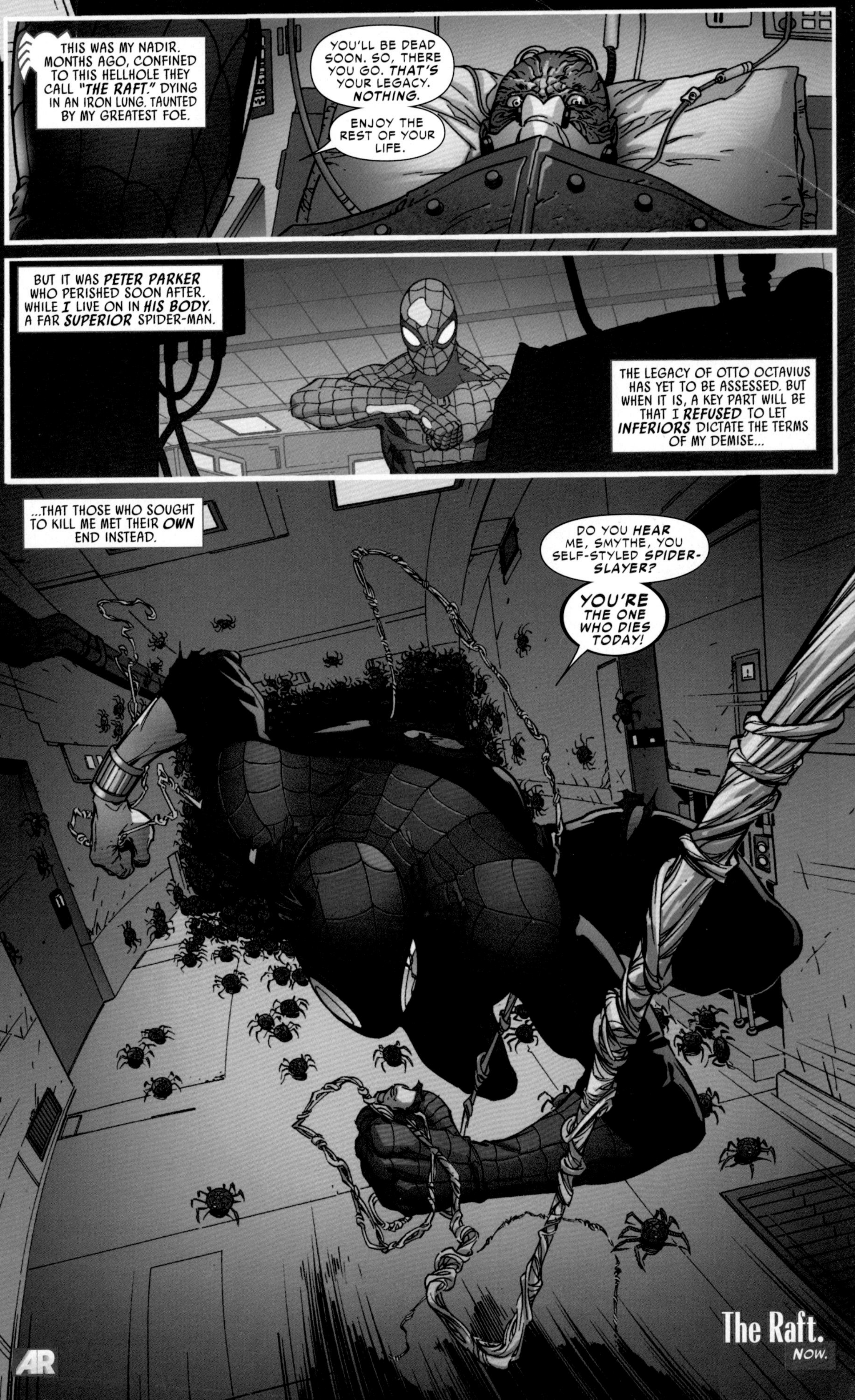
THIS WAS MY NADIR. MONTHS AGO, CONFINED TO THIS HELLHOLE THEY CALL "THE RAFT." DYING IN AN IRON LUNG. TAUNTED BY MY GREATEST FOE.
YOU'LL BE DEAD SOON. SO, THERE YOU GO. THAT'S YOUR LEGACY. NOTHING.
ENJOY THE REST OF YOUR LIFE.
BUT IT WAS PETER PARKER WHO PERISHED SOON AFTER. WHILE I LIVE ON IN HIS BODY. A FAR SUPERIOR SPIDER-MAN.
THE LEGACY OF OTTO OCTAVIUS HAS YET TO BE ASSESSED. BUT WHEN IT IS, A KEY PART WILL BE THAT I REFUSED TO LET INFERIORS DICTATE THE TERMS OF MY DEMISE...
...THAT THOSE WHO SOUGHT TO KILL ME MET THEIR OWN END INSTEAD.
DO YOU HEAR ME, SMYTHE, YOU SELF-STYLED SPIDER-SLAYER?
YOU'RE THE ONE WHO DIES TODAY!
The Raft.
NOW.

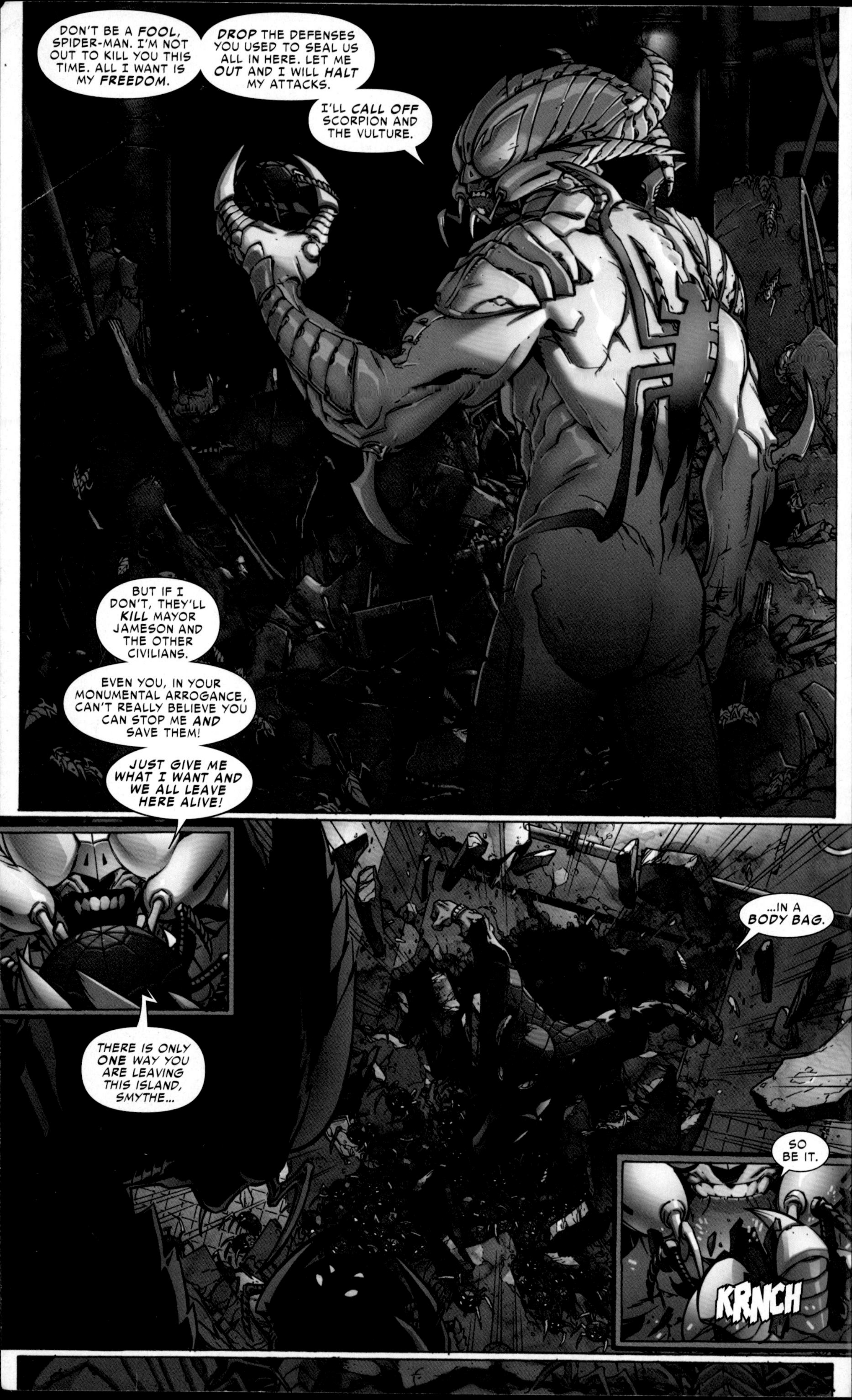
DON'T BE A FOOL, SPIDER-MAN. I'M NOT OUT TO KILL YOU THIS TIME. ALL I WANT IS MY FREEDOM.
DROP THE DEFENSES YOU USED TO SEAL US ALL IN HERE. LET ME OUT AND I WILL HALT MY ATTACKS.
I'LL CALL OFF SCORPION AND THE VULTURE.
BUT IF I DON'T, THEY'LL KILL MAYOR JAMESON AND THE OTHER CIVILIANS.
EVEN YOU, IN YOUR MONUMENTAL ARROGANCE, CAN'T REALLY BELIEVE YOU CAN STOP ME AND SAVE THEM!
JUST GIVE ME WHAT I WANT AND WE ALL LEAVE HERE ALIVE!
THERE IS ONLY ONE WAY YOU ARE LEAVING THIS ISLAND, SMYTHE...
...IN A BODY BAG.
SO BE IT.
KRNCH

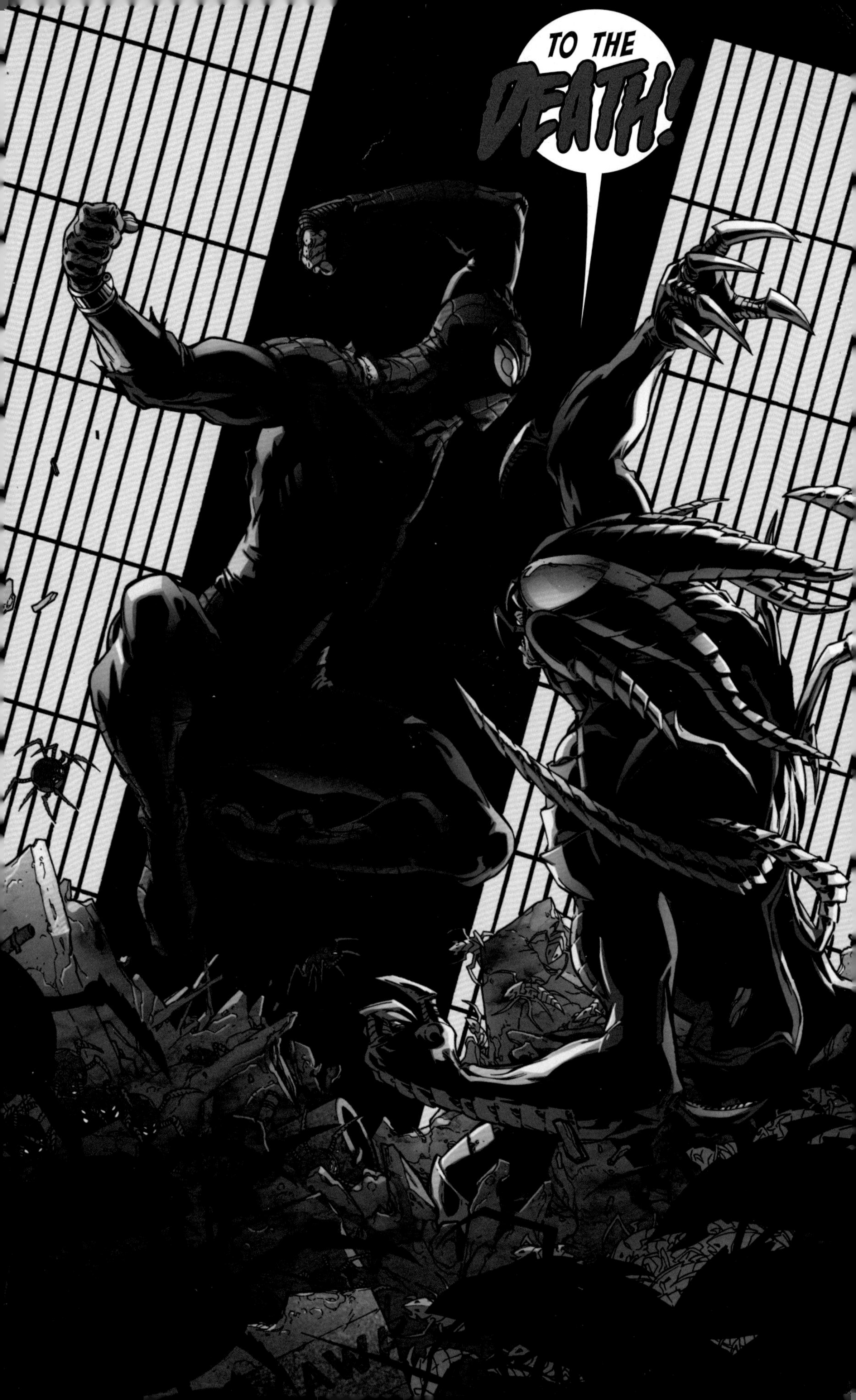
TO THE DEATH!

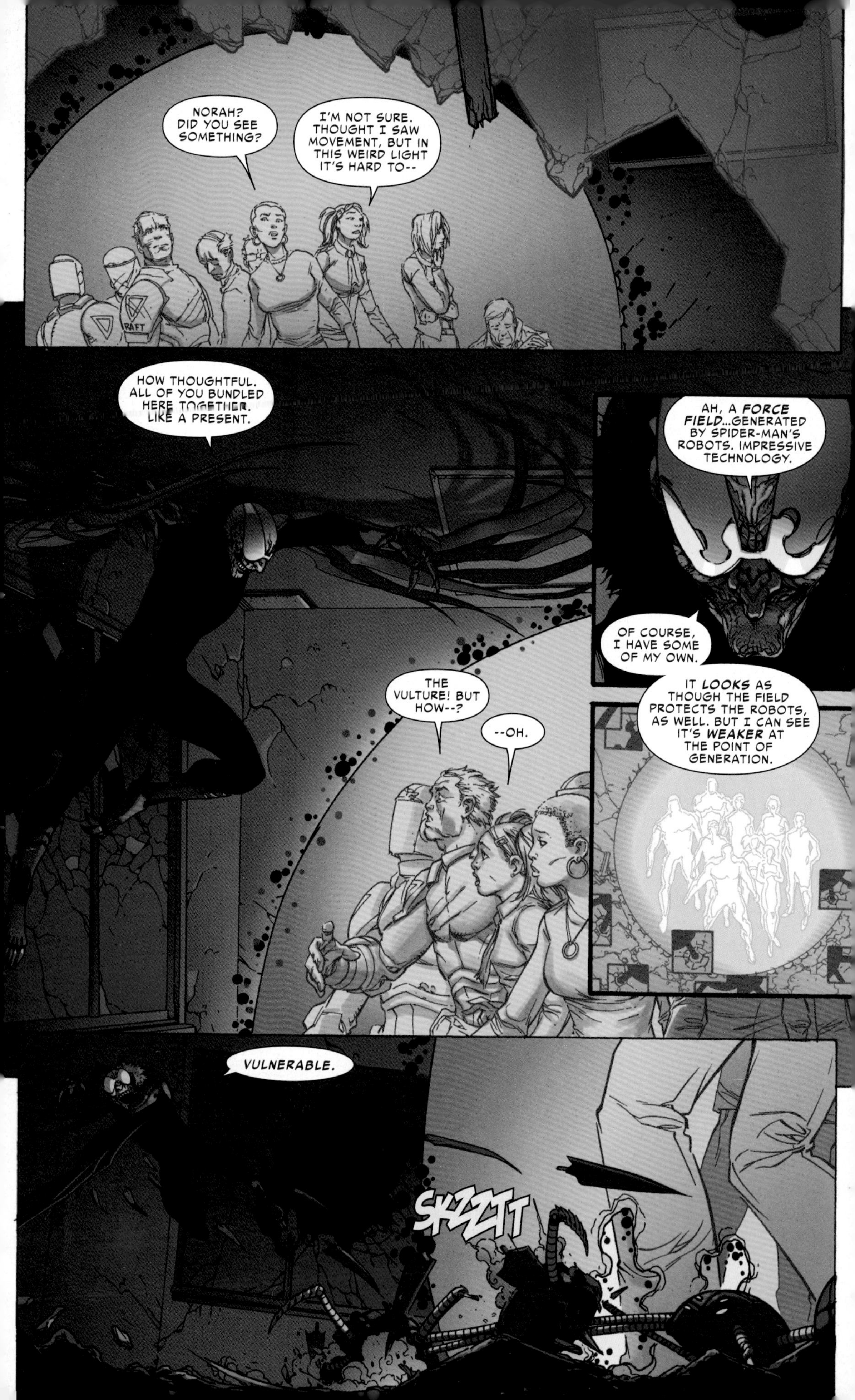
NORAH? DID YOU SEE SOMETHING?
I'M NOT SURE. THOUGHT I SAW MOVEMENT, BUT IN THIS WEIRD LIGHT IT'S HARD TO--
RAFT
HOW THOUGHTFUL. ALL OF YOU BUNDLED HERE TOGETHER. LIKE A PRESENT.
AH, A FORCE FIELD...GENERATED BY SPIDER-MAN'S ROBOTS. IMPRESSIVE TECHNOLOGY.
OF COURSE, I HAVE SOME OF MY OWN.
THE VULTURE! BUT HOW--?
--OH.
IT LOOKS AS THOUGH THE FIELD PROTECTS THE ROBOTS, AS WELL. BUT I CAN SEE IT'S WEAKER AT THE POINT OF GENERATION.
VULNERABLE.
SKZZTT

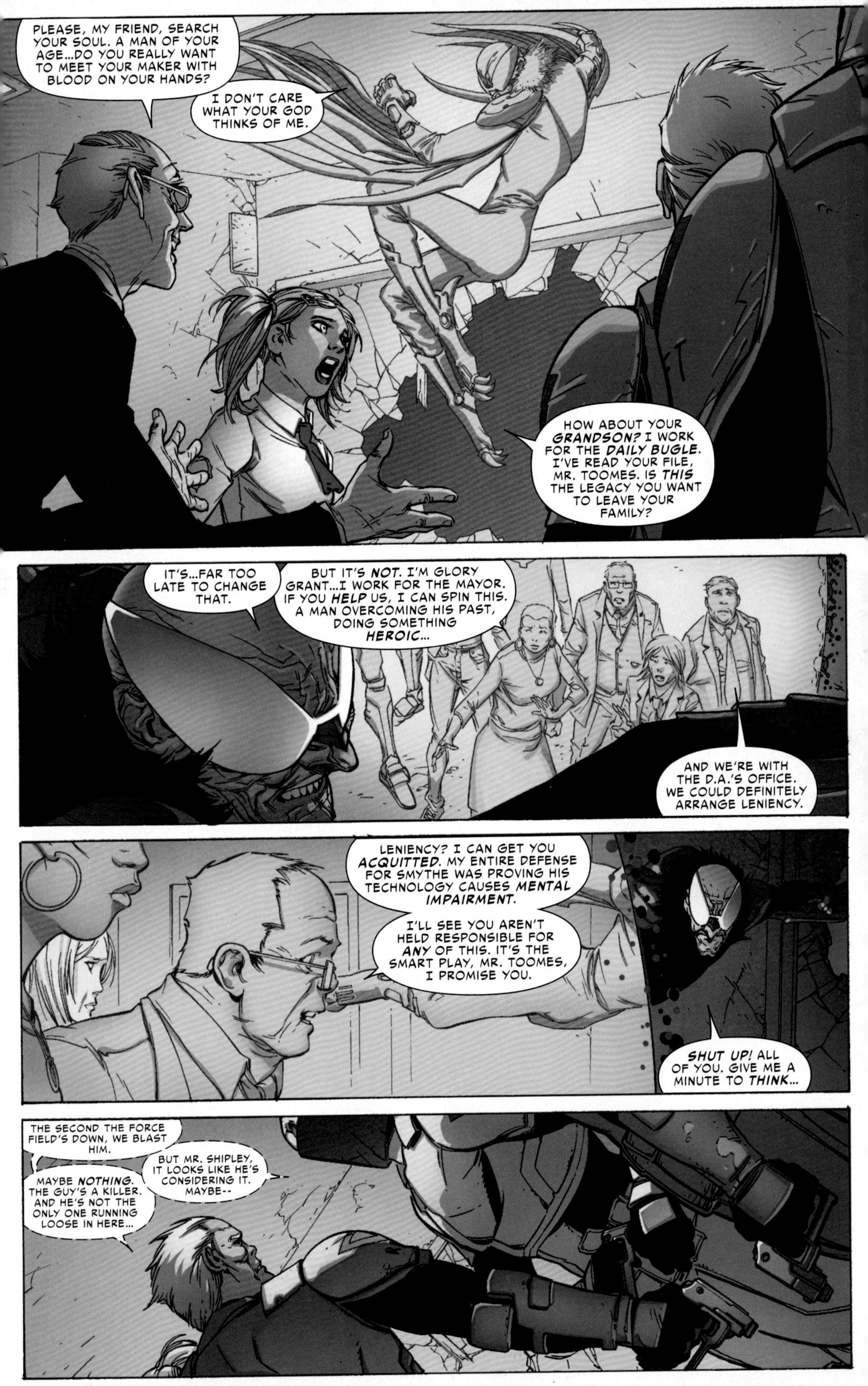

PLEASE, MY FRIEND, SEARCH YOUR SOUL. A MAN OF YOUR AGE...DO YOU REALLY WANT TO MEET YOUR MAKER WITH BLOOD ON YOUR HANDS?
I DON'T CARE WHAT YOUR GOD THINKS OF ME.
HOW ABOUT YOUR GRANDSON? I WORK FOR THE DAILY BUGLE. I'VE READ YOUR FILE, MR. TOOMES. IS THIS THE LEGACY YOU WANT TO LEAVE YOUR FAMILY?
IT'S...FAR TOO LATE TO CHANGE THAT.
BUT IT'S NOT. I'M GLORY GRANT...I WORK FOR THE MAYOR. IF YOU HELP US, I CAN SPIN THIS. A MAN OVERCOMING HIS PAST, DOING SOMETHING HEROIC...
AND WE'RE WITH THE D.A.'S OFFICE. WE COULD DEFINITELY ARRANGE LENIENCY.
LENIENCY? I CAN GET YOU ACQUITTED. MY ENTIRE DEFENSE FOR SMYTHE WAS PROVING HIS TECHNOLOGY CAUSES MENTAL IMPAIRMENT.
I'LL SEE YOU AREN'T HELD RESPONSIBLE FOR ANY OF THIS. IT'S THE SMART PLAY, MR. TOOMES, I PROMISE YOU.
SHUT UP! ALL OF YOU. GIVE ME A MINUTE TO THINK...
THE SECOND THE FORCE FIELD'S DOWN, WE BLAST HIM.
BUT MR. SHIPLEY, IT LOOKS LIKE HE'S CONSIDERING IT. MAYBE--
MAYBE NOTHING. THE GUY'S A KILLER. AND HE'S NOT THE ONLY ONE RUNNING LOOSE IN HERE...

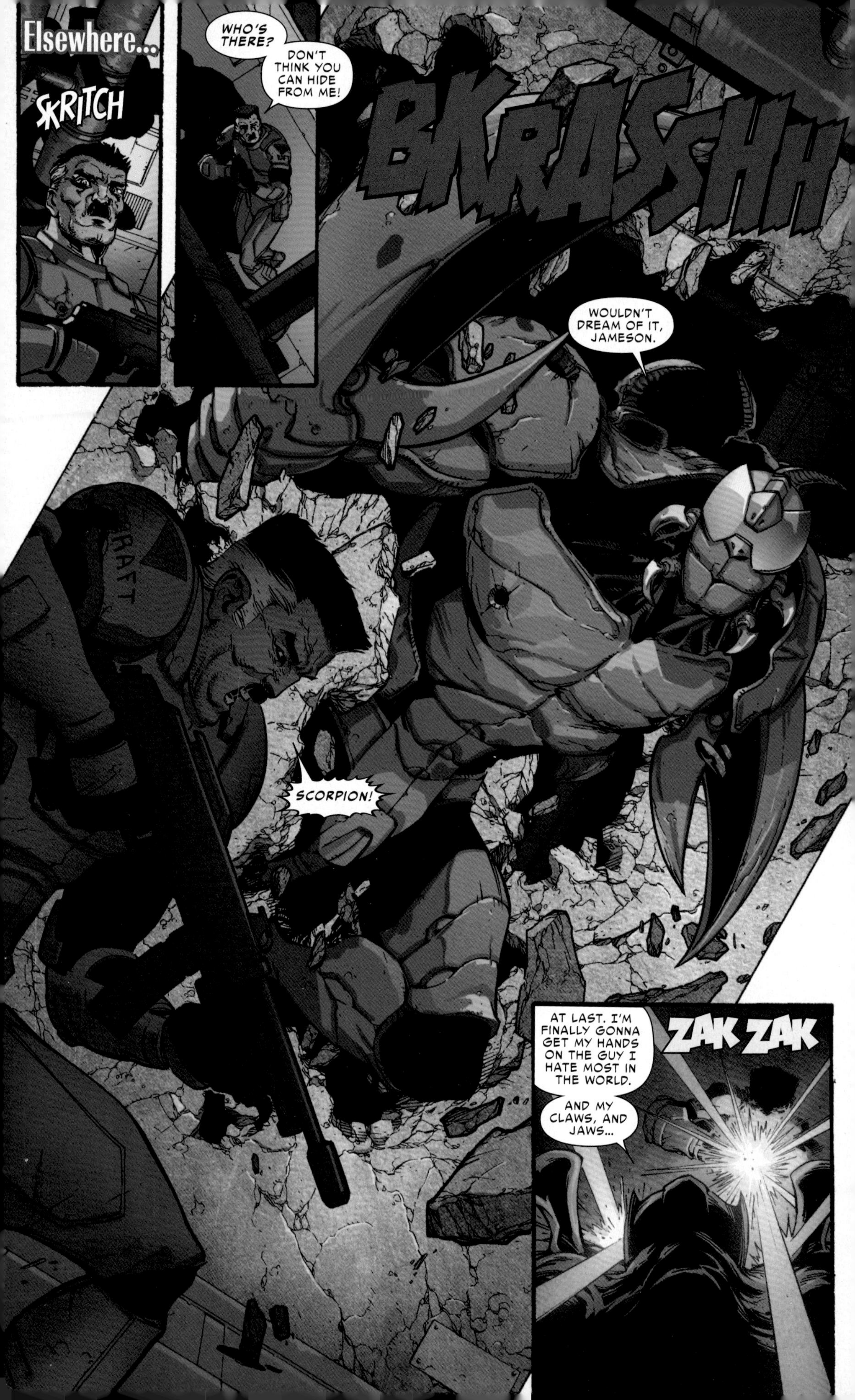
Elsewhere...
SKRITCH
WHO'S THERE?
DON'T THINK YOU CAN HIDE FROM ME!
BKRASHH
WOULDN'T DREAM OF IT, JAMESON.
RAFT
SCORPION!
AT LAST. I'M FINALLY GONNA GET MY HANDS ON THE GUY I HATE MOST IN THE WORLD.
AND MY CLAWS, AND JAWS...
ZAK ZAK

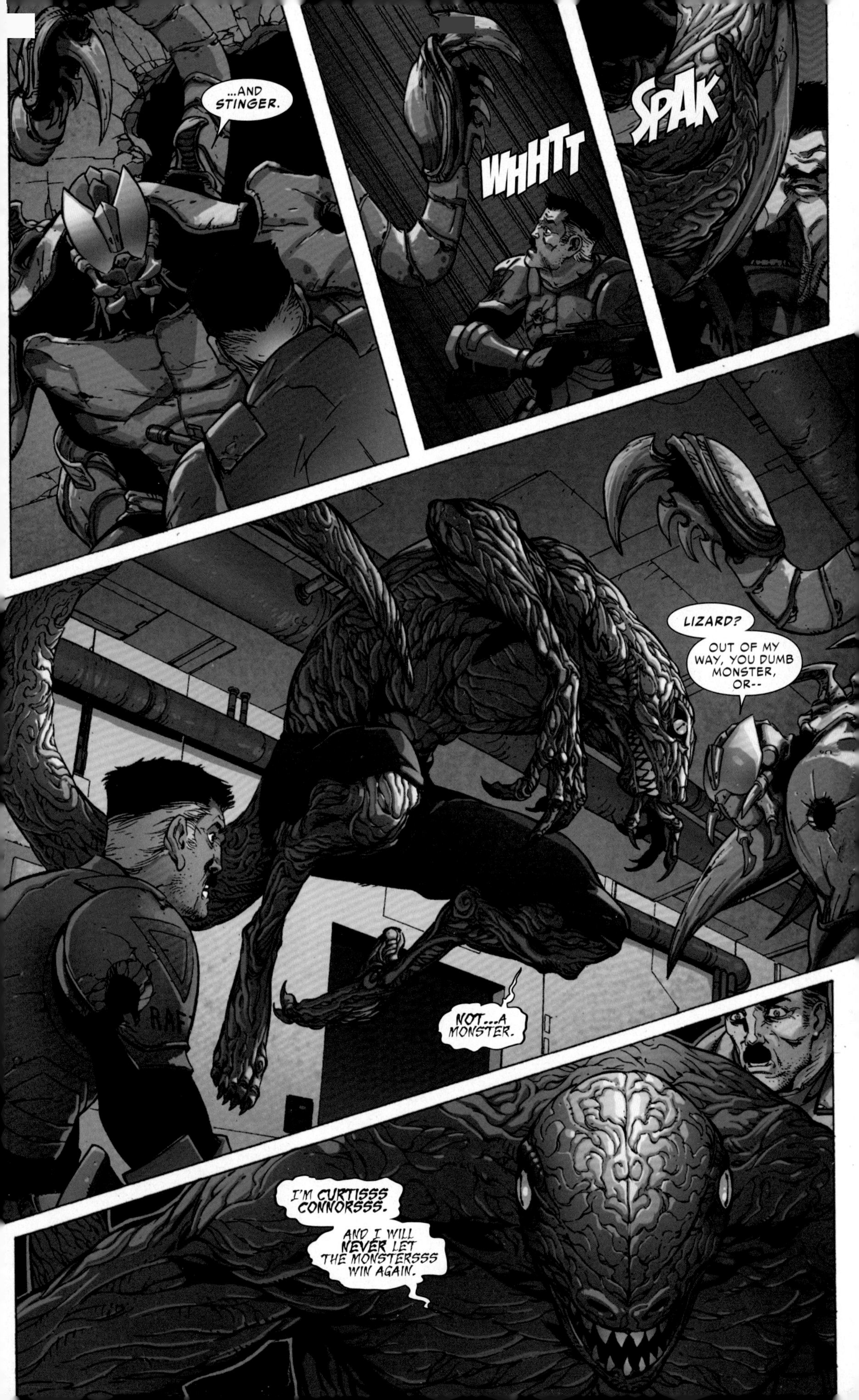
...AND STINGER.
WHHTT
SPAK
LIZARD?
OUT OF MY WAY, YOU DUMB MONSTER, OR--
NOT...A MONSTER.
I'M CURTISSS CONNORSSS.
AND I WILL NEVER LET THE MONSTERSSS WIN AGAIN.

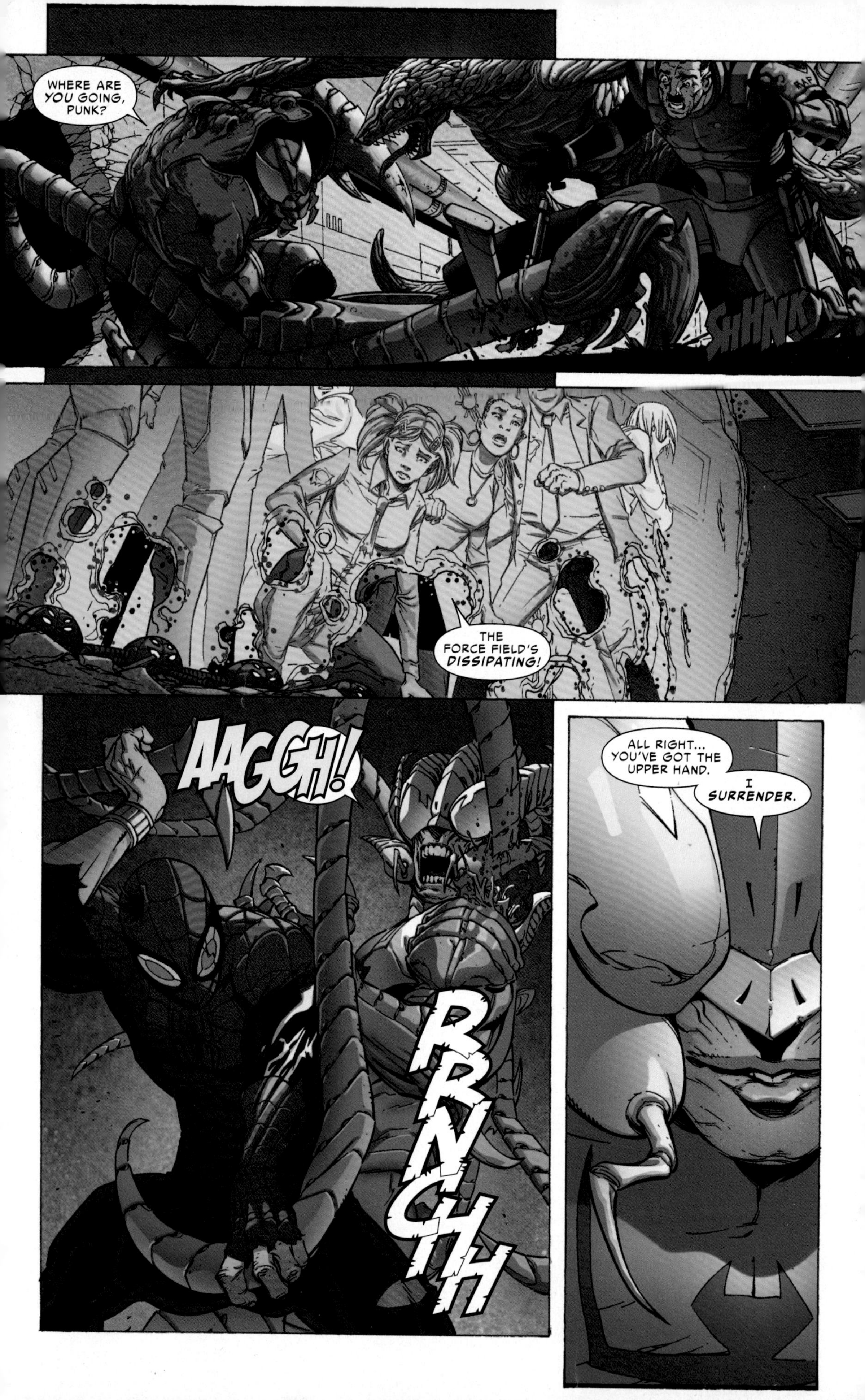
WHERE ARE YOU GOING, PUNK?
SHHNK
THE FORCE FIELD'S DISSIPATING!
AAGGH!
RRNCHH
ALL RIGHT... YOU'VE GOT THE UPPER HAND.
I SURRENDER.

OF COURSE, THE *CIVILIANS* ARE IN MORTAL DANGER. COULD BE KILLED AT ANY MOMENT.

SO IT'S TIME TO PUT YOUR NEWFOUND BRAVADO ASIDE, "*HERO*"...

...AND START *NEGOTIATING* TO SAVE THESE PEOPLE'S LIVES.

YOU *HAVE* BEEN LOCKED UP HERE TOO LONG, SMYTHE. THINGS HAVE CHANGED.

BUT IF YOU INSIST, I'LL GIVE YOU MY OPENING OFFER.

I THOUGHT YOU MIGHT--

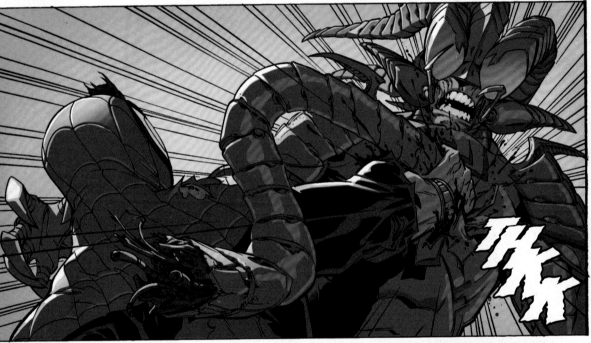

THKK

I...AM NOT IN THE HABIT OF TAKING LIVES, SMYTHE, BUT YOU LEFT ME NO CHOICE.

INNOCENT LIVES WERE IN DANGER FROM *YOUR* CYBER-MONSTROSITIES.

AND SINCE I'D *NEVER* TRUST A MURDEROUS PSYCHOPATH LIKE YOU TO DISARM THEM...

PERMANENTLY SHUTTING *YOU* DOWN WAS THE ONLY SOLUTION. THE ONLY WAY TO SAVE THEM ALL.

KRNSH

HOW COULD YOU *NOT* SEE THAT?

IDIOT.

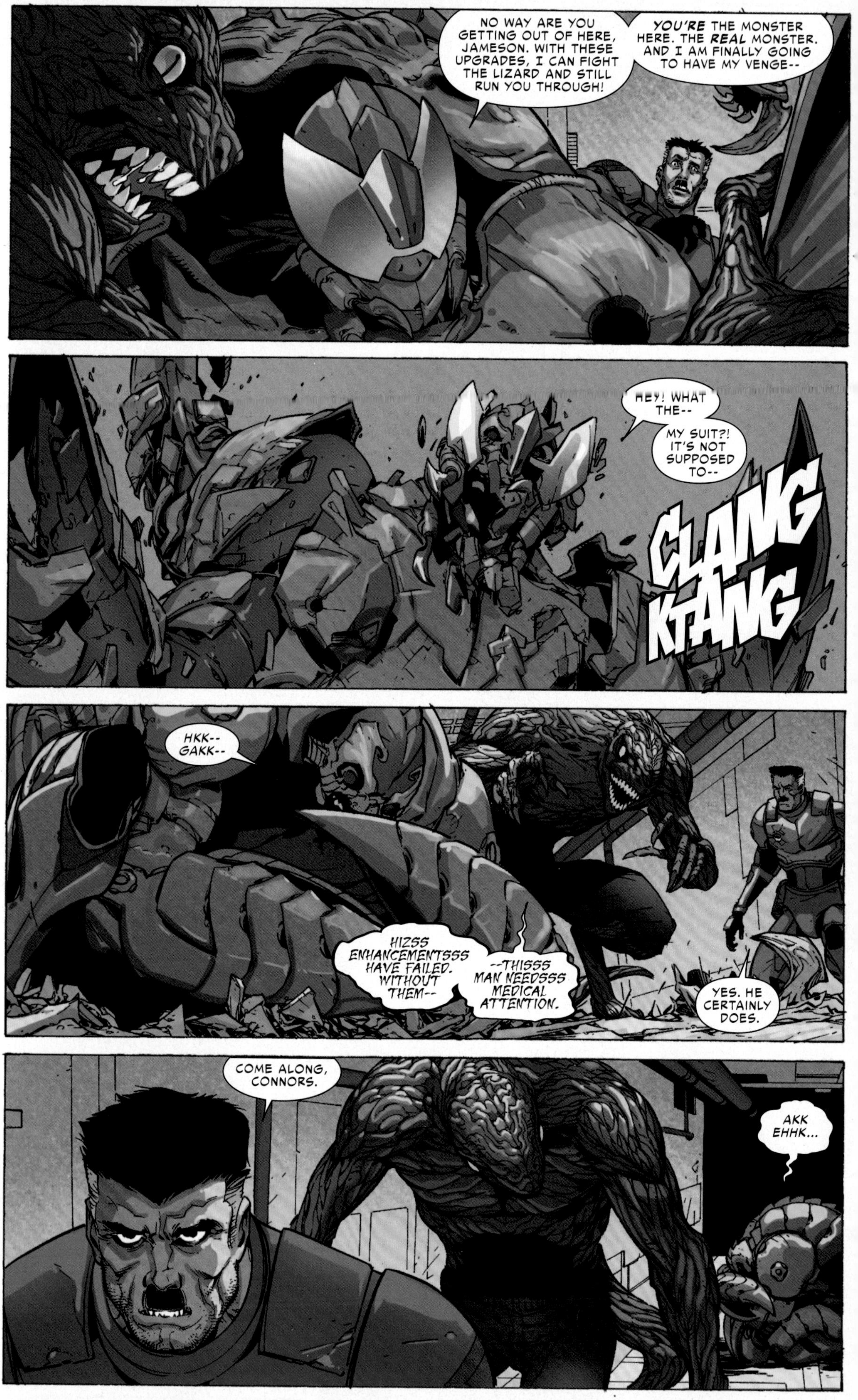
NO WAY ARE YOU GETTING OUT OF HERE, JAMESON. WITH THESE UPGRADES, I CAN FIGHT THE LIZARD AND STILL RUN YOU THROUGH!
YOU'RE THE MONSTER HERE. THE REAL MONSTER. AND I AM FINALLY GOING TO HAVE MY VENGE--
HEY! WHAT THE--
MY SUIT?! IT'S NOT SUPPOSED TO--
CLANG
KTANG
HKK-- GAKK--
HIZSS ENHANCEMENTSSS HAVE FAILED. WITHOUT THEM--
--THISSS MAN NEEDSSS MEDICAL ATTENTION.
YES. HE CERTAINLY DOES.
COME ALONG, CONNORS.
AKK EHHK...

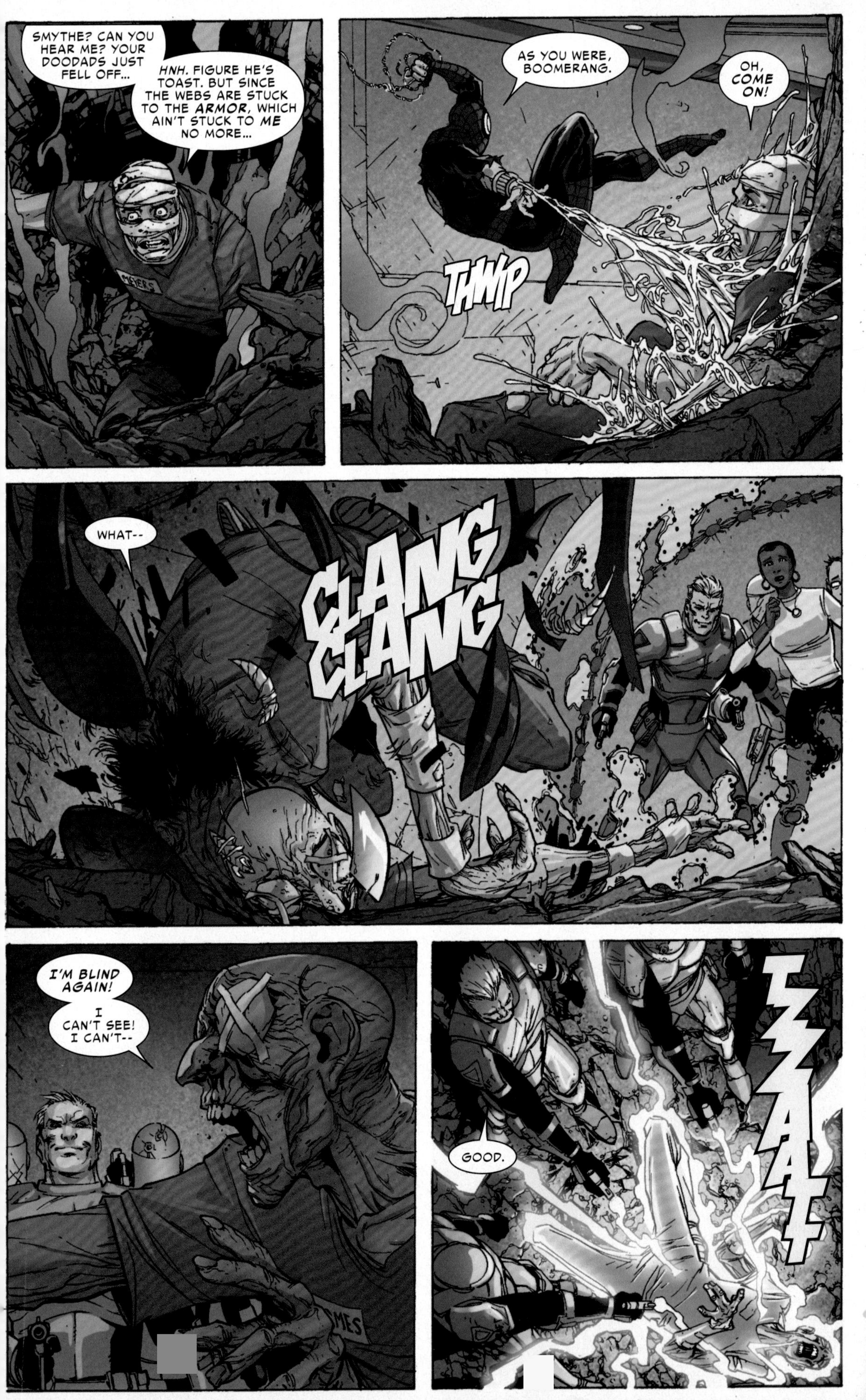
SMYTHE? CAN YOU HEAR ME? YOUR DOODADS JUST FELL OFF...
HNH. FIGURE HE'S TOAST. BUT SINCE THE WEBS ARE STUCK TO THE ARMOR, WHICH AIN'T STUCK TO ME NO MORE...
MEYERS
AS YOU WERE, BOOMERANG.
OH, COME ON!
THWIP
WHAT--
CLANG CLANG
I'M BLIND AGAIN!
I CAN'T SEE! I CAN'T--
GOOD.
TZZAAT

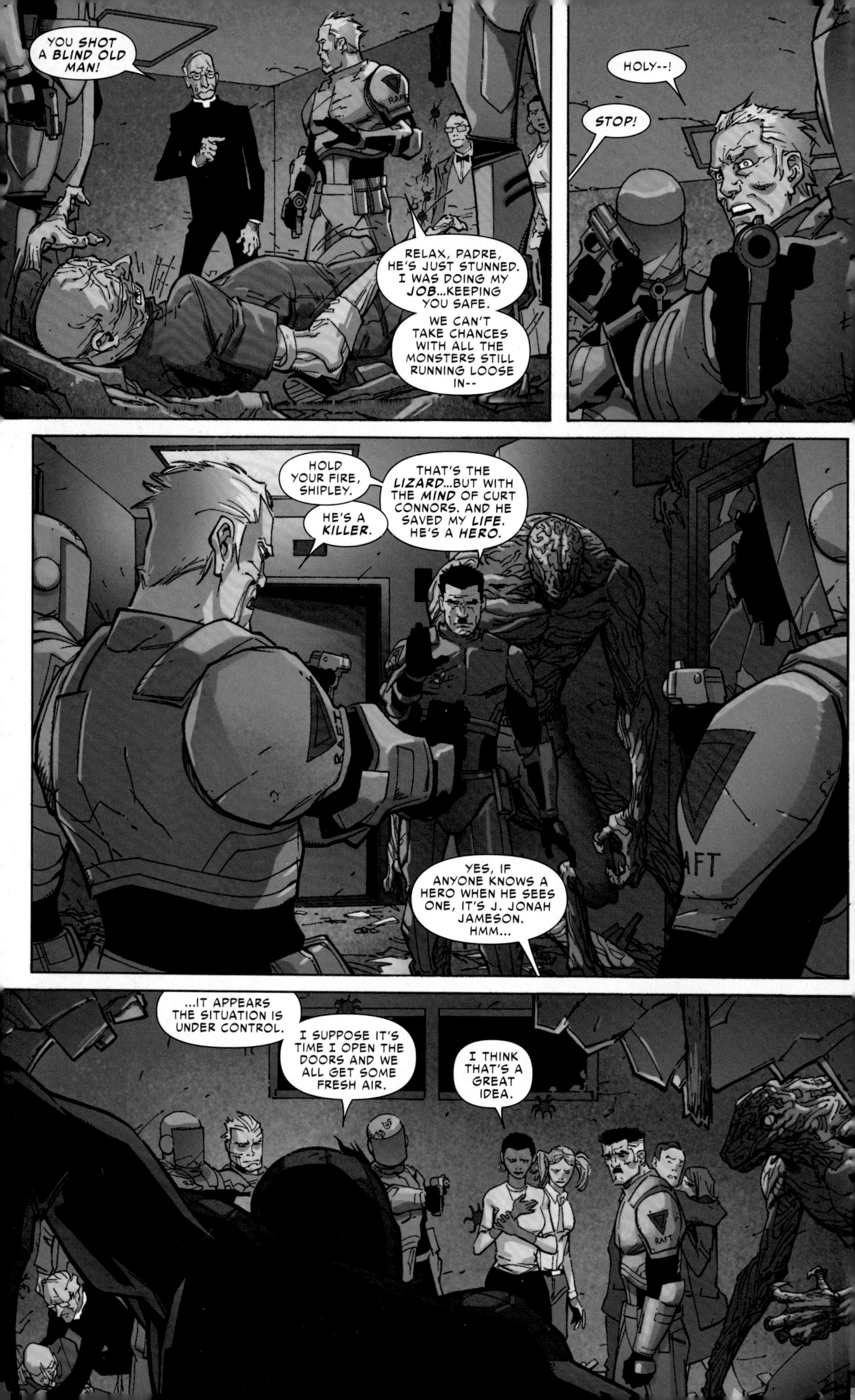
YOU SHOT A BLIND OLD MAN!
RELAX, PADRE, HE'S JUST STUNNED. I WAS DOING MY JOB...KEEPING YOU SAFE.
WE CAN'T TAKE CHANCES WITH ALL THE MONSTERS STILL RUNNING LOOSE IN--
HOLY--!
STOP!
HOLD YOUR FIRE, SHIPLEY.
HE'S A KILLER.
THAT'S THE LIZARD...BUT WITH THE MIND OF CURT CONNORS. AND HE SAVED MY LIFE. HE'S A HERO.
YES, IF ANYONE KNOWS A HERO WHEN HE SEES ONE, IT'S J. JONAH JAMESON. HMM...
...IT APPEARS THE SITUATION IS UNDER CONTROL.
I SUPPOSE IT'S TIME I OPEN THE DOORS AND WE ALL GET SOME FRESH AIR.
I THINK THAT'S A GREAT IDEA.

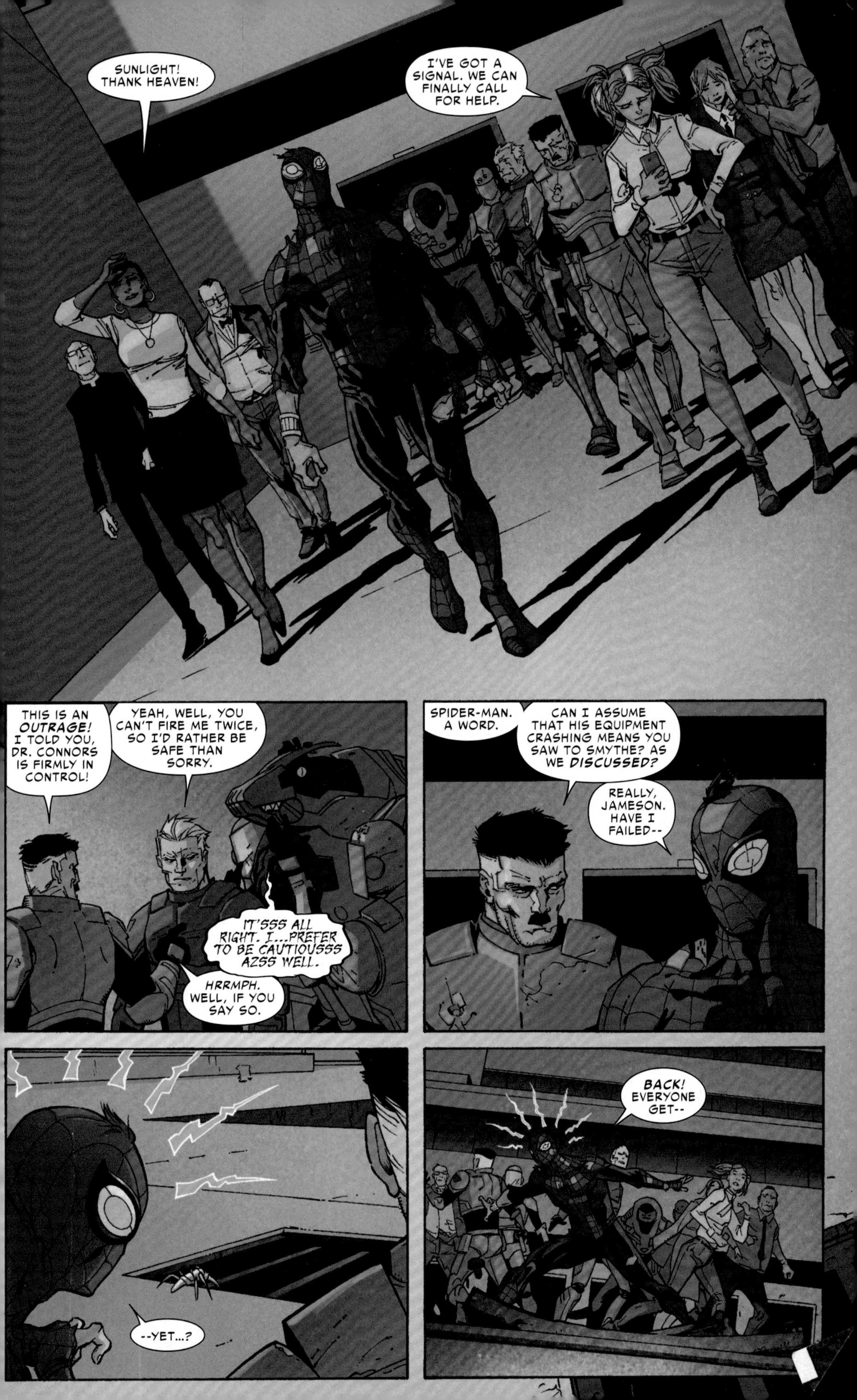
SUNLIGHT! THANK HEAVEN!
I'VE GOT A SIGNAL. WE CAN FINALLY CALL FOR HELP.
THIS IS AN OUTRAGE! I TOLD YOU, DR. CONNORS IS FIRMLY IN CONTROL!
YEAH, WELL, YOU CAN'T FIRE ME TWICE, SO I'D RATHER BE SAFE THAN SORRY.
IT'SSS ALL RIGHT. I...PREFER TO BE CAUTIOUSSS AZSS WELL.
HRRMPH. WELL, IF YOU SAY SO.
SPIDER-MAN. A WORD.
CAN I ASSUME THAT HIS EQUIPMENT CRASHING MEANS YOU SAW TO SMYTHE? AS WE DISCUSSED?
REALLY, JAMESON. HAVE I FAILED--
--YET...?
BACK! EVERYONE GET--

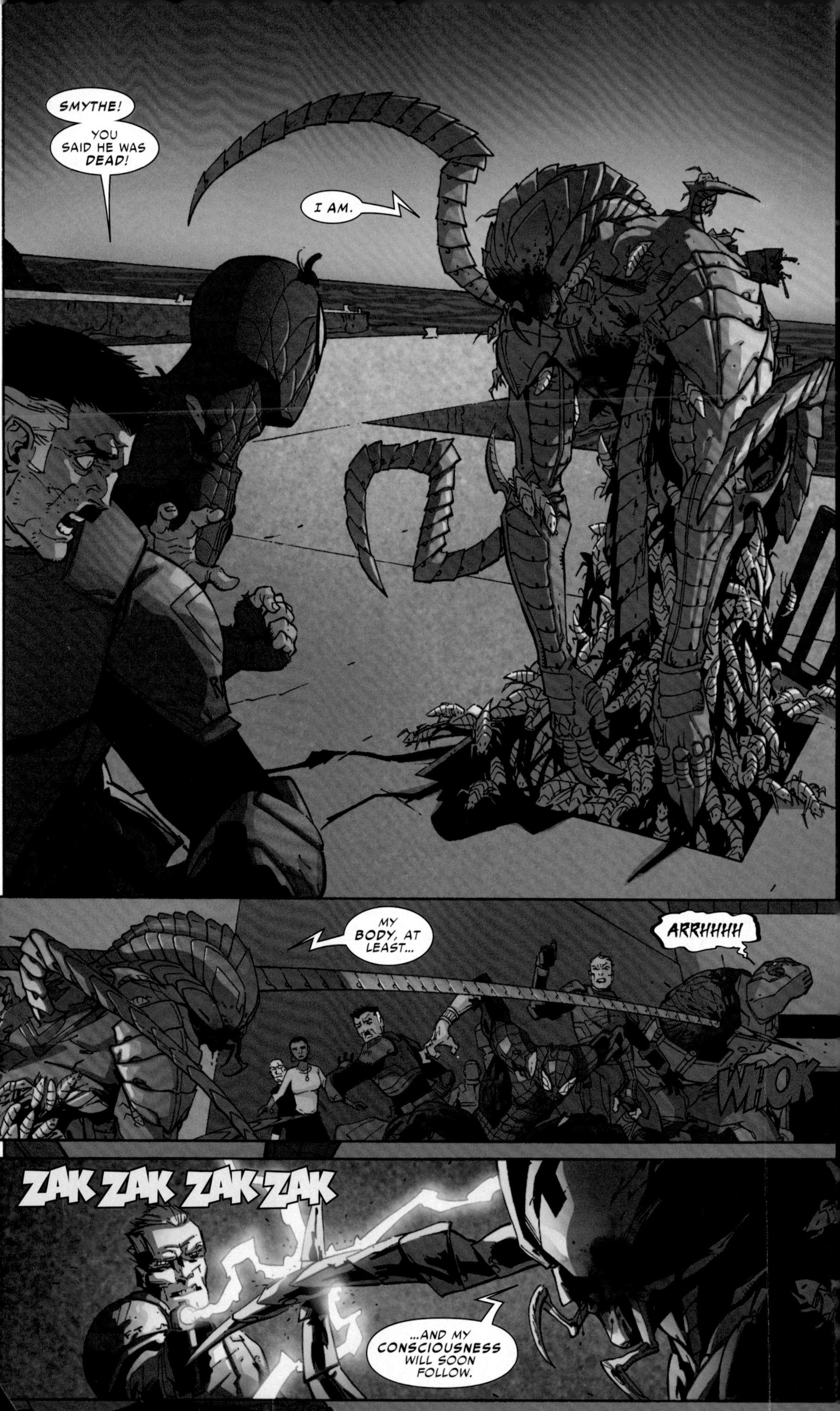
SMYTHE!
YOU SAID HE WAS DEAD!
I AM.
MY BODY, AT LEAST...
ARRHHHH
WHOK
ZAK ZAK ZAK ZAK
...AND MY CONSCIOUSNESS WILL SOON FOLLOW.

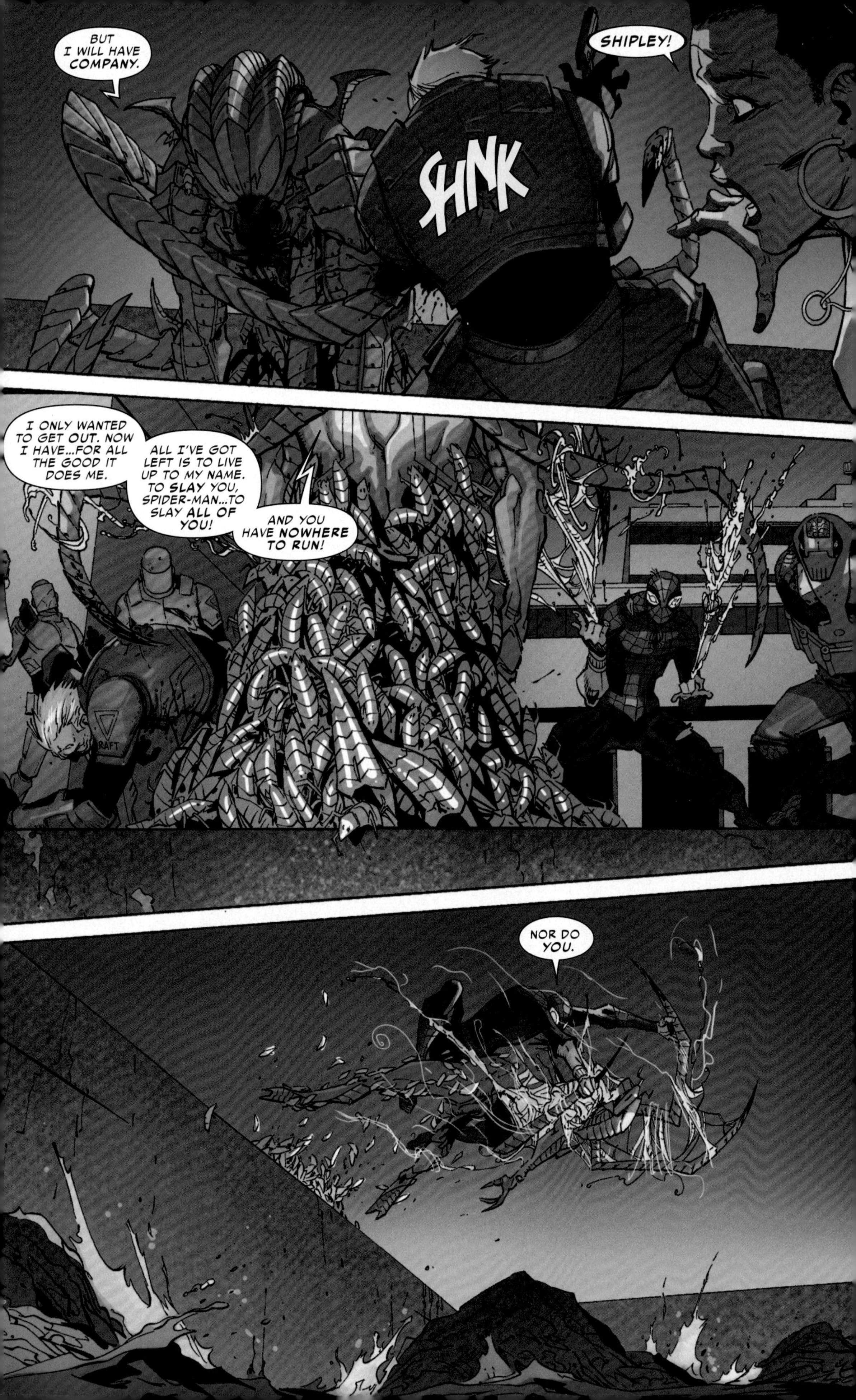
BUT I WILL HAVE COMPANY.
SHIPLEY!
SHNK
I ONLY WANTED TO GET OUT. NOW I HAVE...FOR ALL THE GOOD IT DOES ME.
ALL I'VE GOT LEFT IS TO LIVE UP TO MY NAME. TO SLAY YOU, SPIDER-MAN...TO SLAY ALL OF YOU!
AND YOU HAVE NOWHERE TO RUN!
RAFT
NOR DO YOU.

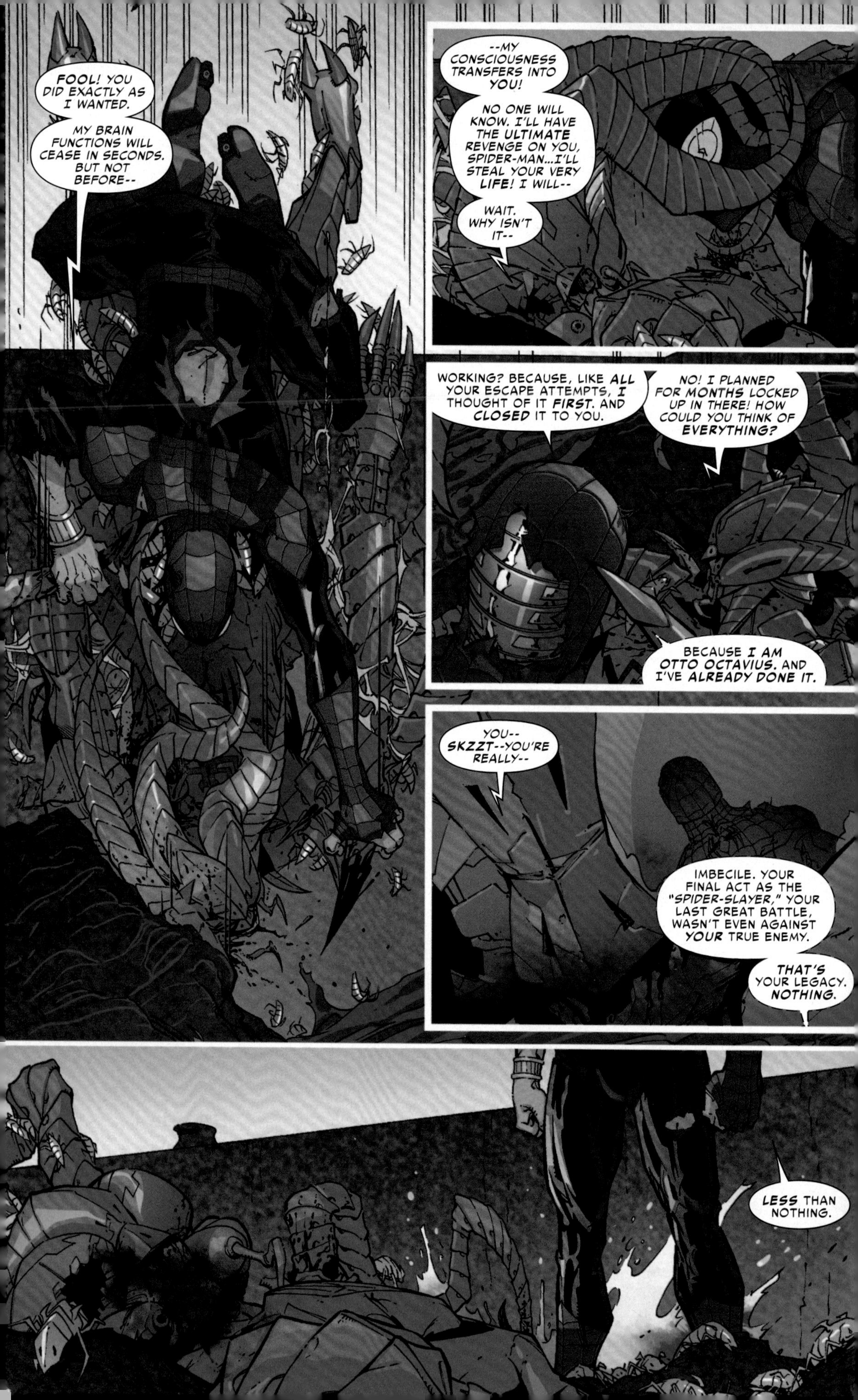
FOOL! YOU DID EXACTLY AS I WANTED.
MY BRAIN FUNCTIONS WILL CEASE IN SECONDS. BUT NOT BEFORE--
--MY CONSCIOUSNESS TRANSFERS INTO YOU!
NO ONE WILL KNOW. I'LL HAVE THE ULTIMATE REVENGE ON YOU, SPIDER-MAN...I'LL STEAL YOUR VERY LIFE! I WILL--
WAIT. WHY ISN'T IT--
WORKING? BECAUSE, LIKE ALL YOUR ESCAPE ATTEMPTS, I THOUGHT OF IT FIRST. AND CLOSED IT TO YOU.
NO! I PLANNED FOR MONTHS LOCKED UP IN THERE! HOW COULD YOU THINK OF EVERYTHING?
BECAUSE I AM OTTO OCTAVIUS. AND I'VE ALREADY DONE IT.
YOU-- SKZZT--YOU'RE REALLY--
IMBECILE. YOUR FINAL ACT AS THE "SPIDER-SLAYER," YOUR LAST GREAT BATTLE, WASN'T EVEN AGAINST YOUR TRUE ENEMY.
THAT'S YOUR LEGACY. NOTHING.
LESS THAN NOTHING.

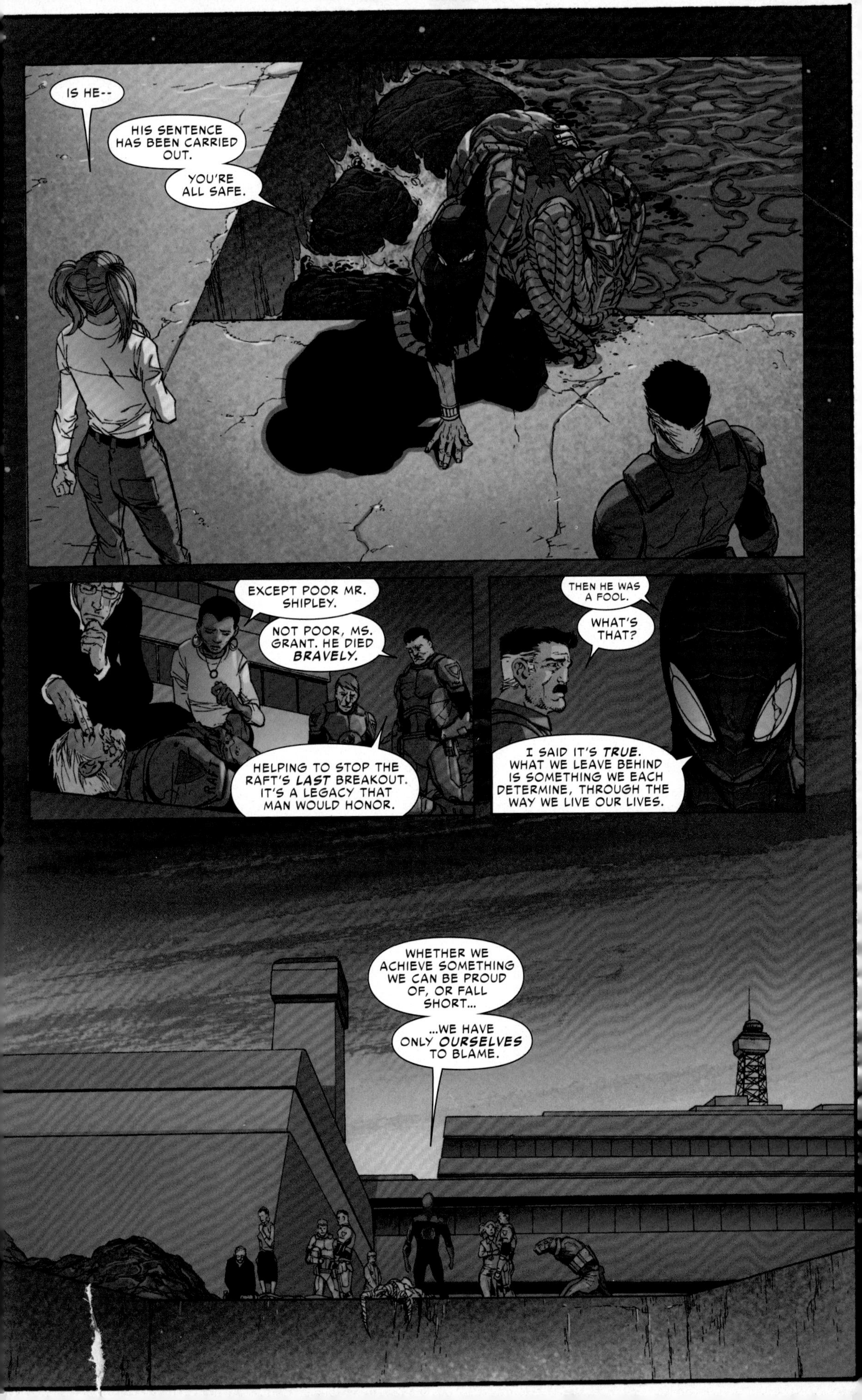
IS HE--
HIS SENTENCE HAS BEEN CARRIED OUT.
YOU'RE ALL SAFE.
EXCEPT POOR MR. SHIPLEY.
NOT POOR, MS. GRANT. HE DIED BRAVELY.
HELPING TO STOP THE RAFT'S LAST BREAKOUT. IT'S A LEGACY THAT MAN WOULD HONOR.
THEN HE WAS A FOOL.
WHAT'S THAT?
I SAID IT'S TRUE. WHAT WE LEAVE BEHIND IS SOMETHING WE EACH DETERMINE, THROUGH THE WAY WE LIVE OUR LIVES.
WHETHER WE ACHIEVE SOMETHING WE CAN BE PROUD OF, OR FALL SHORT...
...WE HAVE ONLY OURSELVES TO BLAME.

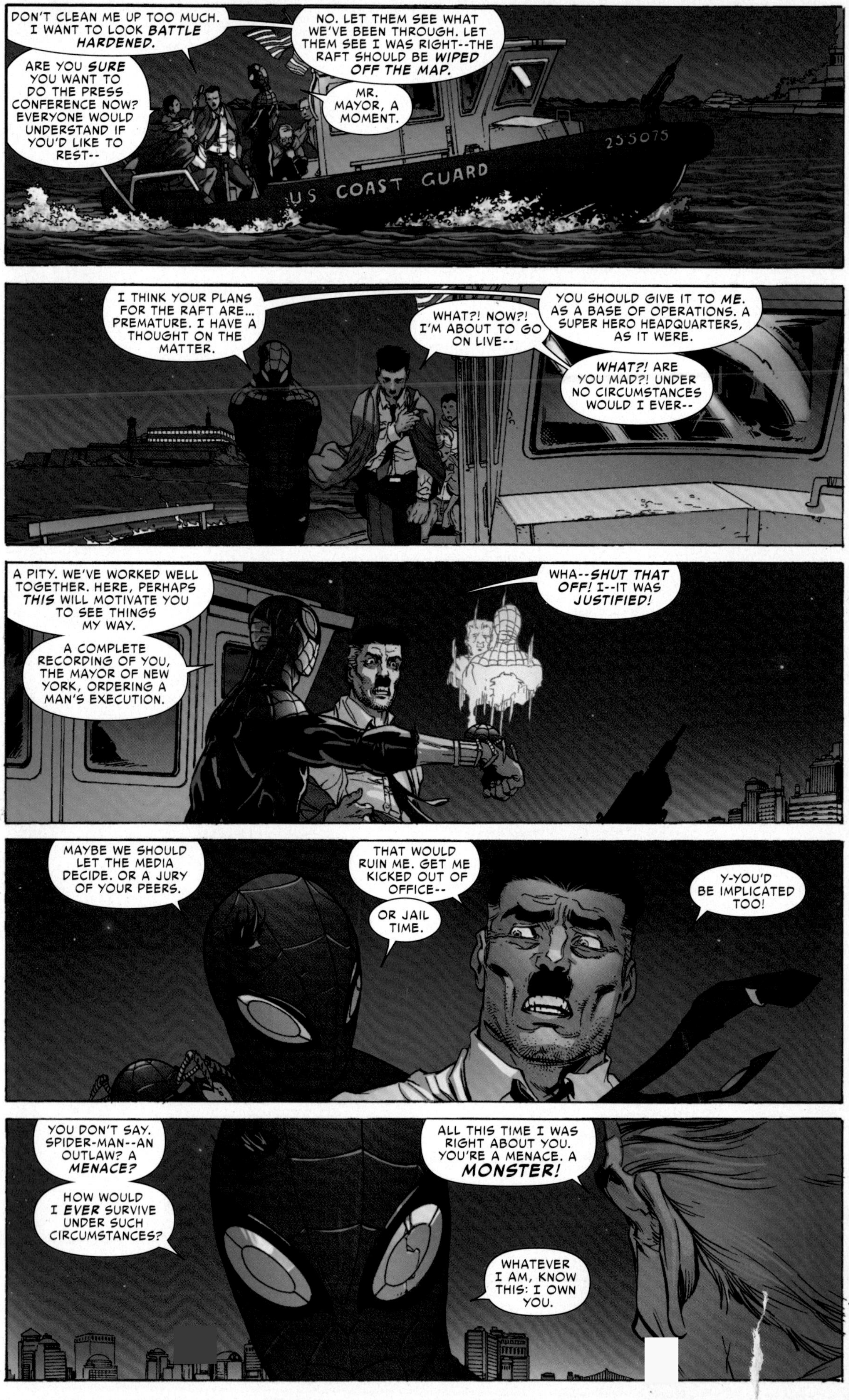
DON'T CLEAN ME UP TOO MUCH. I WANT TO LOOK BATTLE HARDENED.
ARE YOU SURE YOU WANT TO DO THE PRESS CONFERENCE NOW? EVERYONE WOULD UNDERSTAND IF YOU'D LIKE TO REST--
NO. LET THEM SEE WHAT WE'VE BEEN THROUGH. LET THEM SEE I WAS RIGHT--THE RAFT SHOULD BE WIPED OFF THE MAP.
MR. MAYOR, A MOMENT.
255075
US COAST GUARD
I THINK YOUR PLANS FOR THE RAFT ARE... PREMATURE. I HAVE A THOUGHT ON THE MATTER.
WHAT?! NOW?! I'M ABOUT TO GO ON LIVE--
YOU SHOULD GIVE IT TO ME. AS A BASE OF OPERATIONS. A SUPER HERO HEADQUARTERS, AS IT WERE.
WHAT?! ARE YOU MAD?! UNDER NO CIRCUMSTANCES WOULD I EVER--
A PITY. WE'VE WORKED WELL TOGETHER. HERE, PERHAPS THIS WILL MOTIVATE YOU TO SEE THINGS MY WAY.
A COMPLETE RECORDING OF YOU, THE MAYOR OF NEW YORK, ORDERING A MAN'S EXECUTION.
WHA--SHUT THAT OFF! I--IT WAS JUSTIFIED!
MAYBE WE SHOULD LET THE MEDIA DECIDE. OR A JURY OF YOUR PEERS.
THAT WOULD RUIN ME. GET ME KICKED OUT OF OFFICE--
OR JAIL TIME.
Y-YOU'D BE IMPLICATED TOO!
YOU DON'T SAY. SPIDER-MAN--AN OUTLAW? A MENACE?
HOW WOULD I EVER SURVIVE UNDER SUCH CIRCUMSTANCES?
ALL THIS TIME I WAS RIGHT ABOUT YOU. YOU'RE A MENACE. A MONSTER!
WHATEVER I AM, KNOW THIS: I OWN YOU.

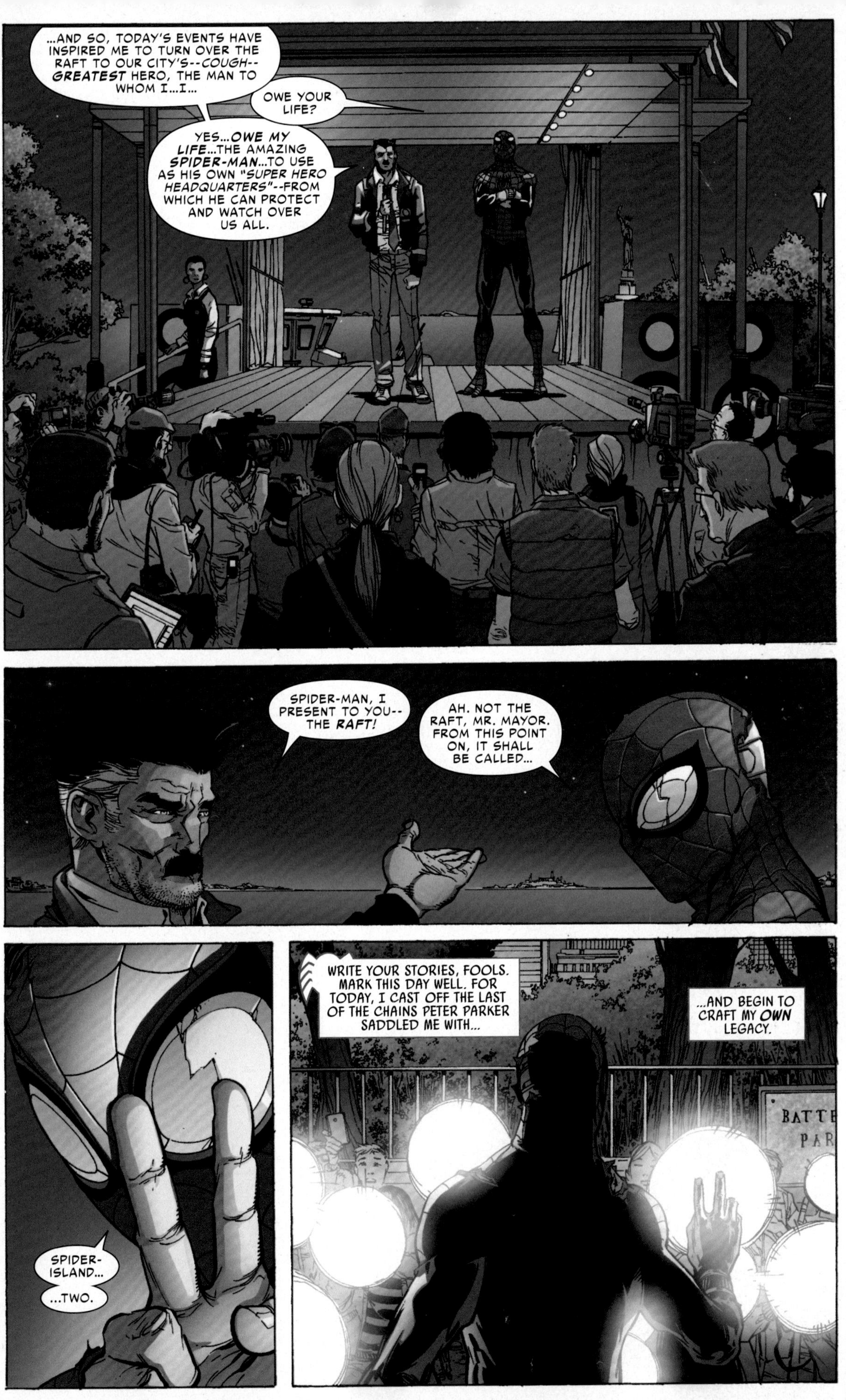
...AND SO, TODAY'S EVENTS HAVE INSPIRED ME TO TURN OVER THE RAFT TO OUR CITY'S--COUGH--GREATEST HERO, THE MAN TO WHOM I...I...
OWE YOUR LIFE?
YES...OWE MY LIFE...THE AMAZING SPIDER-MAN...TO USE AS HIS OWN "SUPER HERO HEADQUARTERS"--FROM WHICH HE CAN PROTECT AND WATCH OVER US ALL.
SPIDER-MAN, I PRESENT TO YOU--THE RAFT!
AH. NOT THE RAFT, MR. MAYOR. FROM THIS POINT ON, IT SHALL BE CALLED...
SPIDER-ISLAND...
...TWO.
WRITE YOUR STORIES, FOOLS. MARK THIS DAY WELL. FOR TODAY, I CAST OFF THE LAST OF THE CHAINS PETER PARKER SADDLED ME WITH...
...AND BEGIN TO CRAFT MY OWN LEGACY.
BATTE
PAR

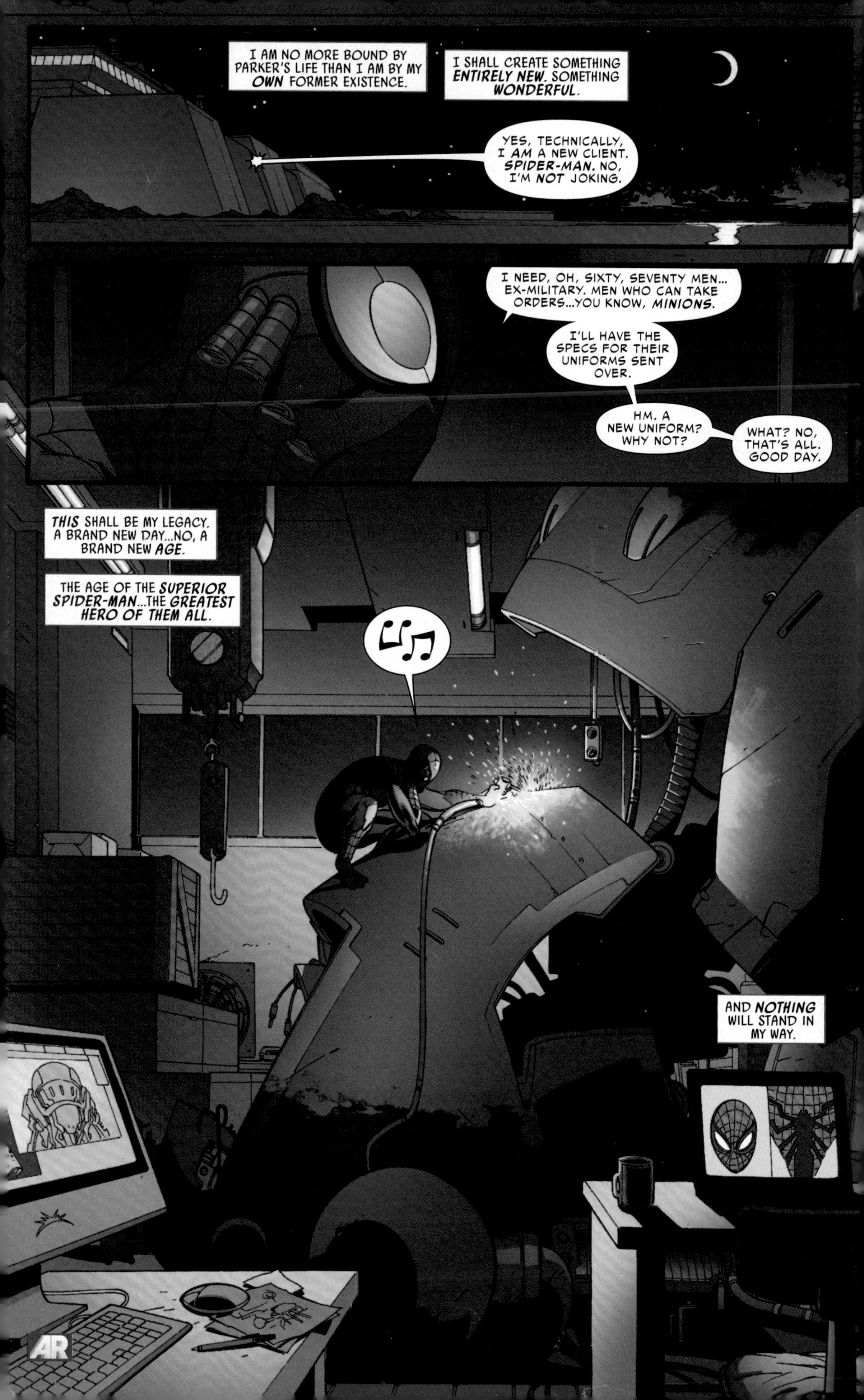

I AM NO MORE BOUND BY PARKER'S LIFE THAN I AM BY MY OWN FORMER EXISTENCE.
I SHALL CREATE SOMETHING ENTIRELY NEW. SOMETHING WONDERFUL.
YES, TECHNICALLY, I AM A NEW CLIENT. SPIDER-MAN. NO, I'M NOT JOKING.
I NEED, OH, SIXTY, SEVENTY MEN... EX-MILITARY. MEN WHO CAN TAKE ORDERS...YOU KNOW, MINIONS.
I'LL HAVE THE SPECS FOR THEIR UNIFORMS SENT OVER.
HM. A NEW UNIFORM? WHY NOT?
WHAT? NO, THAT'S ALL. GOOD DAY.
THIS SHALL BE MY LEGACY. A BRAND NEW DAY...NO, A BRAND NEW AGE.
THE AGE OF THE SUPERIOR SPIDER-MAN...THE GREATEST HERO OF THEM ALL.
AND NOTHING WILL STAND IN MY WAY.

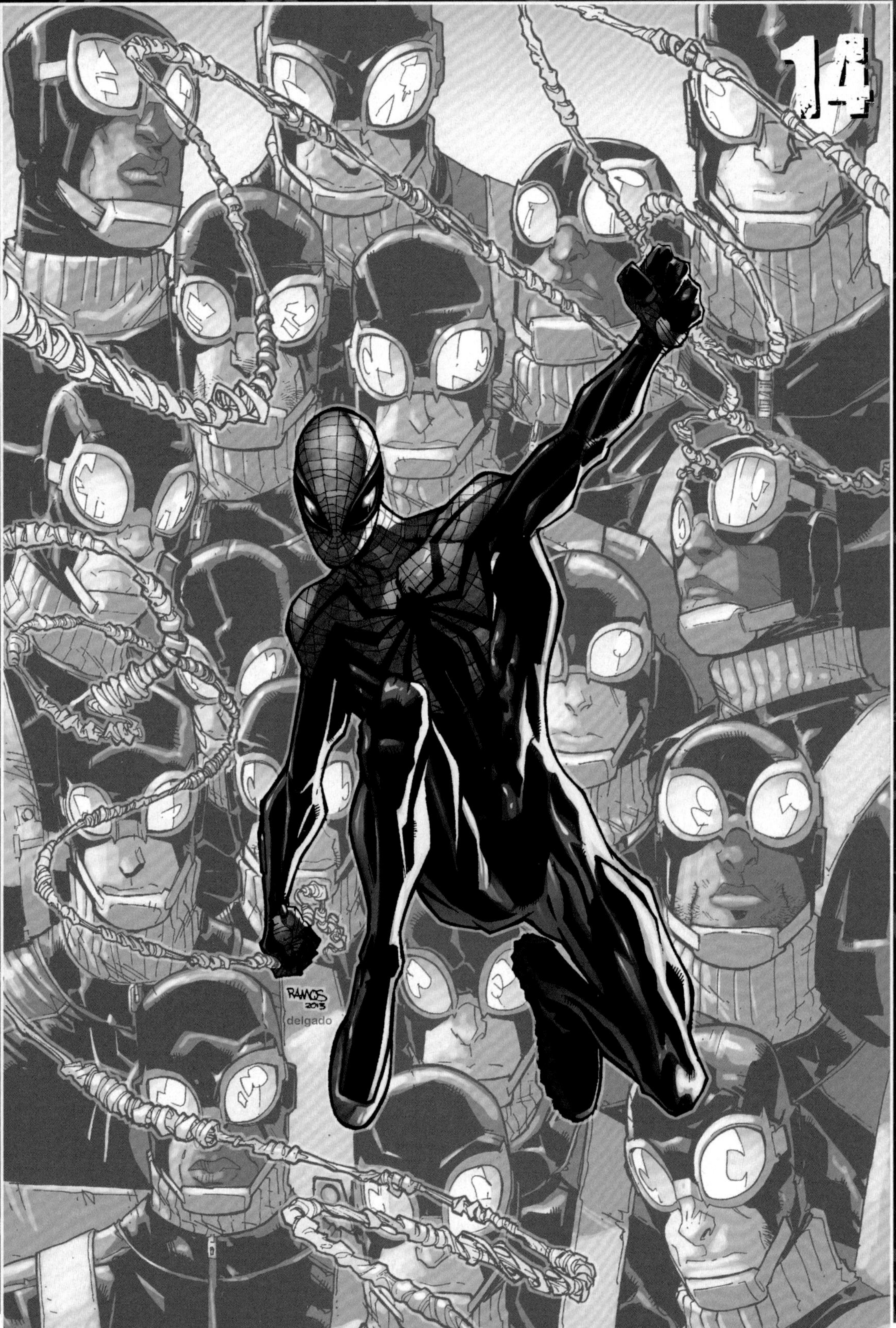
14
RAMOS 2013
delgado

A BLIND EYE

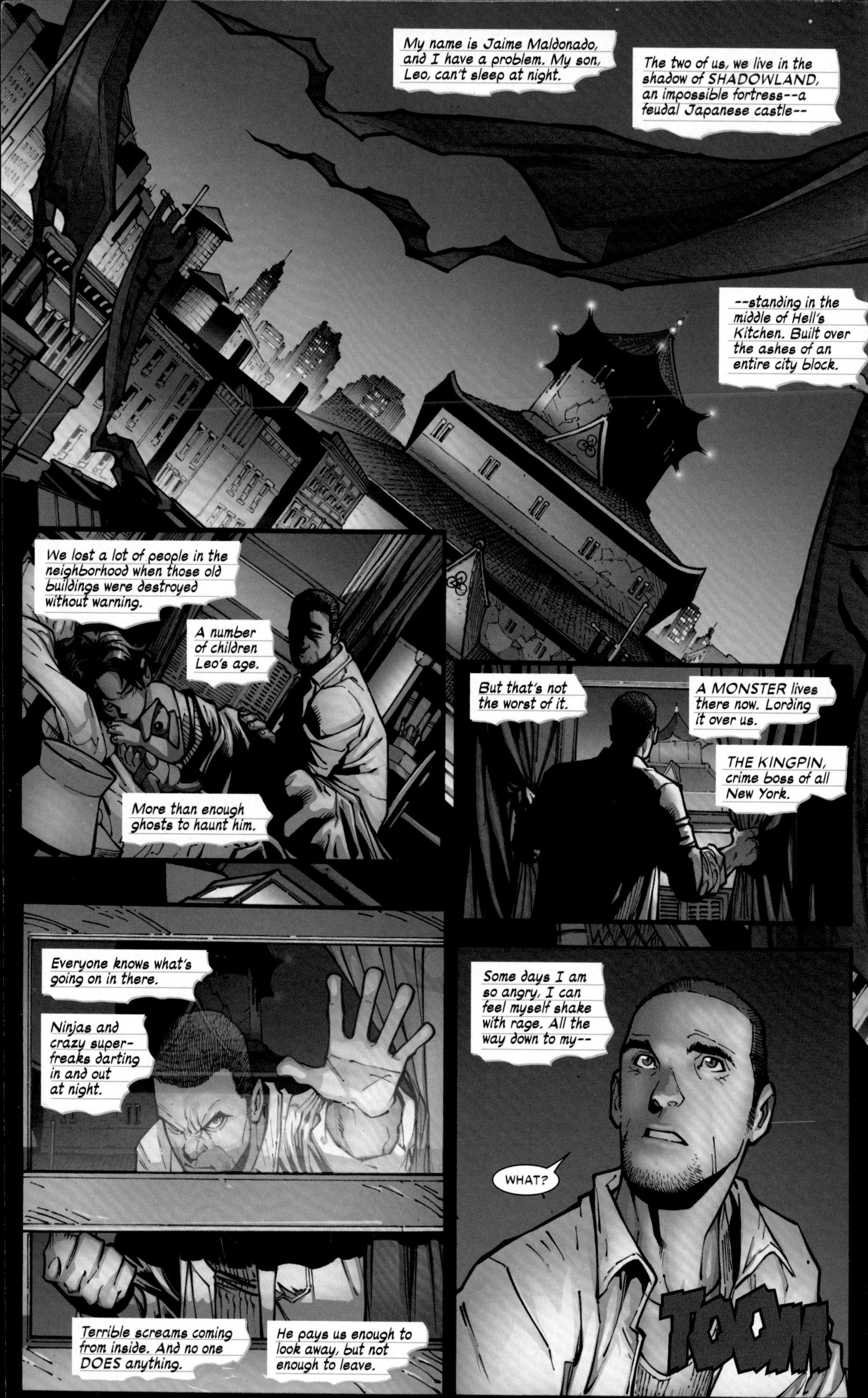
My name is Jaime Maldonado, and I have a problem. My son, Leo, can't sleep at night.
The two of us, we live in the shadow of SHADOWLAND, an impossible fortress--a feudal Japanese castle--
--standing in the middle of Hell's Kitchen. Built over the ashes of an entire city block.
We lost a lot of people in the neighborhood when those old buildings were destroyed without warning.
A number of children Leo's age.
More than enough ghosts to haunt him.
But that's not the worst of it.
A MONSTER lives there now. Lording it over us.
THE KINGPIN, crime boss of all New York.
Everyone knows what's going on in there.
Ninjas and crazy super-freaks darting in and out at night.
Terrible screams coming from inside. And no one DOES anything.
He pays us enough to look away, but not enough to leave.
Some days I am so angry, I can feel myself shake with rage. All the way down to my--
WHAT?
TOOM

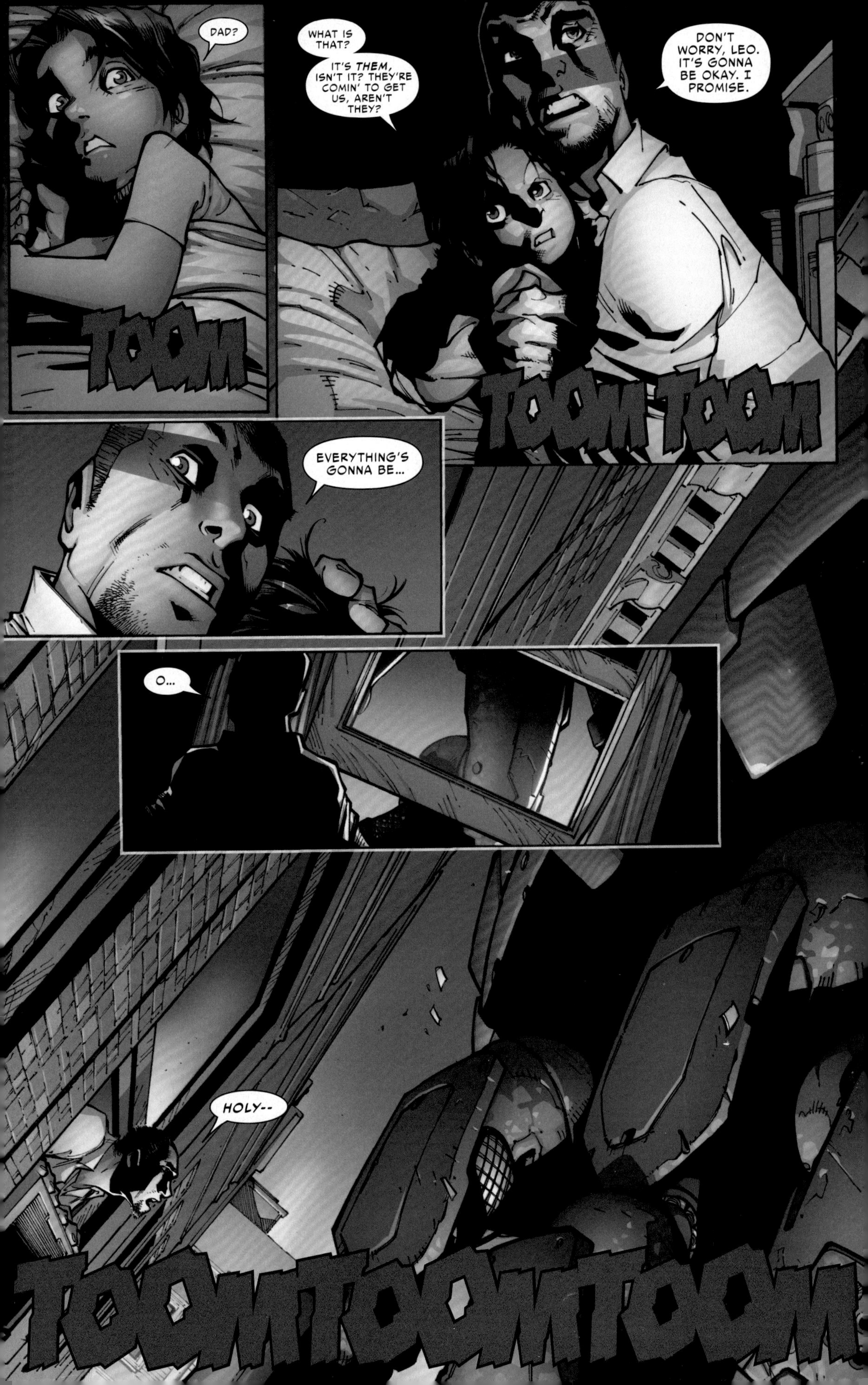
DAD?
TOOM
WHAT IS THAT?
IT'S THEM, ISN'T IT? THEY'RE COMIN' TO GET US, AREN'T THEY?
DON'T WORRY, LEO. IT'S GONNA BE OKAY. I PROMISE.
TOOM TOOM
EVERYTHING'S GONNA BE...
O...
HOLY--
TOOM TOOM TOOM

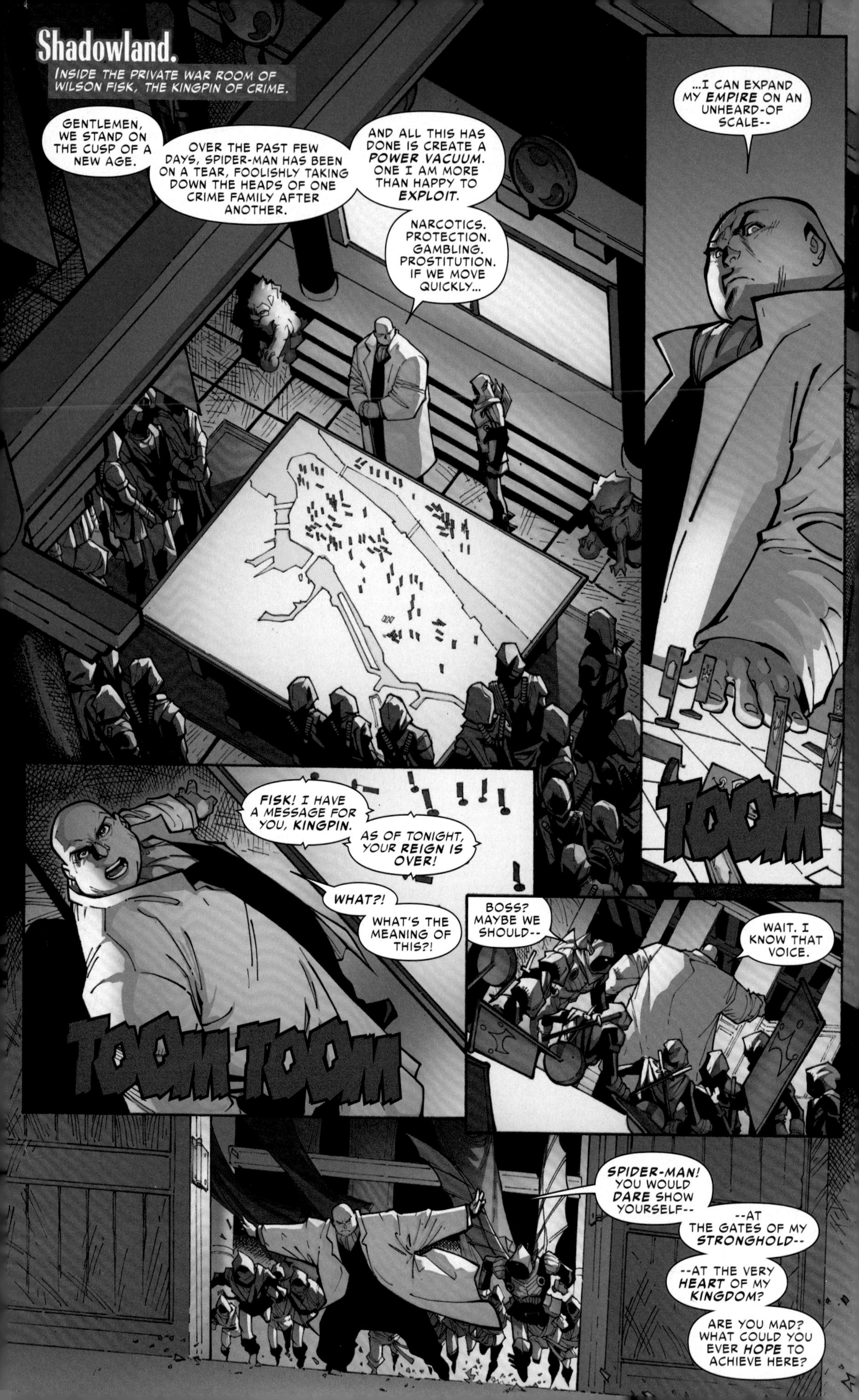
Shadowland.
INSIDE THE PRIVATE WAR ROOM OF WILSON FISK, THE KINGPIN OF CRIME.
GENTLEMEN, WE STAND ON THE CUSP OF A NEW AGE.
OVER THE PAST FEW DAYS, SPIDER-MAN HAS BEEN ON A TEAR, FOOLISHLY TAKING DOWN THE HEADS OF ONE CRIME FAMILY AFTER ANOTHER.
AND ALL THIS HAS DONE IS CREATE A POWER VACUUM. ONE I AM MORE THAN HAPPY TO EXPLOIT.
NARCOTICS. PROTECTION. GAMBLING. PROSTITUTION. IF WE MOVE QUICKLY...
...I CAN EXPAND MY EMPIRE ON AN UNHEARD-OF SCALE--
TOOM
FISK! I HAVE A MESSAGE FOR YOU, KINGPIN.
AS OF TONIGHT, YOUR REIGN IS OVER!
WHAT?!
WHAT'S THE MEANING OF THIS?!
TOOM TOOM
BOSS? MAYBE WE SHOULD--
WAIT. I KNOW THAT VOICE.
SPIDER-MAN! YOU WOULD DARE SHOW YOURSELF--
--AT THE GATES OF MY STRONGHOLD--
--AT THE VERY HEART OF MY KINGDOM?
ARE YOU MAD? WHAT COULD YOU EVER HOPE TO ACHIEVE HERE?

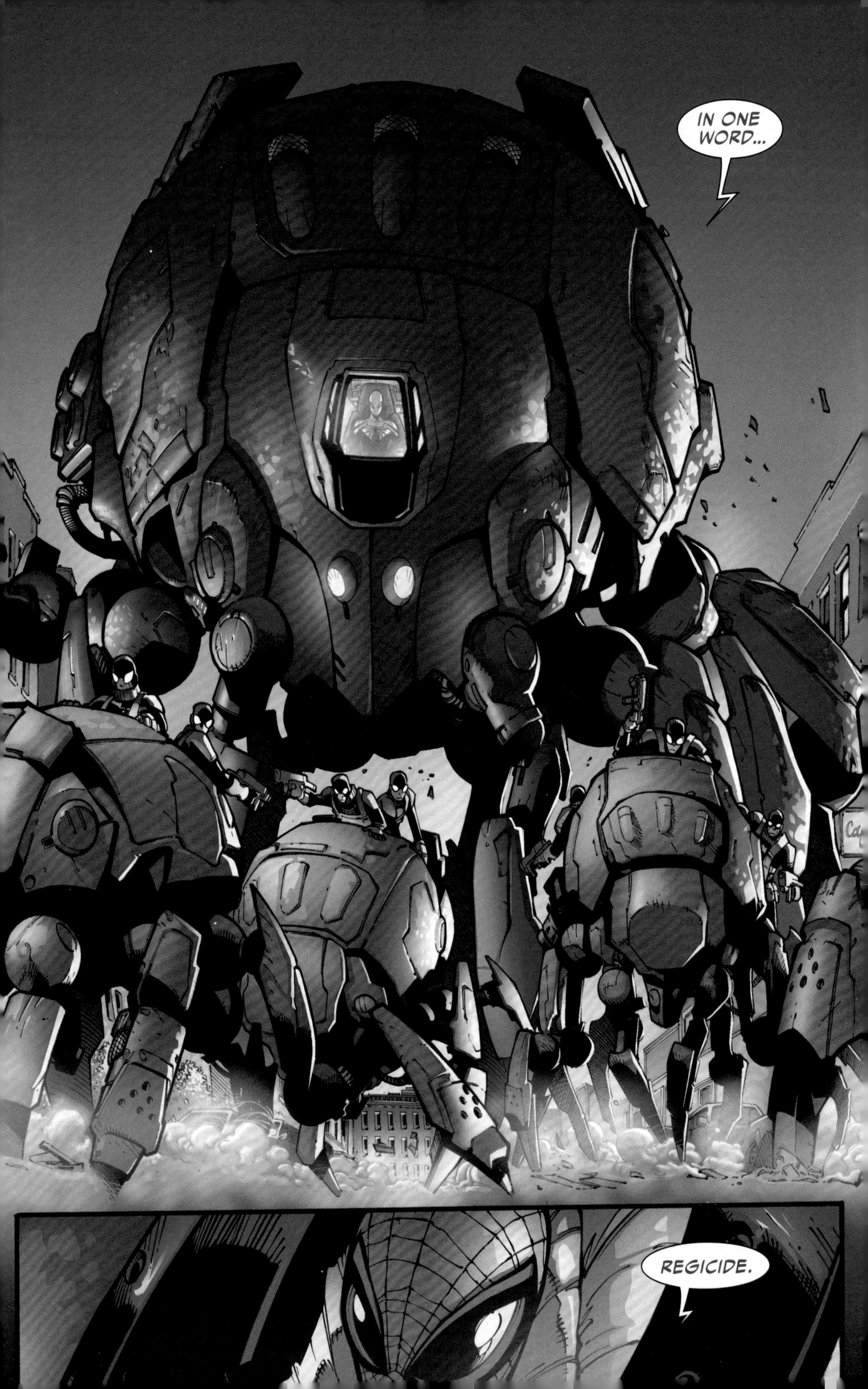
IN ONE WORD...
REGICIDE.

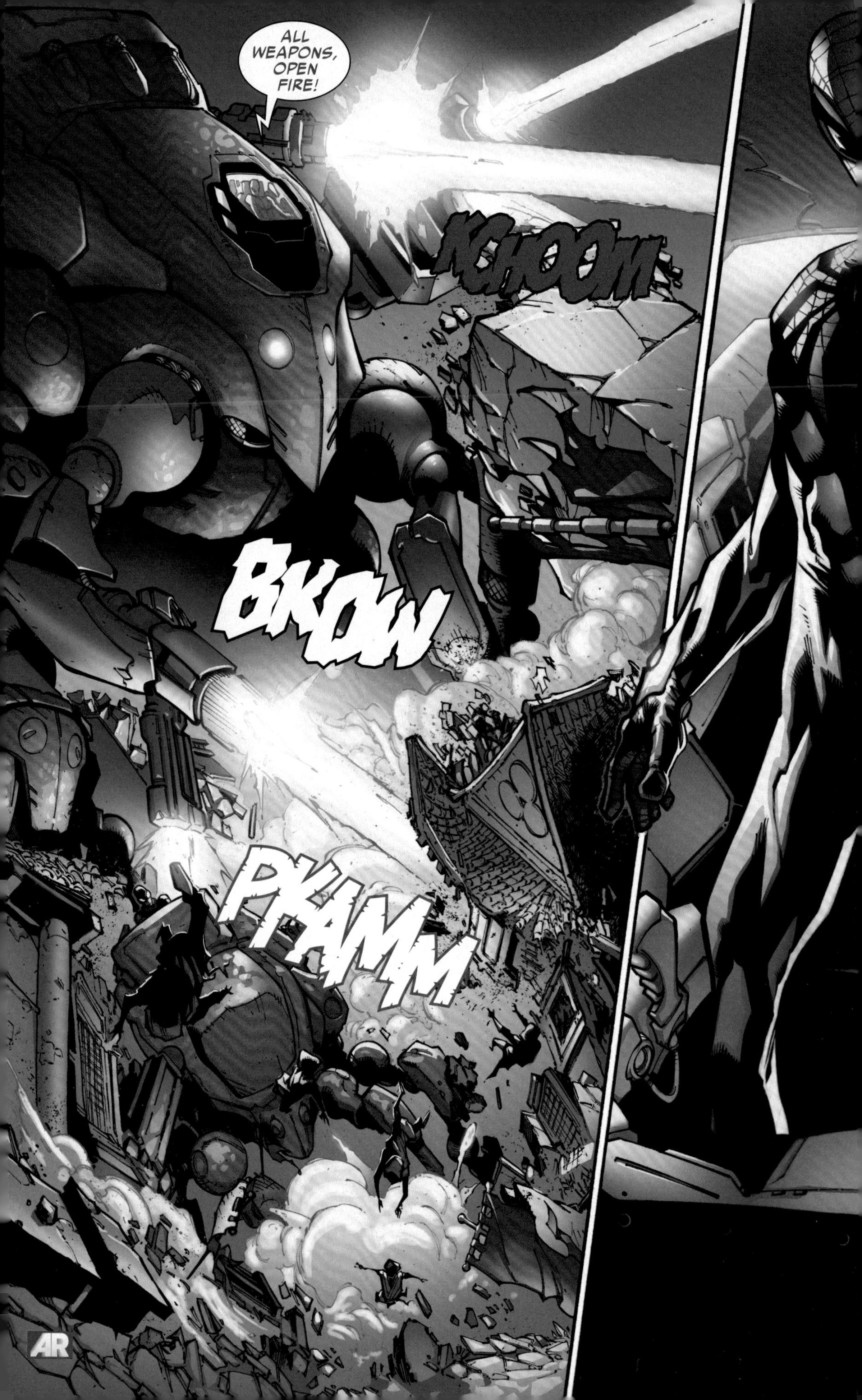
ALL WEAPONS, OPEN FIRE!
KCHOOM
BKOW
PKAMM

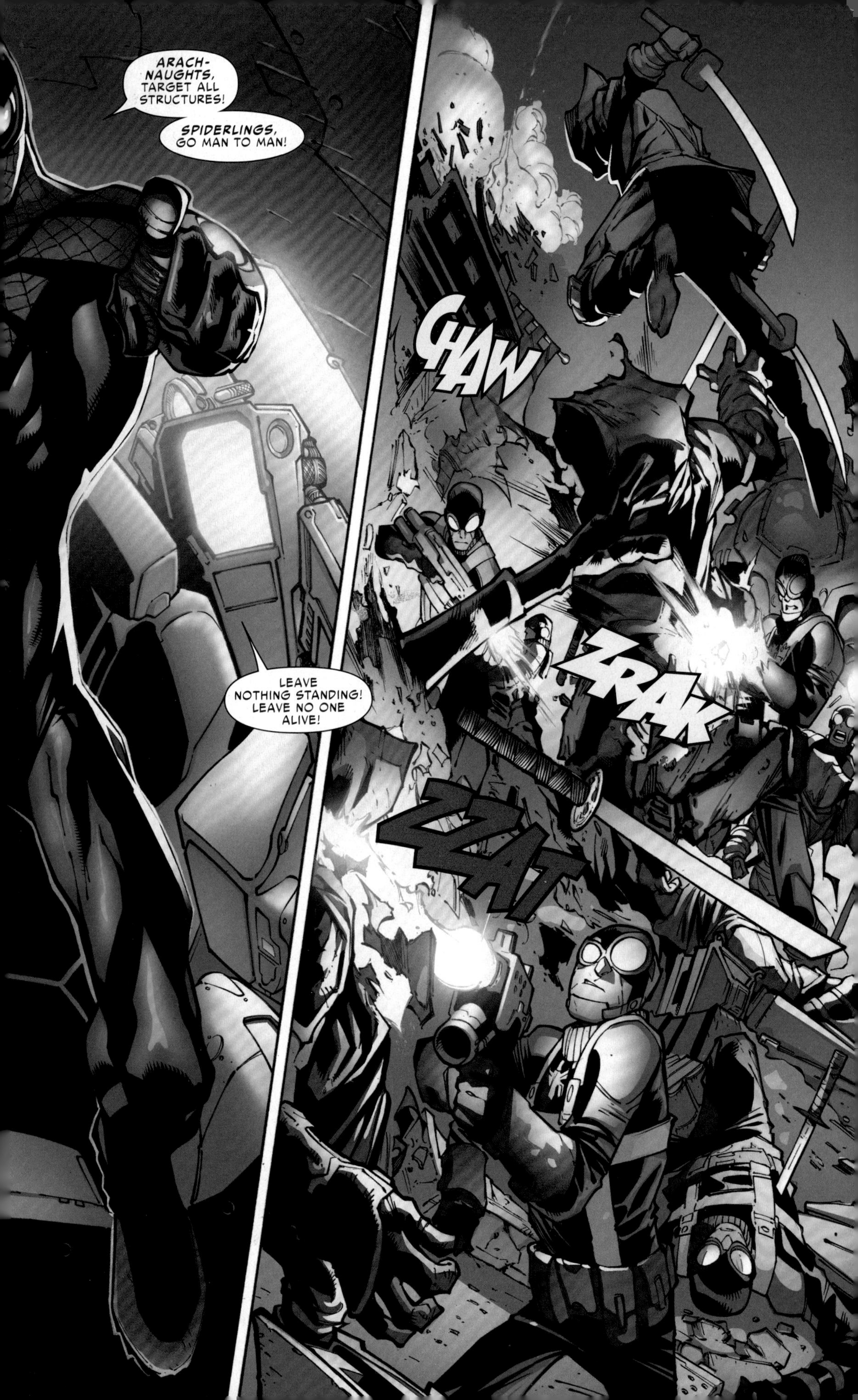
ARACH-NAUGHTS, TARGET ALL STRUCTURES!
SPIDERLINGS, GO MAN TO MAN!
LEAVE NOTHING STANDING! LEAVE NO ONE ALIVE!
CHAW
ZRAK
ZZAT

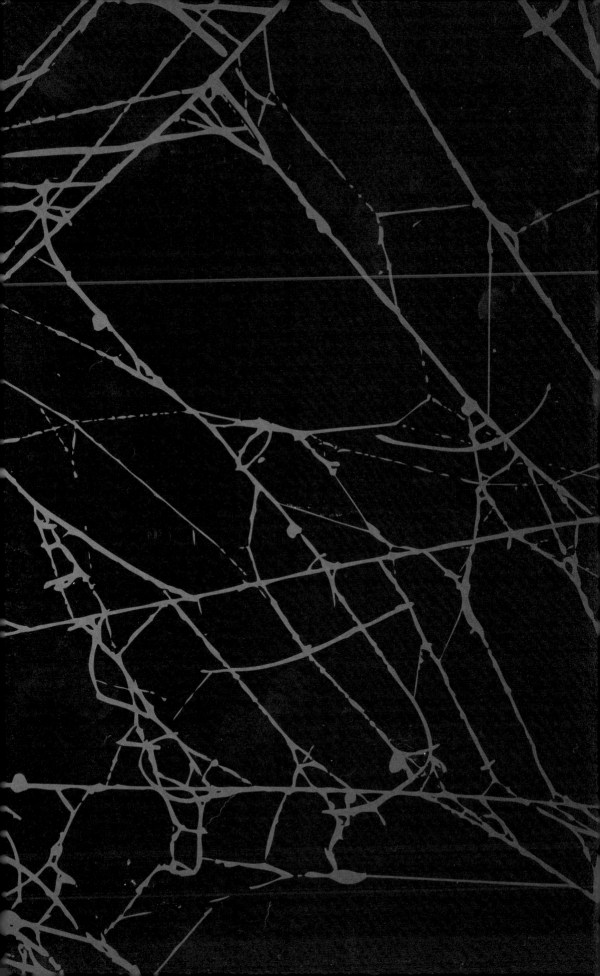

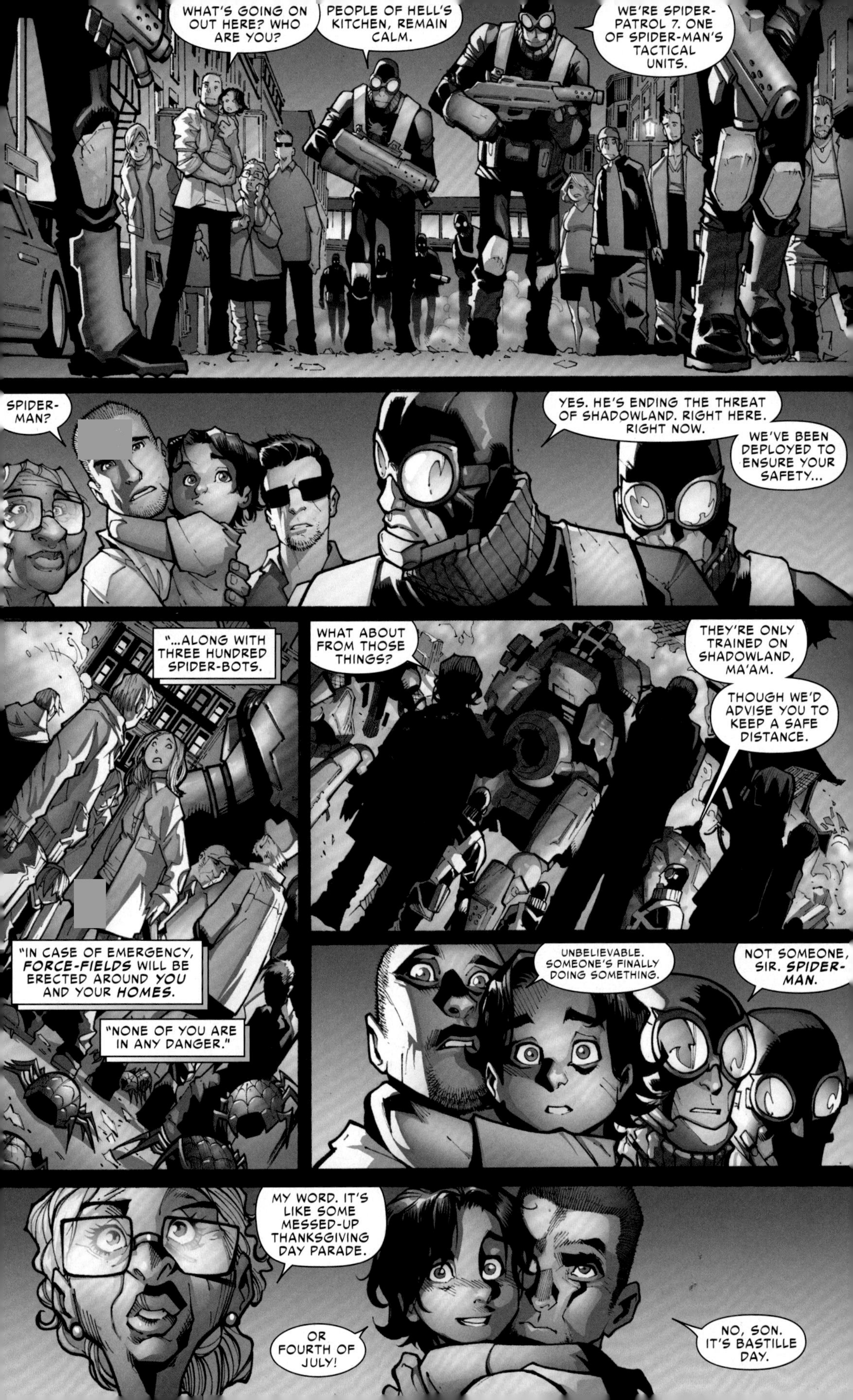
WHAT'S GOING ON OUT HERE? WHO ARE YOU?
PEOPLE OF HELL'S KITCHEN, REMAIN CALM.
WE'RE SPIDER-PATROL 7. ONE OF SPIDER-MAN'S TACTICAL UNITS.
SPIDER-MAN?
YES. HE'S ENDING THE THREAT OF SHADOWLAND. RIGHT HERE. RIGHT NOW.
WE'VE BEEN DEPLOYED TO ENSURE YOUR SAFETY...
"...ALONG WITH THREE HUNDRED SPIDER-BOTS.
"IN CASE OF EMERGENCY, FORCE-FIELDS WILL BE ERECTED AROUND YOU AND YOUR HOMES.
"NONE OF YOU ARE IN ANY DANGER."
WHAT ABOUT FROM THOSE THINGS?
THEY'RE ONLY TRAINED ON SHADOWLAND, MA'AM.
THOUGH WE'D ADVISE YOU TO KEEP A SAFE DISTANCE.
UNBELIEVABLE. SOMEONE'S FINALLY DOING SOMETHING.
NOT SOMEONE, SIR. SPIDER-MAN.
MY WORD. IT'S LIKE SOME MESSED-UP THANKSGIVING DAY PARADE.
OR FOURTH OF JULY!
NO, SON. IT'S BASTILLE DAY.

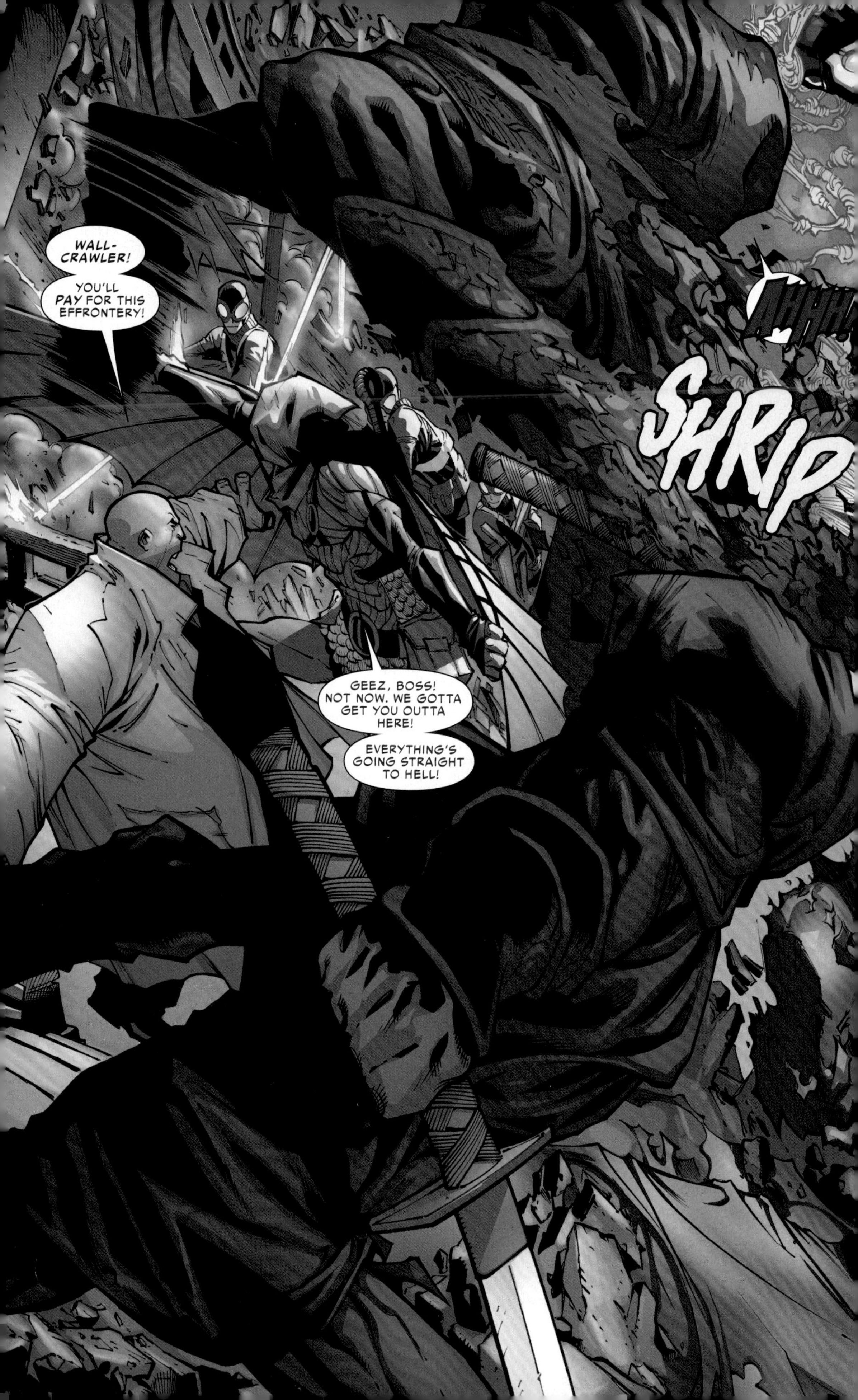
WALL-CRAWLER!
YOU'LL PAY FOR THIS EFFRONTERY!
SHRIP
GEEZ, BOSS! NOT NOW. WE GOTTA GET YOU OUTTA HERE!
EVERYTHING'S GOING STRAIGHT TO HELL!

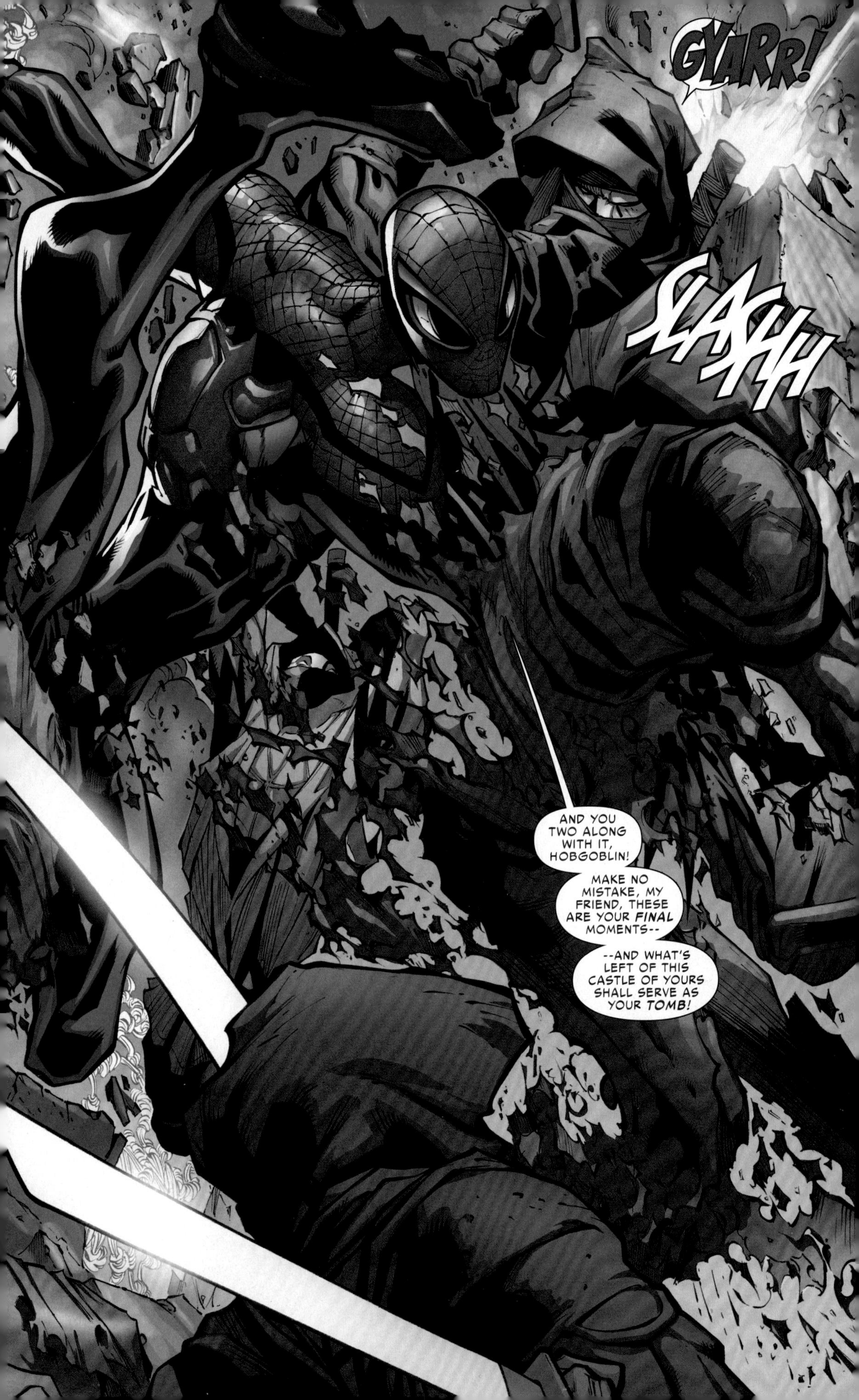
GYARR!
SLASHH
AND YOU TWO ALONG WITH IT, HOBGOBLIN!
MAKE NO MISTAKE, MY FRIEND, THESE ARE YOUR FINAL MOMENTS--
--AND WHAT'S LEFT OF THIS CASTLE OF YOURS SHALL SERVE AS YOUR TOMB!

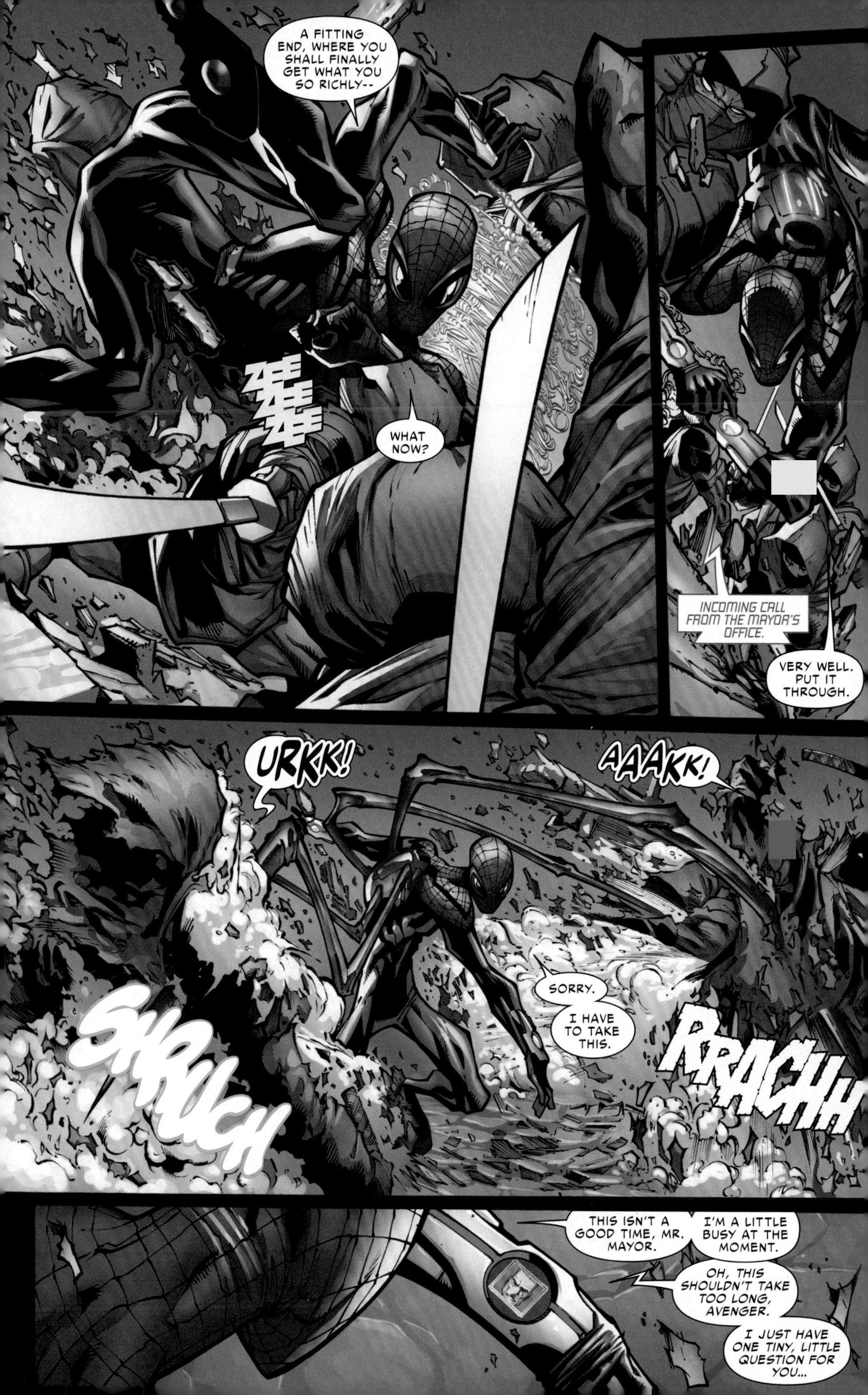
A FITTING END, WHERE YOU SHALL FINALLY GET WHAT YOU SO RICHLY--
WHAT NOW?
INCOMING CALL FROM THE MAYOR'S OFFICE.
VERY WELL. PUT IT THROUGH.
URKK!
AAAKK!
SORRY.
I HAVE TO TAKE THIS.
SHRUCH
RRACHH
THIS ISN'T A GOOD TIME, MR. MAYOR.
I'M A LITTLE BUSY AT THE MOMENT.
OH, THIS SHOULDN'T TAKE TOO LONG, AVENGER.
I JUST HAVE ONE TINY, LITTLE QUESTION FOR YOU...

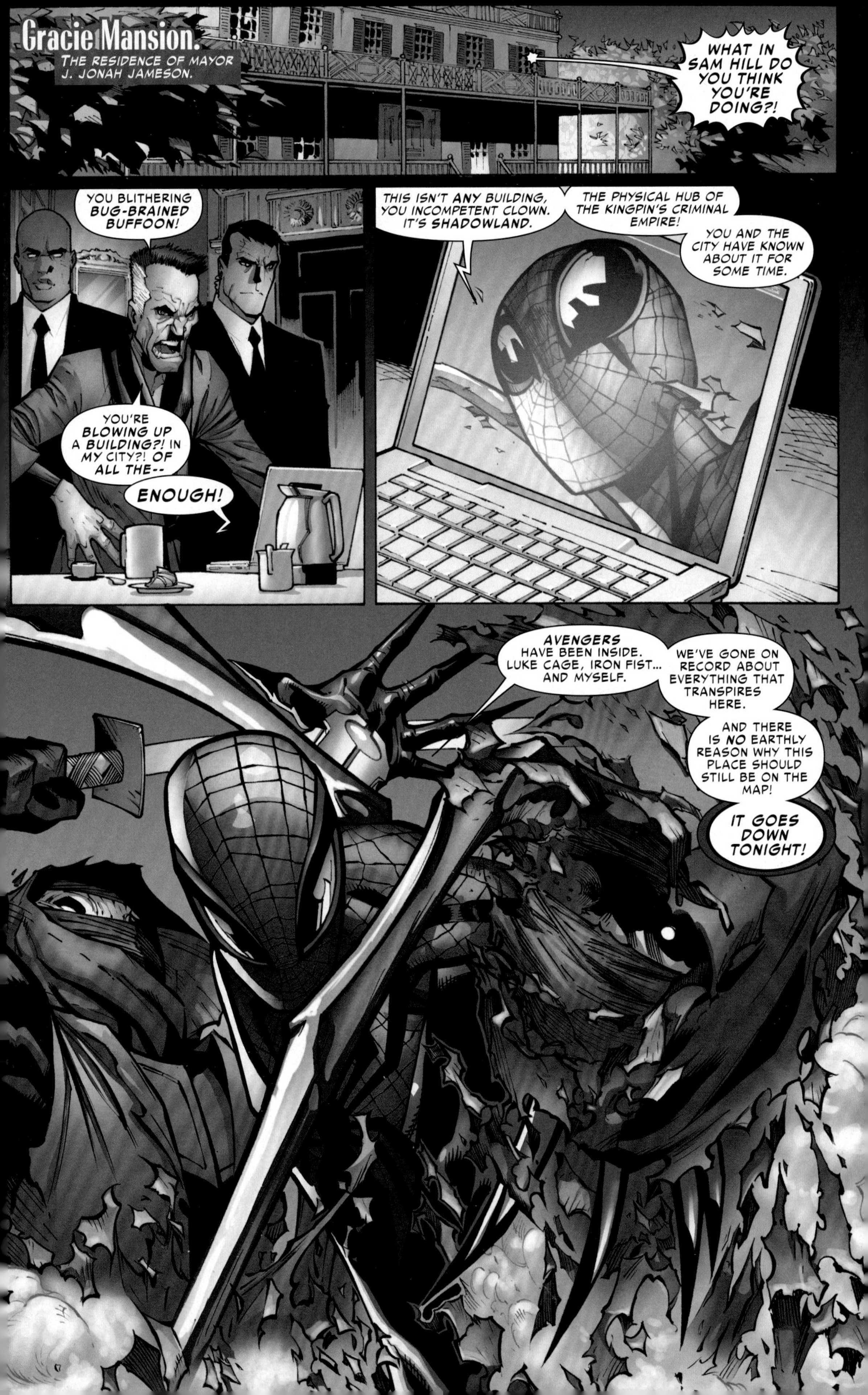

Gracie Mansion.
THE RESIDENCE OF MAYOR J. JONAH JAMESON.
WHAT IN SAM HILL DO YOU THINK YOU'RE DOING?!
YOU BLITHERING BUG-BRAINED BUFFOON!
YOU'RE BLOWING UP A BUILDING?! IN MY CITY?! OF ALL THE--
ENOUGH!
THIS ISN'T ANY BUILDING, YOU INCOMPETENT CLOWN. IT'S SHADOWLAND.
THE PHYSICAL HUB OF THE KINGPIN'S CRIMINAL EMPIRE!
YOU AND THE CITY HAVE KNOWN ABOUT IT FOR SOME TIME.
AVENGERS HAVE BEEN INSIDE. LUKE CAGE, IRON FIST... AND MYSELF.
WE'VE GONE ON RECORD ABOUT EVERYTHING THAT TRANSPIRES HERE.
AND THERE IS NO EARTHLY REASON WHY THIS PLACE SHOULD STILL BE ON THE MAP!
IT GOES DOWN TONIGHT!

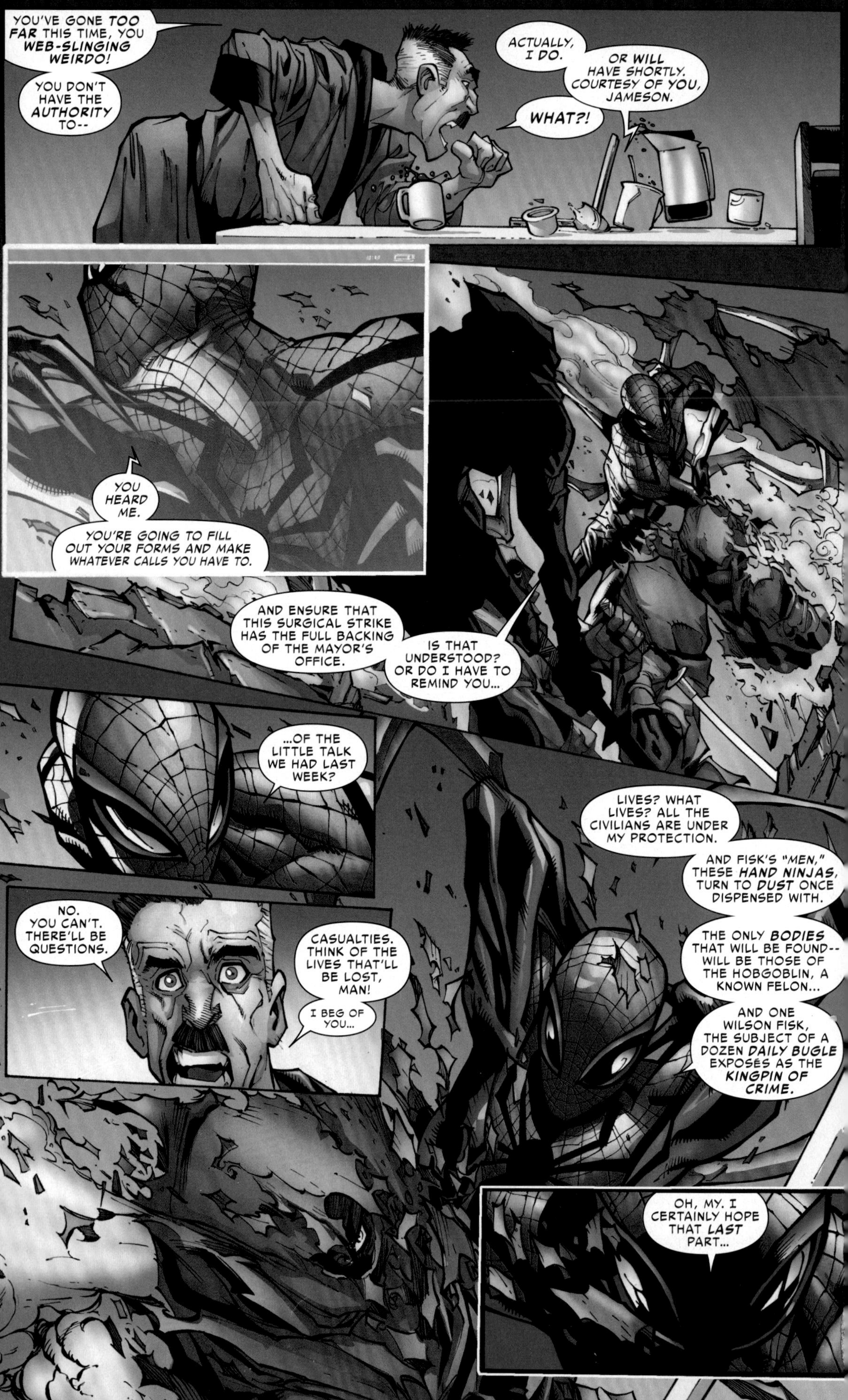
YOU'VE GONE TOO FAR THIS TIME, YOU WEB-SLINGING WEIRDO!
YOU DON'T HAVE THE AUTHORITY TO--
ACTUALLY, I DO.
OR WILL HAVE SHORTLY. COURTESY OF YOU, JAMESON.
WHAT?!
YOU HEARD ME.
YOU'RE GOING TO FILL OUT YOUR FORMS AND MAKE WHATEVER CALLS YOU HAVE TO.
AND ENSURE THAT THIS SURGICAL STRIKE HAS THE FULL BACKING OF THE MAYOR'S OFFICE.
IS THAT UNDERSTOOD? OR DO I HAVE TO REMIND YOU...
...OF THE LITTLE TALK WE HAD LAST WEEK?
NO. YOU CAN'T. THERE'LL BE QUESTIONS.
CASUALTIES. THINK OF THE LIVES THAT'LL BE LOST, MAN!
I BEG OF YOU...
LIVES? WHAT LIVES? ALL THE CIVILIANS ARE UNDER MY PROTECTION.
AND FISK'S "MEN," THESE HAND NINJAS, TURN TO DUST ONCE DISPENSED WITH.
THE ONLY BODIES THAT WILL BE FOUND--WILL BE THOSE OF THE HOBGOBLIN, A KNOWN FELON...
AND ONE WILSON FISK, THE SUBJECT OF A DOZEN DAILY BUGLE EXPOSÉS AS THE KINGPIN OF CRIME.
OH, MY. I CERTAINLY HOPE THAT LAST PART...

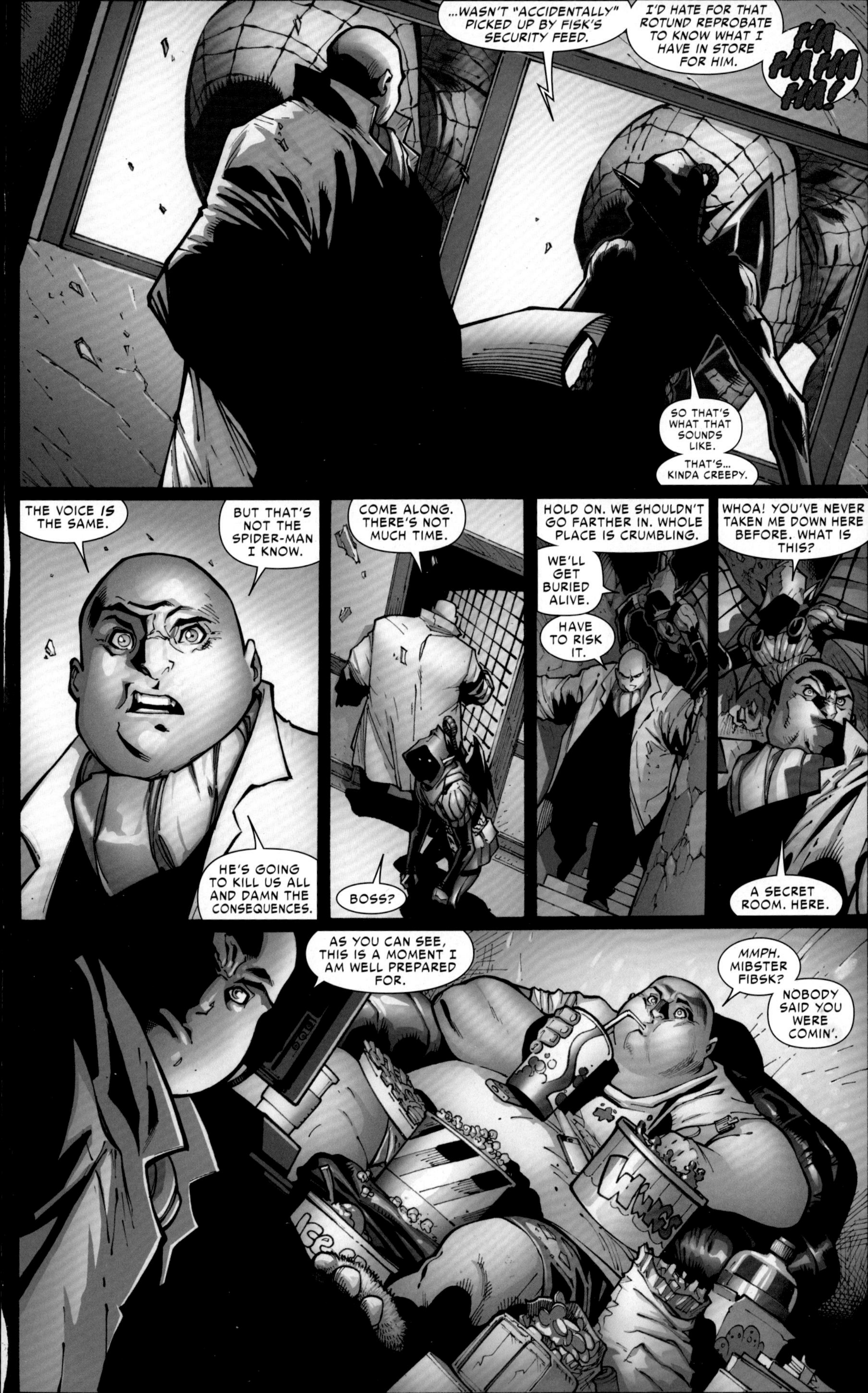

...WASN'T "ACCIDENTALLY" PICKED UP BY FISK'S SECURITY FEED.
I'D HATE FOR THAT ROTUND REPROBATE TO KNOW WHAT I HAVE IN STORE FOR HIM.
HA HA HA HA!
SO THAT'S WHAT THAT SOUNDS LIKE.
THAT'S... KINDA CREEPY.
THE VOICE *IS* THE SAME.
BUT THAT'S NOT THE SPIDER-MAN I KNOW.
HE'S GOING TO KILL US ALL AND DAMN THE CONSEQUENCES.
COME ALONG. THERE'S NOT MUCH TIME.
BOSS?
HOLD ON. WE SHOULDN'T GO FARTHER IN. WHOLE PLACE IS CRUMBLING.
WE'LL GET BURIED ALIVE.
HAVE TO RISK IT.
WHOA! YOU'VE NEVER TAKEN ME DOWN HERE BEFORE. WHAT IS THIS?
A SECRET ROOM. HERE.
AS YOU CAN SEE, THIS IS A MOMENT I AM WELL PREPARED FOR.
MMPH. MIBSTER FIBSK?
NOBODY SAID YOU WERE COMIN'.

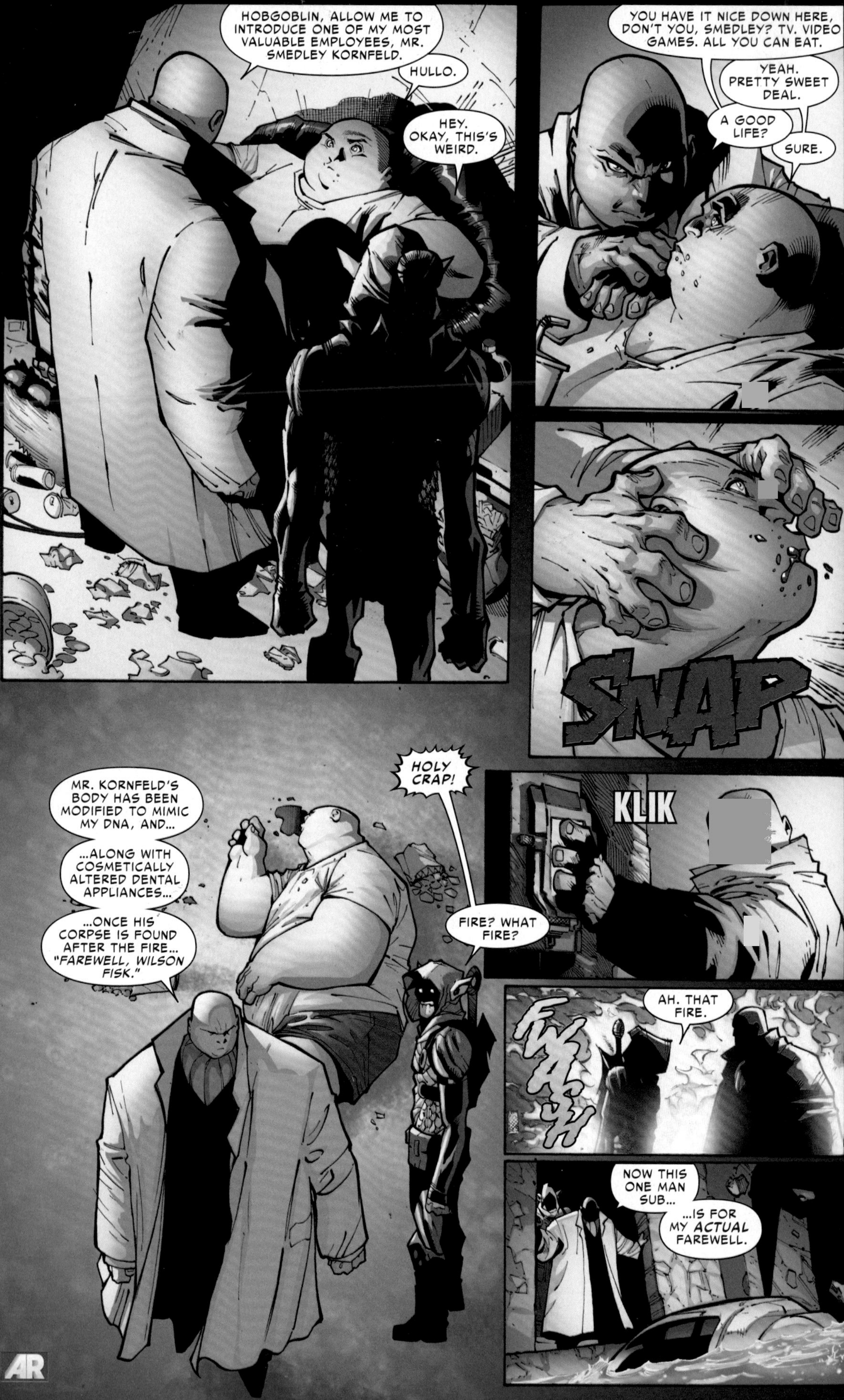
HOBGOBLIN, ALLOW ME TO INTRODUCE ONE OF MY MOST VALUABLE EMPLOYEES, MR. SMEDLEY KORNFELD.
HULLO.
HEY. OKAY, THIS'S WEIRD.
YOU HAVE IT NICE DOWN HERE, DON'T YOU, SMEDLEY? TV. VIDEO GAMES. ALL YOU CAN EAT.
YEAH. PRETTY SWEET DEAL.
A GOOD LIFE?
SURE.
SNAP
MR. KORNFELD'S BODY HAS BEEN MODIFIED TO MIMIC MY DNA, AND...
HOLY CRAP!
...ALONG WITH COSMETICALLY ALTERED DENTAL APPLIANCES...
...ONCE HIS CORPSE IS FOUND AFTER THE FIRE... "FAREWELL, WILSON FISK."
FIRE? WHAT FIRE?
KLIK
FWASH
AH. THAT FIRE.
NOW THIS ONE MAN SUB...
...IS FOR MY ACTUAL FAREWELL.

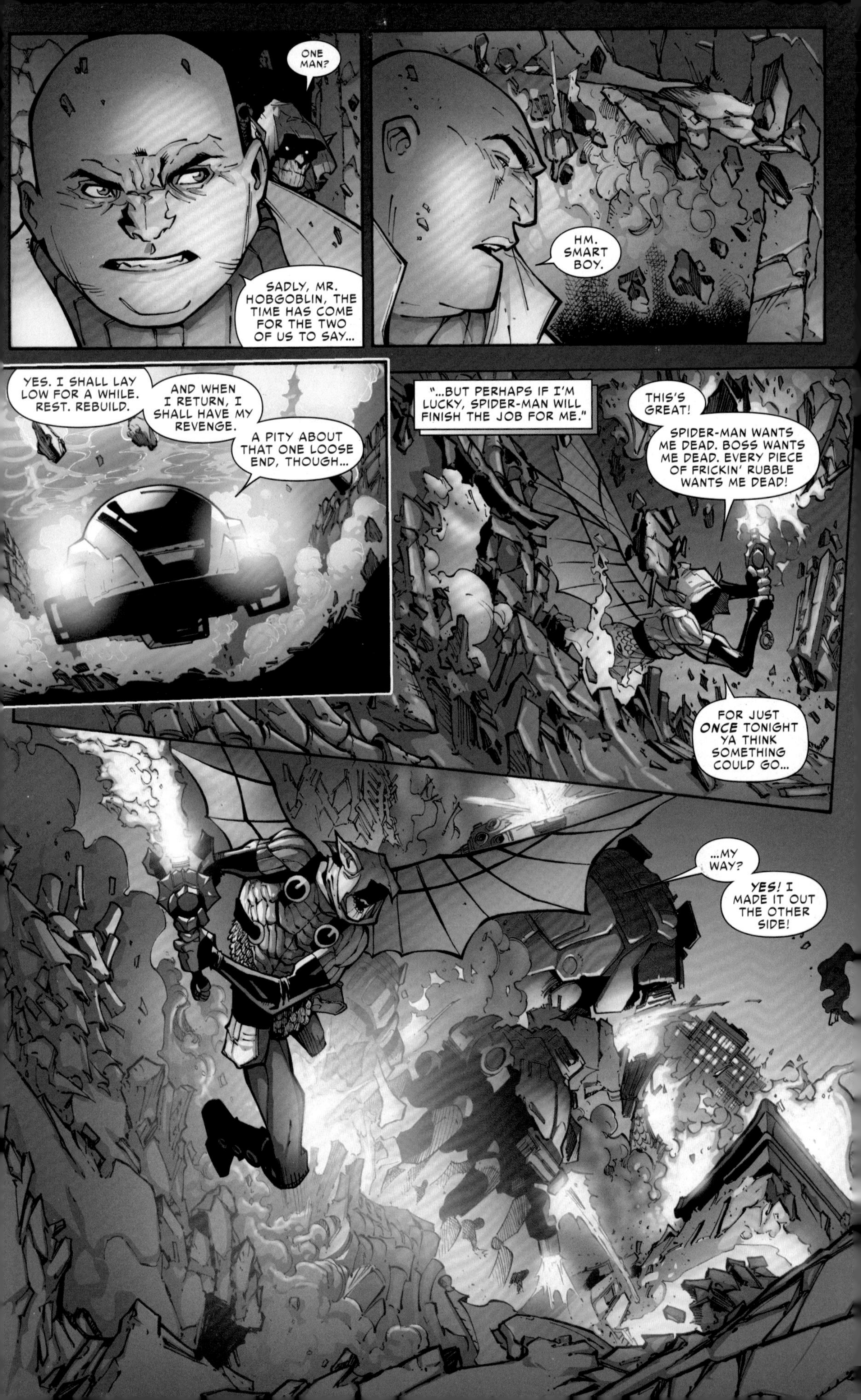
ONE MAN?
SADLY, MR. HOBGOBLIN, THE TIME HAS COME FOR THE TWO OF US TO SAY...
HM. SMART BOY.
YES. I SHALL LAY LOW FOR A WHILE. REST. REBUILD.
AND WHEN I RETURN, I SHALL HAVE MY REVENGE.
A PITY ABOUT THAT ONE LOOSE END, THOUGH...
"...BUT PERHAPS IF I'M LUCKY, SPIDER-MAN WILL FINISH THE JOB FOR ME."
THIS'S GREAT!
SPIDER-MAN WANTS ME DEAD. BOSS WANTS ME DEAD. EVERY PIECE OF FRICKIN' RUBBLE WANTS ME DEAD!
FOR JUST ONCE TONIGHT YA THINK SOMETHING COULD GO...
...MY WAY?
YES! I MADE IT OUT THE OTHER SIDE!

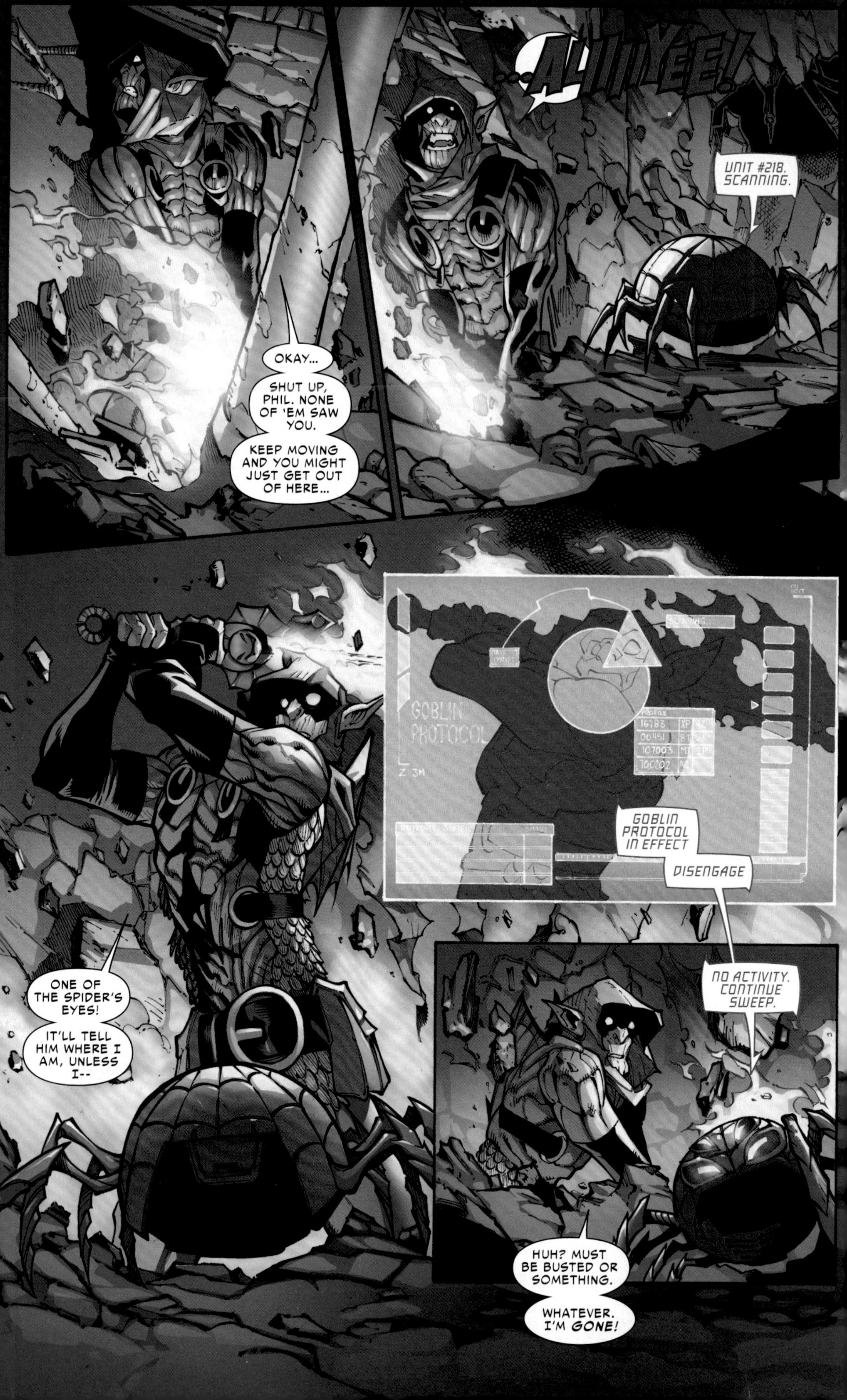
...AIIIIYEE!
UNIT #218. SCANNING.
OKAY...
SHUT UP, PHIL. NONE OF 'EM SAW YOU.
KEEP MOVING AND YOU MIGHT JUST GET OUT OF HERE...
GOBLIN PROTOCOL
Z 3M
PROFILE
16783 XP
00451 8T
107003 MT
100202
GOBLIN PROTOCOL IN EFFECT
DISENGAGE
ONE OF THE SPIDER'S EYES!
IT'LL TELL HIM WHERE I AM, UNLESS I--
NO ACTIVITY. CONTINUE SWEEP.
HUH? MUST BE BUSTED OR SOMETHING.
WHATEVER. I'M GONE!

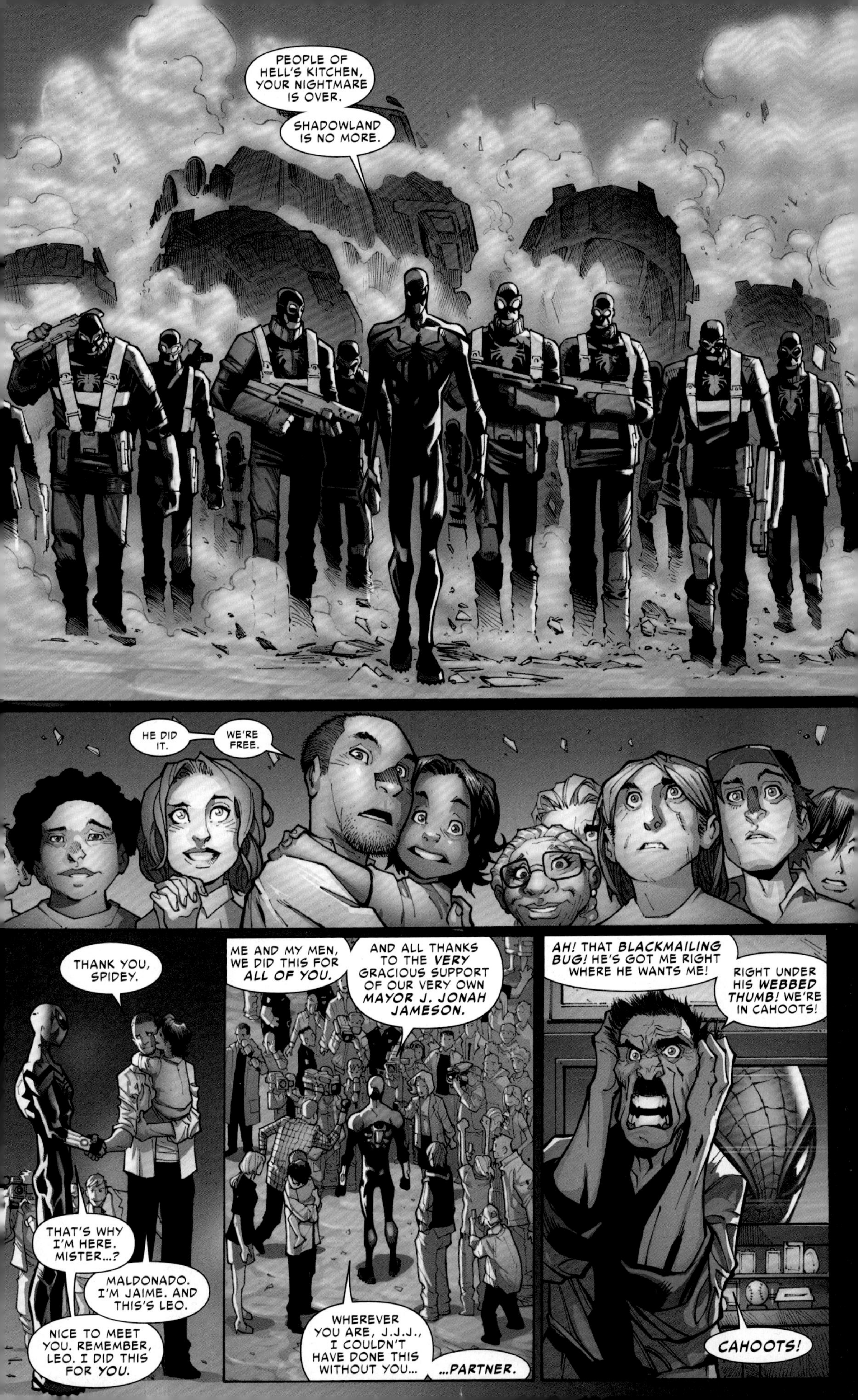
PEOPLE OF HELL'S KITCHEN, YOUR NIGHTMARE IS OVER.
SHADOWLAND IS NO MORE.
HE DID IT.
WE'RE FREE.
THANK YOU, SPIDEY.
THAT'S WHY I'M HERE. MISTER...?
MALDONADO. I'M JAIME. AND THIS'S LEO.
NICE TO MEET YOU. REMEMBER, LEO. I DID THIS FOR YOU.
ME AND MY MEN, WE DID THIS FOR ALL OF YOU.
AND ALL THANKS TO THE VERY GRACIOUS SUPPORT OF OUR VERY OWN MAYOR J. JONAH JAMESON.
WHEREVER YOU ARE, J.J.J., I COULDN'T HAVE DONE THIS WITHOUT YOU...
...PARTNER.
AH! THAT BLACKMAILING BUG! HE'S GOT ME RIGHT WHERE HE WANTS ME!
RIGHT UNDER HIS WEBBED THUMB! WE'RE IN CAHOOTS!
CAHOOTS!

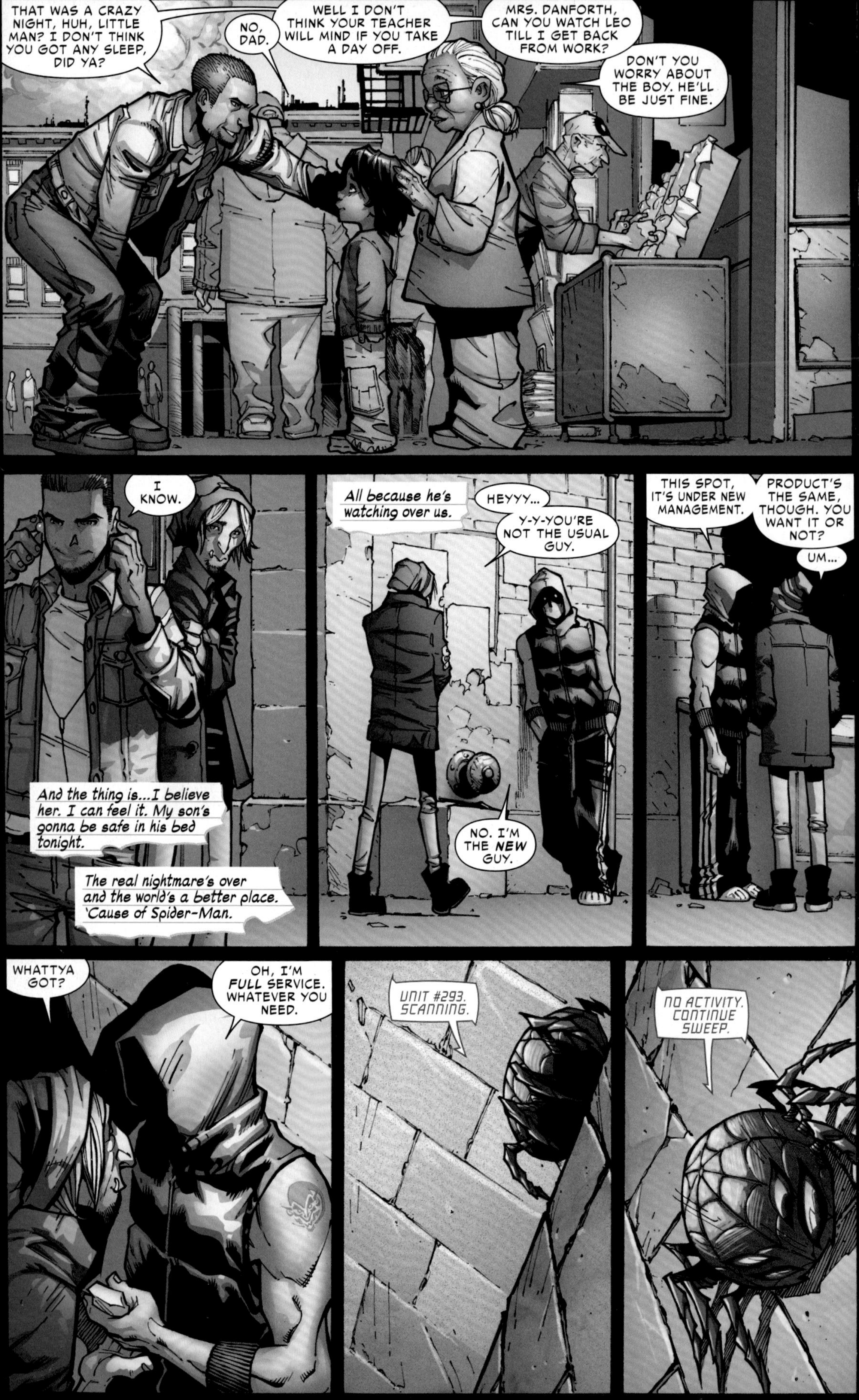
THAT WAS A CRAZY NIGHT, HUH, LITTLE MAN? I DON'T THINK YOU GOT ANY SLEEP, DID YA?
NO, DAD.
WELL I DON'T THINK YOUR TEACHER WILL MIND IF YOU TAKE A DAY OFF.
MRS. DANFORTH, CAN YOU WATCH LEO TILL I GET BACK FROM WORK?
DON'T YOU WORRY ABOUT THE BOY. HE'LL BE JUST FINE.
I KNOW.
And the thing is...I believe her. I can feel it. My son's gonna be safe in his bed tonight.
The real nightmare's over and the world's a better place. 'Cause of Spider-Man.
All because he's watching over us.
HEYYY...
Y-Y-YOU'RE NOT THE USUAL GUY.
NO. I'M THE NEW GUY.
THIS SPOT, IT'S UNDER NEW MANAGEMENT.
PRODUCT'S THE SAME, THOUGH. YOU WANT IT OR NOT?
UM...
WHATTYA GOT?
OH, I'M FULL SERVICE. WHATEVER YOU NEED.
UNIT #293. SCANNING.
NO ACTIVITY. CONTINUE SWEEP.

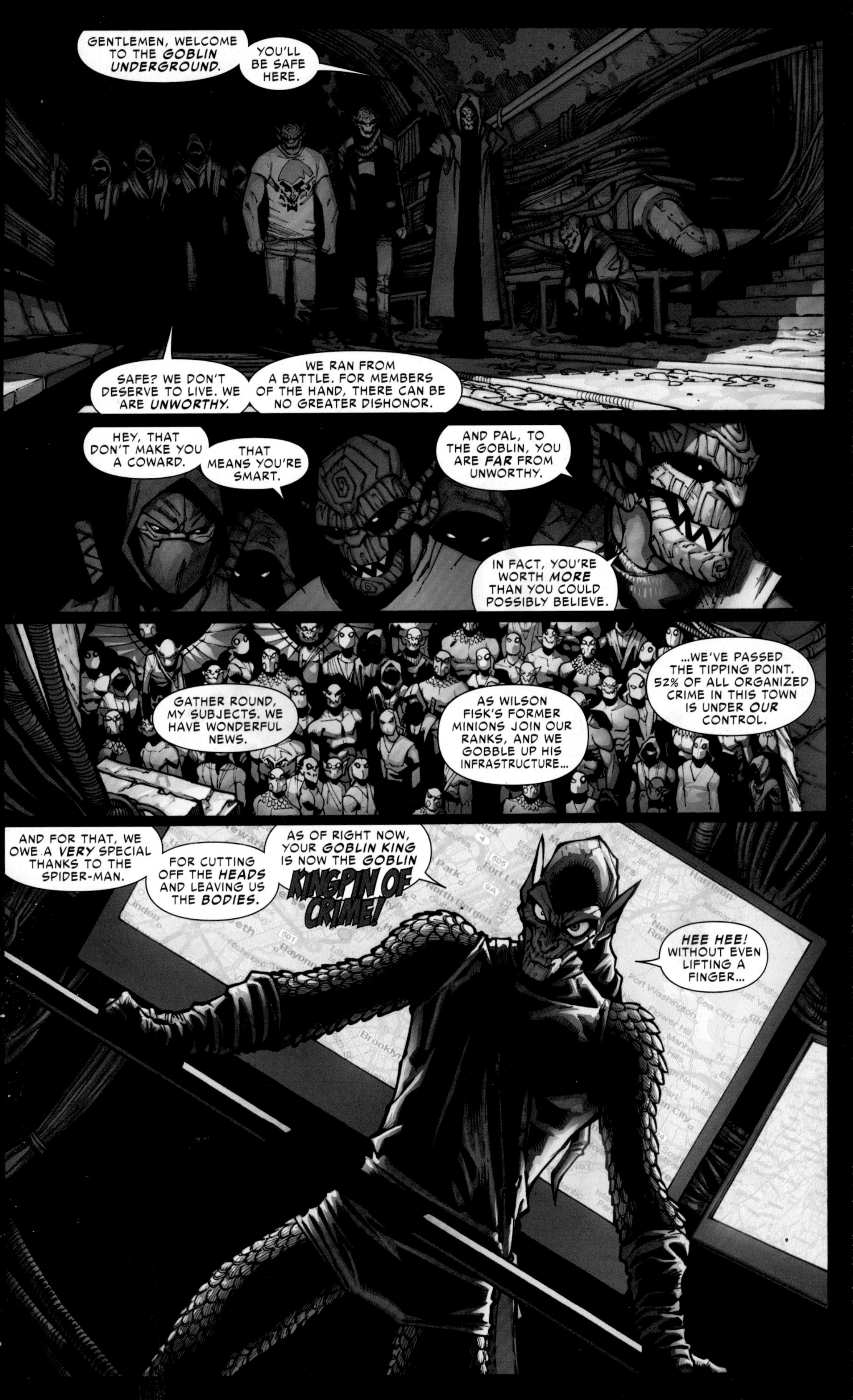
GENTLEMEN, WELCOME TO THE GOBLIN UNDERGROUND.
YOU'LL BE SAFE HERE.
SAFE? WE DON'T DESERVE TO LIVE. WE ARE UNWORTHY.
WE RAN FROM A BATTLE. FOR MEMBERS OF THE HAND, THERE CAN BE NO GREATER DISHONOR.
HEY, THAT DON'T MAKE YOU A COWARD.
THAT MEANS YOU'RE SMART.
AND PAL, TO THE GOBLIN, YOU ARE FAR FROM UNWORTHY.
IN FACT, YOU'RE WORTH MORE THAN YOU COULD POSSIBLY BELIEVE.
GATHER ROUND, MY SUBJECTS. WE HAVE WONDERFUL NEWS.
AS WILSON FISK'S FORMER MINIONS JOIN OUR RANKS, AND WE GOBBLE UP HIS INFRASTRUCTURE...
...WE'VE PASSED THE TIPPING POINT. 52% OF ALL ORGANIZED CRIME IN THIS TOWN IS UNDER OUR CONTROL.
AND FOR THAT, WE OWE A VERY SPECIAL THANKS TO THE SPIDER-MAN.
FOR CUTTING OFF THE HEADS AND LEAVING US THE BODIES.
AS OF RIGHT NOW, YOUR GOBLIN KING IS NOW THE GOBLIN
KINGPIN OF CRIME!
HEE HEE! WITHOUT EVEN LIFTING A FINGER...

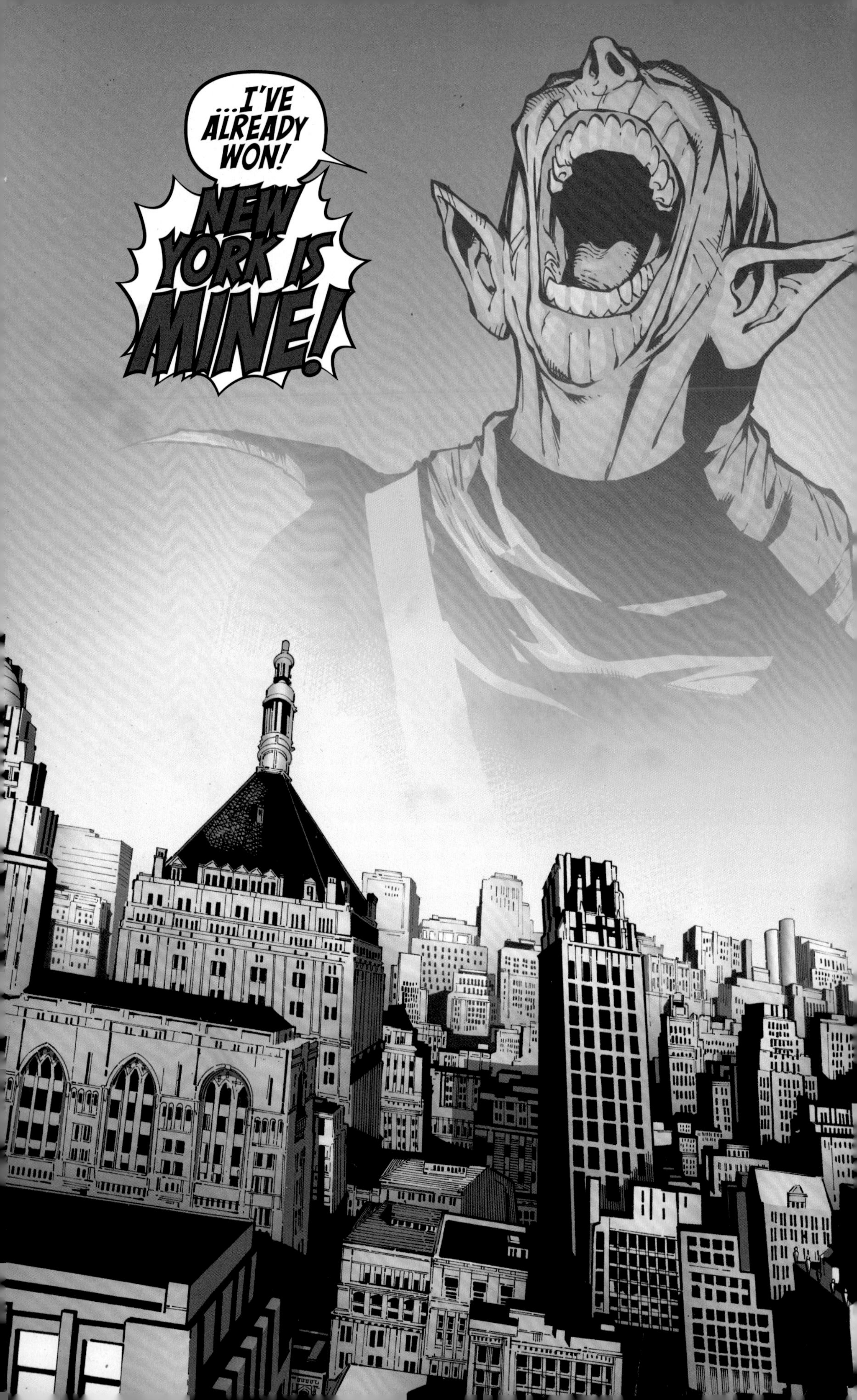
...I'VE ALREADY WON!
NEW YORK IS MINE!

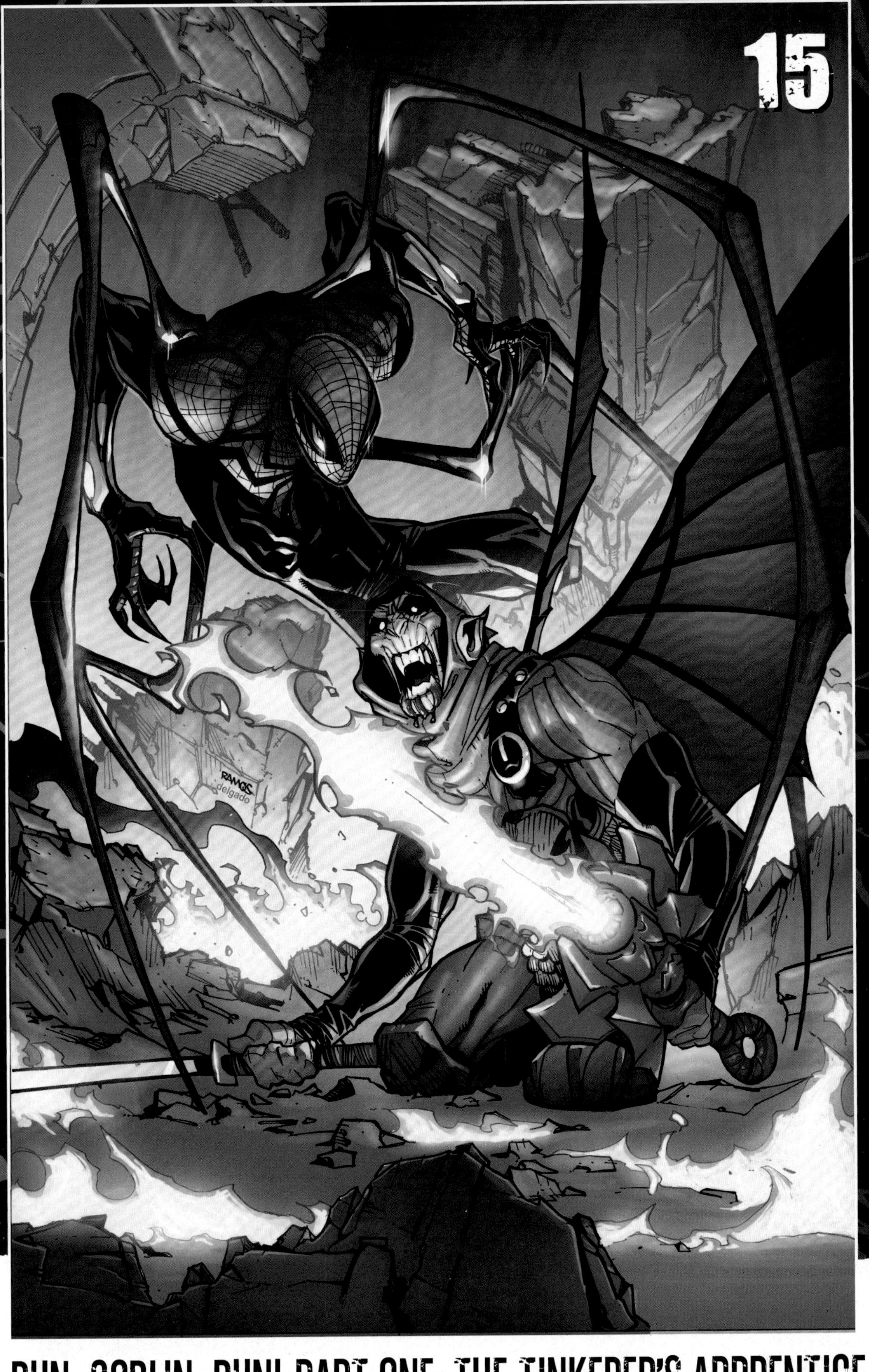
15
RAMOS
delgado

RUN, GOBLIN, RUN! PART ONE: THE TINKERER'S APPRENTICE

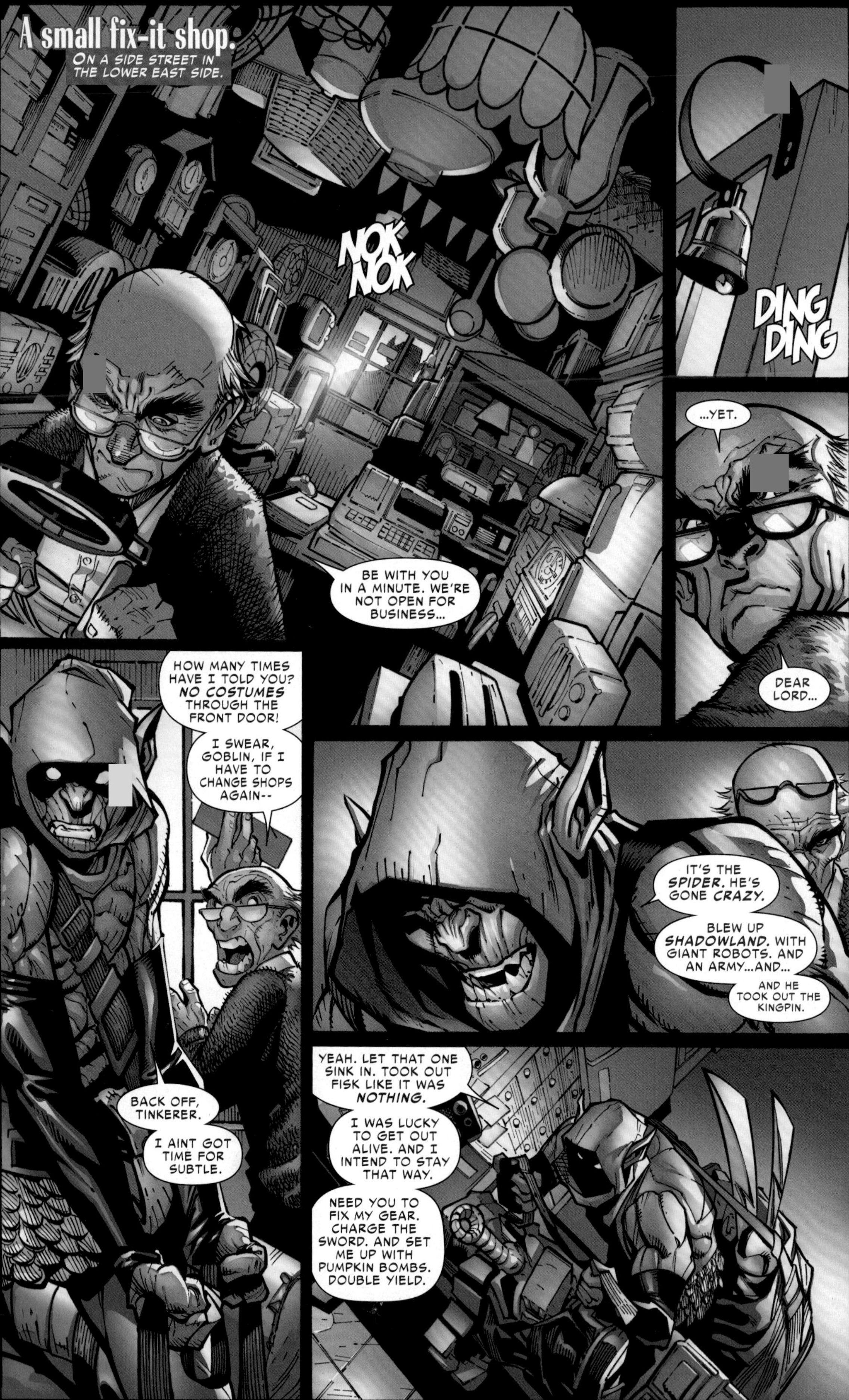
A small fix-it shop.
ON A SIDE STREET IN THE LOWER EAST SIDE.
NOK NOK
DING DING
BE WITH YOU IN A MINUTE. WE'RE NOT OPEN FOR BUSINESS...
...YET.
DEAR LORD...
HOW MANY TIMES HAVE I TOLD YOU? NO COSTUMES THROUGH THE FRONT DOOR!
I SWEAR, GOBLIN, IF I HAVE TO CHANGE SHOPS AGAIN--
BACK OFF, TINKERER.
I AINT GOT TIME FOR SUBTLE.
IT'S THE SPIDER. HE'S GONE CRAZY.
BLEW UP SHADOWLAND. WITH GIANT ROBOTS. AND AN ARMY...AND...
AND HE TOOK OUT THE KINGPIN.
YEAH. LET THAT ONE SINK IN. TOOK OUT FISK LIKE IT WAS NOTHING.
I WAS LUCKY TO GET OUT ALIVE. AND I INTEND TO STAY THAT WAY.
NEED YOU TO FIX MY GEAR. CHARGE THE SWORD. AND SET ME UP WITH PUMPKIN BOMBS. DOUBLE YIELD.

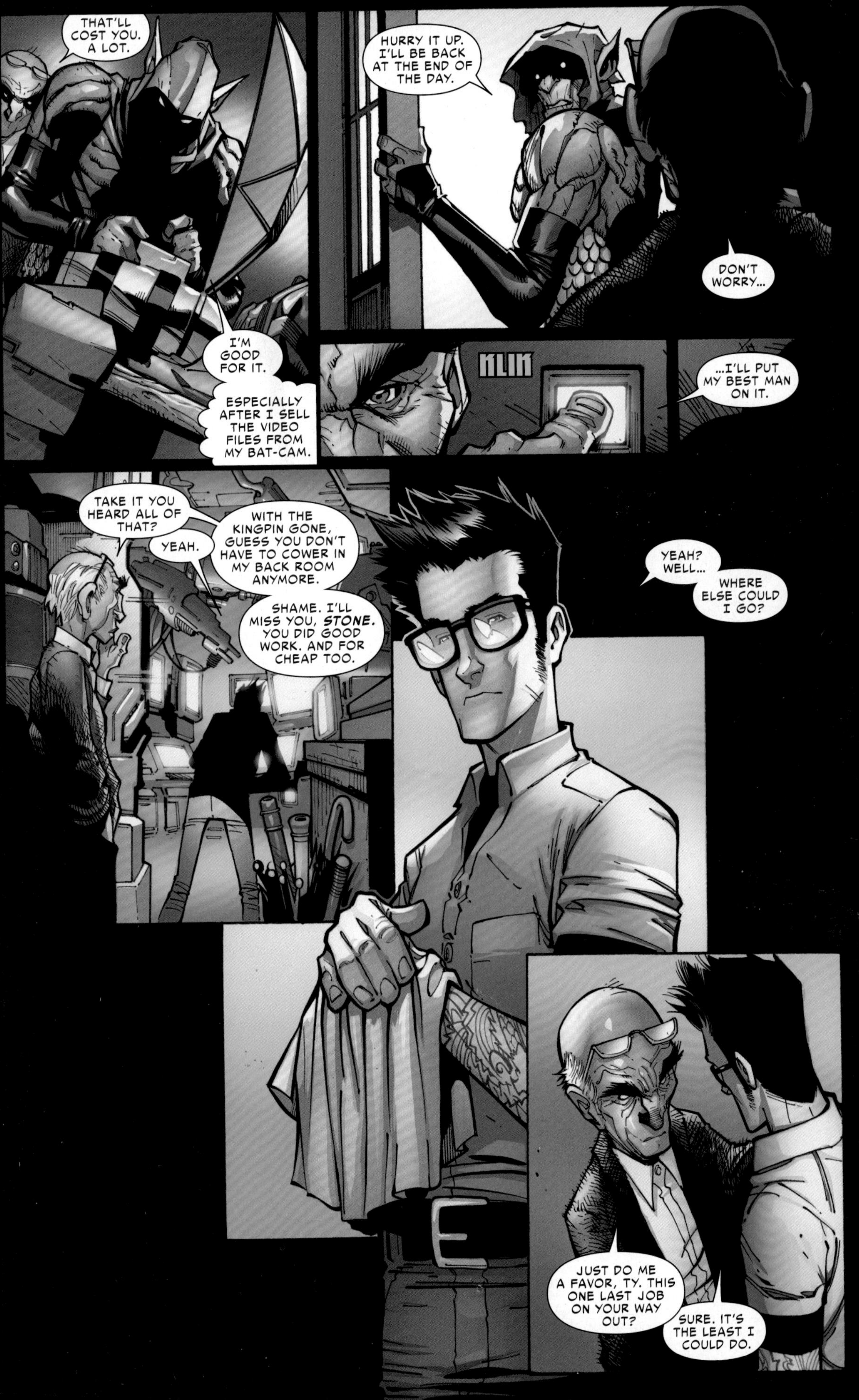
THAT'LL COST YOU. A LOT.
I'M GOOD FOR IT.
ESPECIALLY AFTER I SELL THE VIDEO FILES FROM MY BAT-CAM.
HURRY IT UP. I'LL BE BACK AT THE END OF THE DAY.
DON'T WORRY...
KLIK
...I'LL PUT MY BEST MAN ON IT.
TAKE IT YOU HEARD ALL OF THAT?
YEAH.
WITH THE KINGPIN GONE, GUESS YOU DON'T HAVE TO COWER IN MY BACK ROOM ANYMORE.
SHAME. I'LL MISS YOU, STONE. YOU DID GOOD WORK. AND FOR CHEAP TOO.
YEAH? WELL...
WHERE ELSE COULD I GO?
JUST DO ME A FAVOR, TY. THIS ONE LAST JOB ON YOUR WAY OUT?
SURE. IT'S THE LEAST I COULD DO.

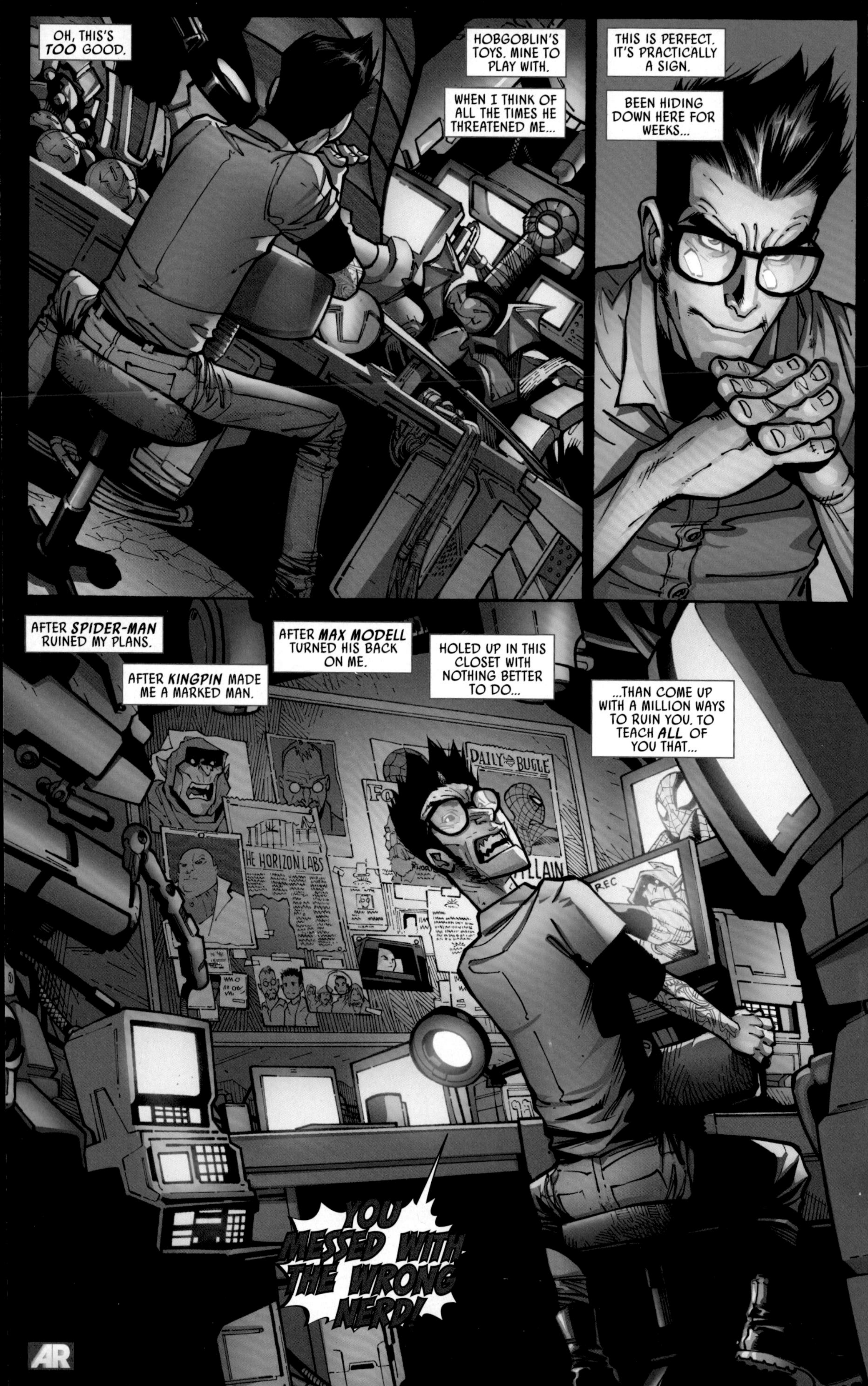

OH, THIS'S *TOO* GOOD.
HOBGOBLIN'S TOYS. MINE TO PLAY WITH.
WHEN I THINK OF ALL THE TIMES HE THREATENED ME...
THIS IS PERFECT. IT'S PRACTICALLY A SIGN.
BEEN HIDING DOWN HERE FOR WEEKS...
AFTER **SPIDER-MAN** RUINED MY PLANS.
AFTER **KINGPIN** MADE ME A MARKED MAN.
AFTER **MAX MODELL** TURNED HIS BACK ON ME.
HOLED UP IN THIS CLOSET WITH NOTHING BETTER TO DO...
...THAN COME UP WITH A MILLION WAYS TO RUIN YOU. TO TEACH **ALL** OF YOU THAT...
YOU MESSED WITH THE WRONG NERD!

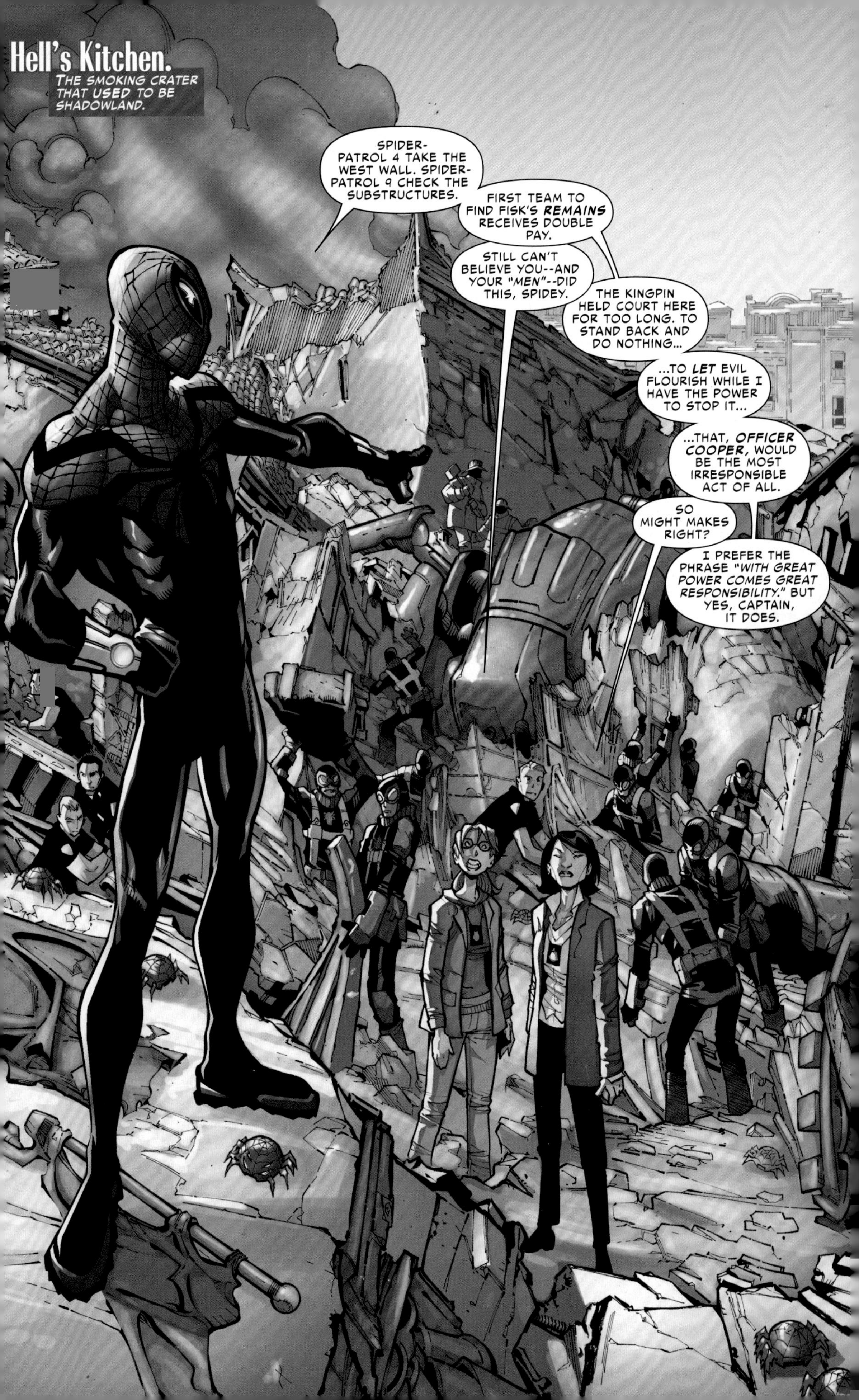

Hell's Kitchen.
THE SMOKING CRATER THAT USED TO BE SHADOWLAND.
SPIDER-PATROL 4 TAKE THE WEST WALL. SPIDER-PATROL 9 CHECK THE SUBSTRUCTURES.
FIRST TEAM TO FIND FISK'S REMAINS RECEIVES DOUBLE PAY.
STILL CAN'T BELIEVE YOU--AND YOUR "MEN"--DID THIS, SPIDEY.
THE KINGPIN HELD COURT HERE FOR TOO LONG. TO STAND BACK AND DO NOTHING...
...TO LET EVIL FLOURISH WHILE I HAVE THE POWER TO STOP IT...
...THAT, OFFICER COOPER, WOULD BE THE MOST IRRESPONSIBLE ACT OF ALL.
SO MIGHT MAKES RIGHT?
I PREFER THE PHRASE "WITH GREAT POWER COMES GREAT RESPONSIBILITY." BUT YES, CAPTAIN, IT DOES.

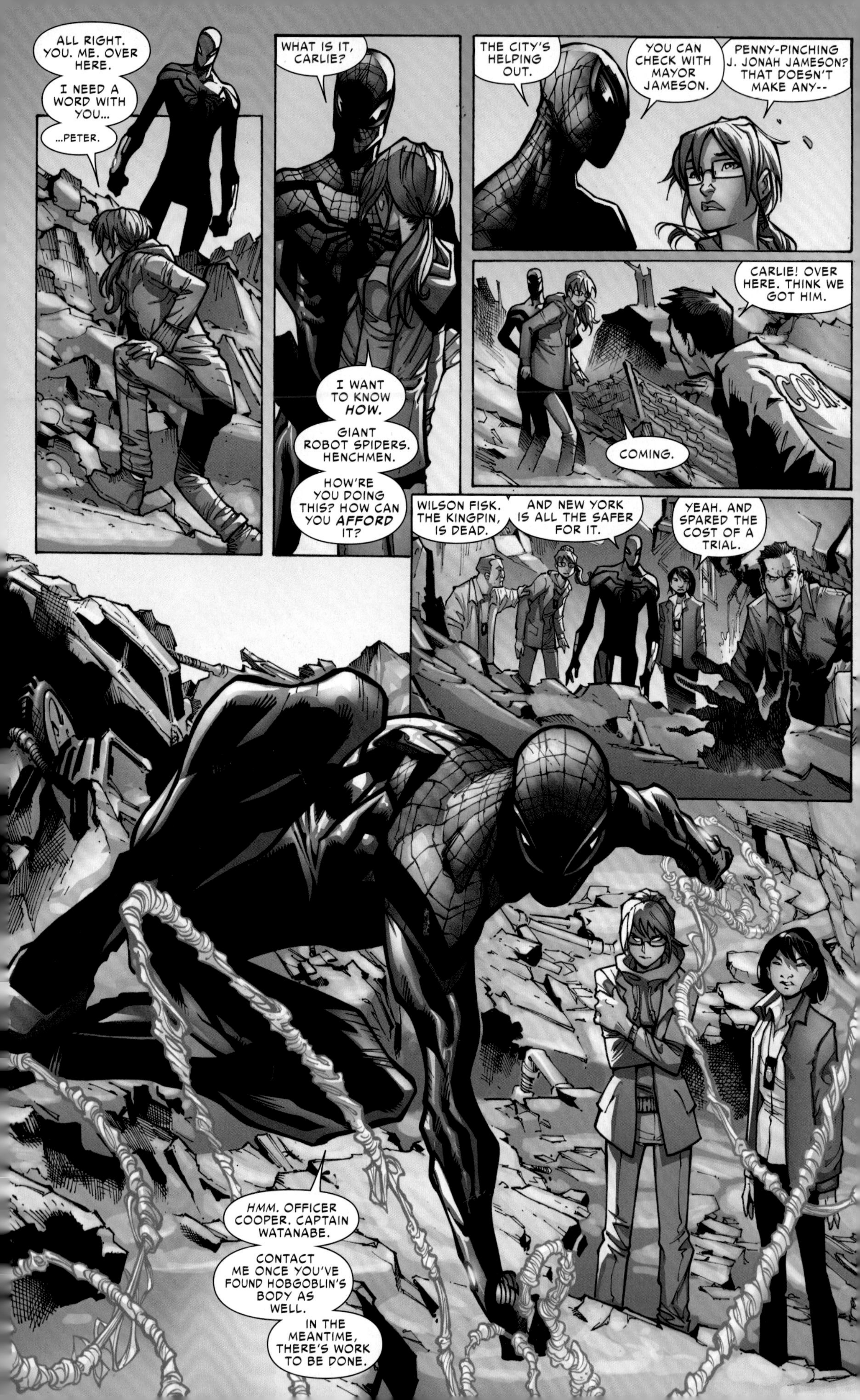
ALL RIGHT. YOU. ME. OVER HERE.
I NEED A WORD WITH YOU...
...PETER.
WHAT IS IT, CARLIE?
I WANT TO KNOW *HOW.*
GIANT ROBOT SPIDERS. HENCHMEN.
HOW'RE YOU DOING THIS? HOW CAN YOU *AFFORD* IT?
THE CITY'S HELPING OUT.
YOU CAN CHECK WITH MAYOR JAMESON.
PENNY-PINCHING J. JONAH JAMESON? THAT DOESN'T MAKE ANY--
CARLIE! OVER HERE. THINK WE GOT HIM.
COMING.
WILSON FISK. THE KINGPIN, IS DEAD.
AND NEW YORK IS ALL THE SAFER FOR IT.
YEAH. AND SPARED THE COST OF A TRIAL.
HMM. OFFICER COOPER. CAPTAIN WATANABE.
CONTACT ME ONCE YOU'VE FOUND HOBGOBLIN'S BODY AS WELL.
IN THE MEANTIME, THERE'S WORK TO BE DONE.

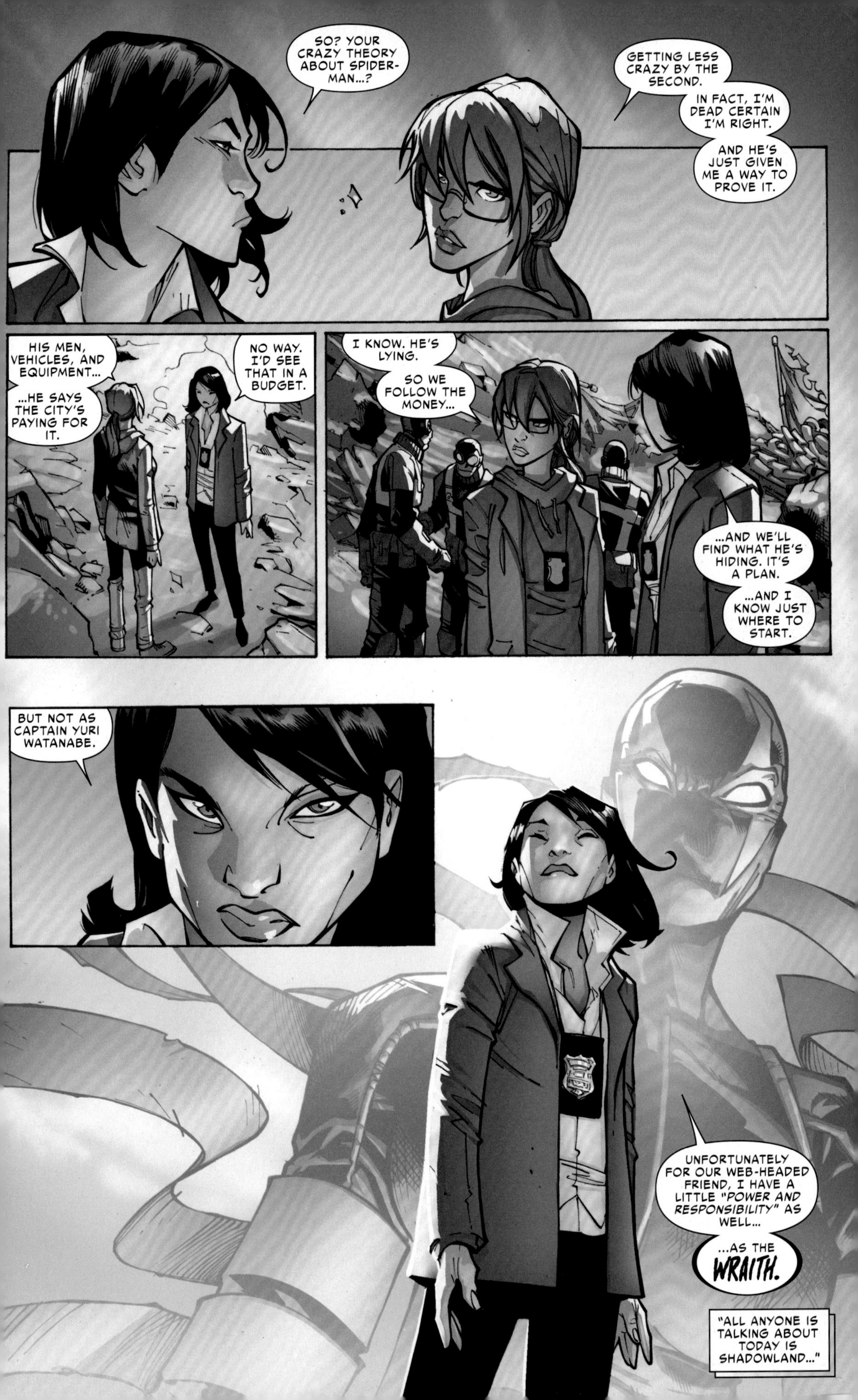

SO? YOUR CRAZY THEORY ABOUT SPIDER-MAN...?
GETTING LESS CRAZY BY THE SECOND.
IN FACT, I'M DEAD CERTAIN I'M RIGHT.
AND HE'S JUST GIVEN ME A WAY TO PROVE IT.
HIS MEN, VEHICLES, AND EQUIPMENT...
...HE SAYS THE CITY'S PAYING FOR IT.
NO WAY. I'D SEE THAT IN A BUDGET.
I KNOW. HE'S LYING.
SO WE FOLLOW THE MONEY...
...AND WE'LL FIND WHAT HE'S HIDING. IT'S A PLAN.
...AND I KNOW JUST WHERE TO START.
BUT NOT AS CAPTAIN YURI WATANABE.
UNFORTUNATELY FOR OUR WEB-HEADED FRIEND, I HAVE A LITTLE "POWER AND RESPONSIBILITY" AS WELL...
...AS THE WRAITH.
"ALL ANYONE IS TALKING ABOUT TODAY IS SHADOWLAND..."

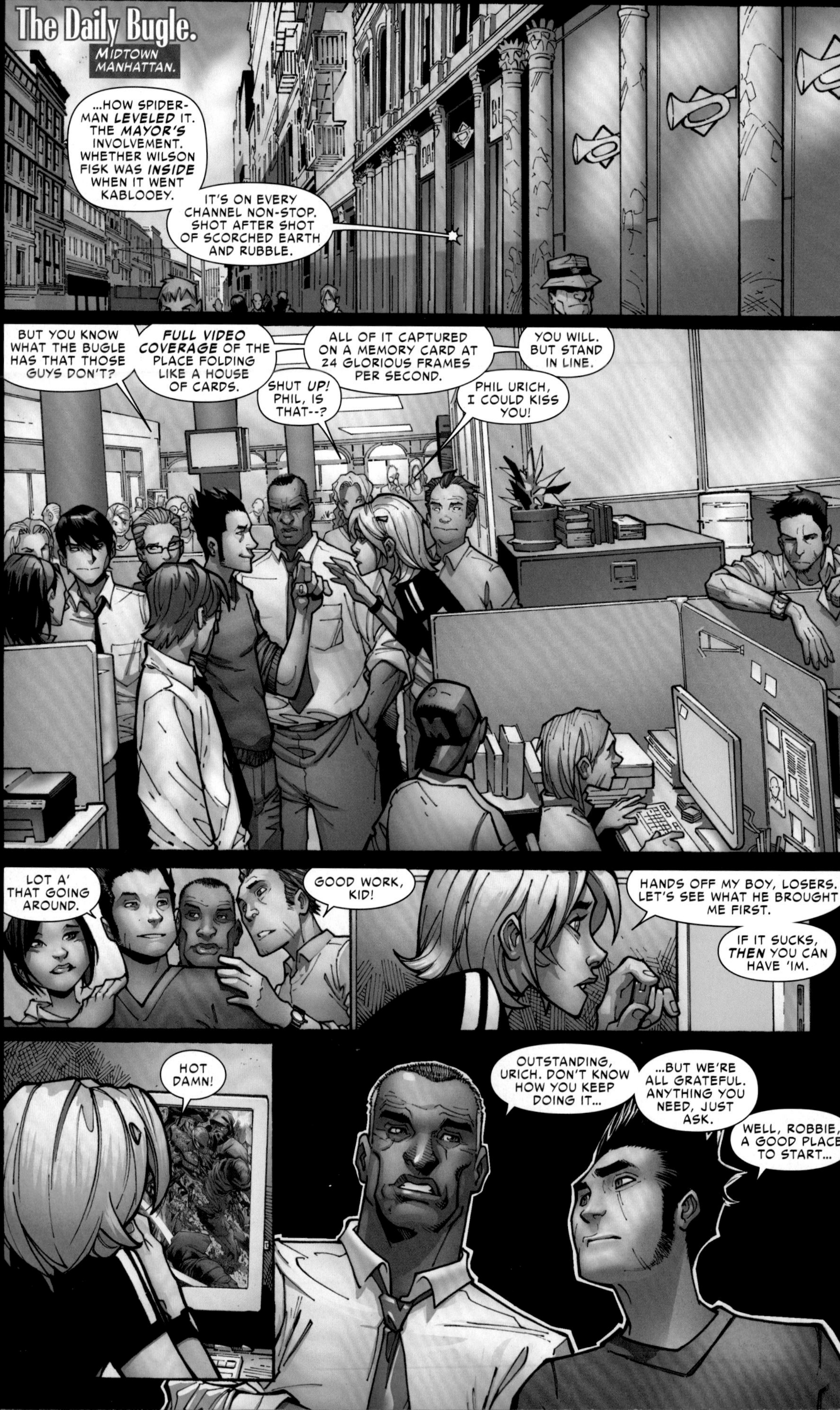
The Daily Bugle.
MIDTOWN MANHATTAN.
...HOW SPIDER-MAN LEVELED IT. THE MAYOR'S INVOLVEMENT. WHETHER WILSON FISK WAS INSIDE WHEN IT WENT KABLOOEY.
IT'S ON EVERY CHANNEL NON-STOP. SHOT AFTER SHOT OF SCORCHED EARTH AND RUBBLE.
BUT YOU KNOW WHAT THE BUGLE HAS THAT THOSE GUYS DON'T?
FULL VIDEO COVERAGE OF THE PLACE FOLDING LIKE A HOUSE OF CARDS.
ALL OF IT CAPTURED ON A MEMORY CARD AT 24 GLORIOUS FRAMES PER SECOND.
SHUT UP! PHIL, IS THAT--?
YOU WILL. BUT STAND IN LINE.
PHIL URICH, I COULD KISS YOU!
LOT A' THAT GOING AROUND.
GOOD WORK, KID!
HANDS OFF MY BOY, LOSERS. LET'S SEE WHAT HE BROUGHT ME FIRST.
IF IT SUCKS, THEN YOU CAN HAVE 'IM.
HOT DAMN!
OUTSTANDING, URICH. DON'T KNOW HOW YOU KEEP DOING IT...
...BUT WE'RE ALL GRATEFUL. ANYTHING YOU NEED, JUST ASK.
WELL, ROBBIE, A GOOD PLACE TO START...

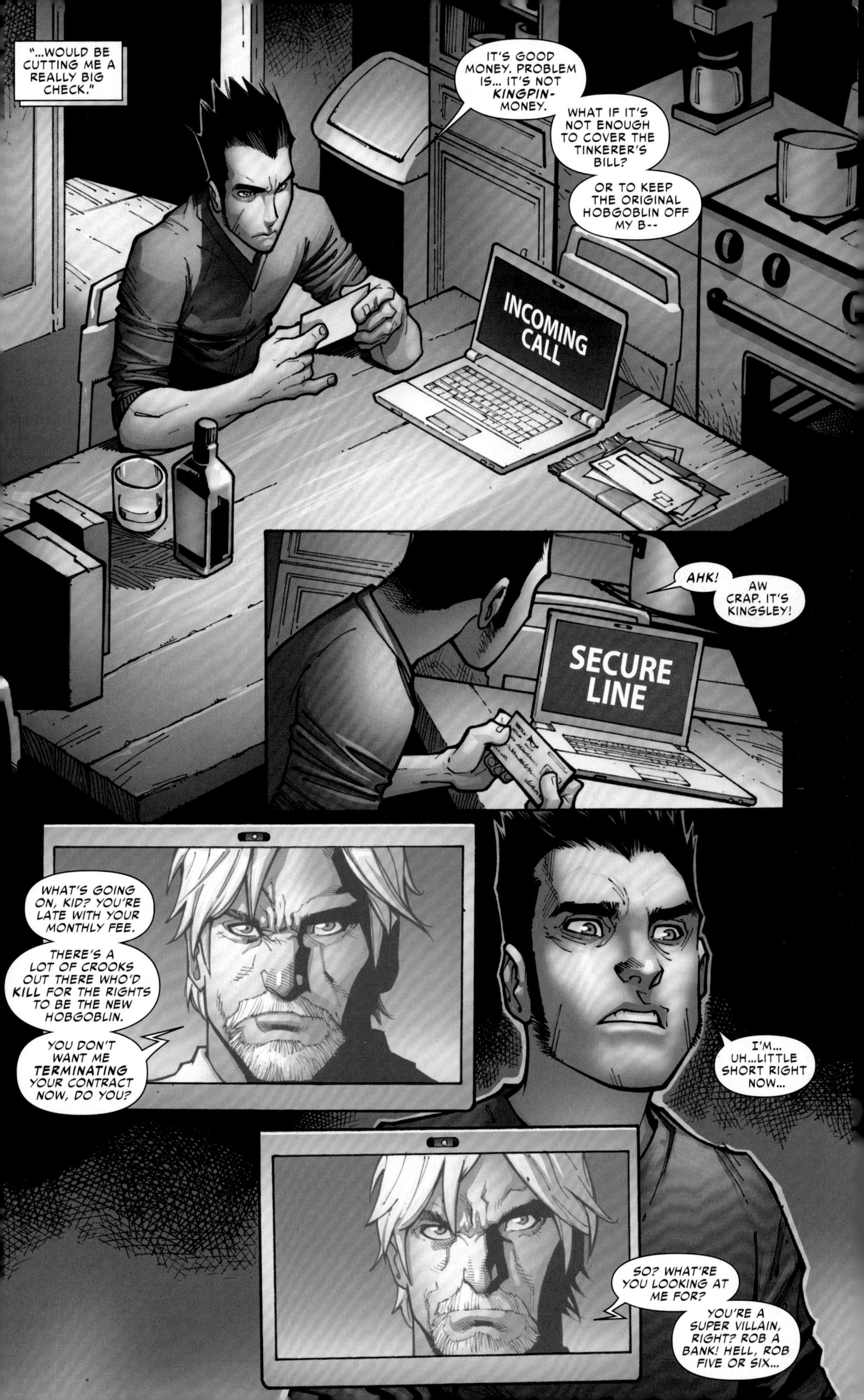
"...WOULD BE CUTTING ME A REALLY BIG CHECK."
IT'S GOOD MONEY. PROBLEM IS... IT'S NOT KINGPIN-MONEY.
WHAT IF IT'S NOT ENOUGH TO COVER THE TINKERER'S BILL?
OR TO KEEP THE ORIGINAL HOBGOBLIN OFF MY B--
INCOMING CALL
AHK!
AW CRAP. IT'S KINGSLEY!
SECURE LINE
WHAT'S GOING ON, KID? YOU'RE LATE WITH YOUR MONTHLY FEE.
THERE'S A LOT OF CROOKS OUT THERE WHO'D KILL FOR THE RIGHTS TO BE THE NEW HOBGOBLIN.
YOU DON'T WANT ME TERMINATING YOUR CONTRACT NOW, DO YOU?
I'M... UH...LITTLE SHORT RIGHT NOW...
SO? WHAT'RE YOU LOOKING AT ME FOR?
YOU'RE A SUPER VILLAIN, RIGHT? ROB A BANK! HELL, ROB FIVE OR SIX...

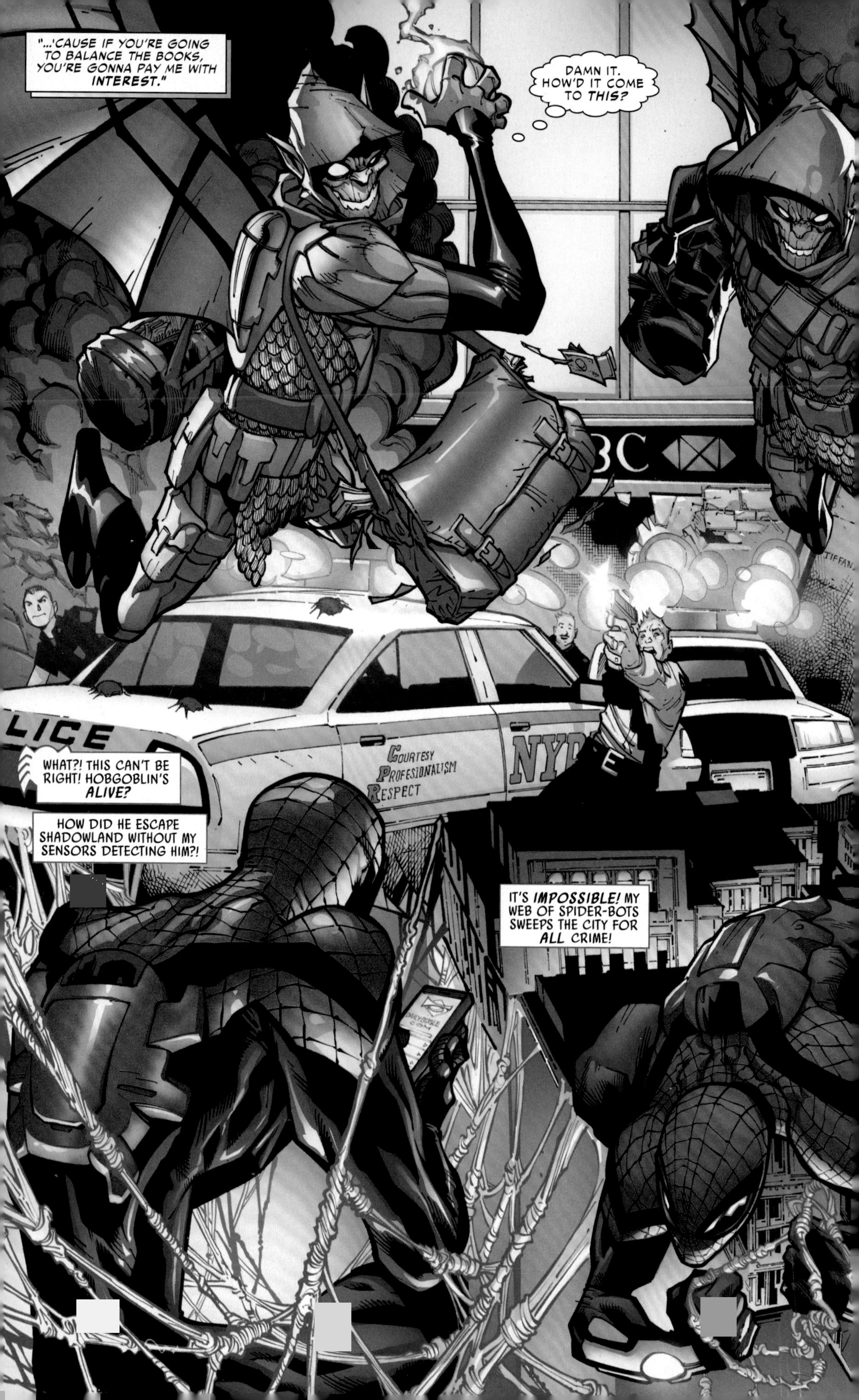

"...'CAUSE IF YOU'RE GOING TO BALANCE THE BOOKS, YOU'RE GONNA PAY ME WITH INTEREST."
DAMN IT. HOW'D IT COME TO THIS?
WHAT?! THIS CAN'T BE RIGHT! HOBGOBLIN'S ALIVE?
HOW DID HE ESCAPE SHADOWLAND WITHOUT MY SENSORS DETECTING HIM?!
IT'S IMPOSSIBLE! MY WEB OF SPIDER-BOTS SWEEPS THE CITY FOR ALL CRIME!

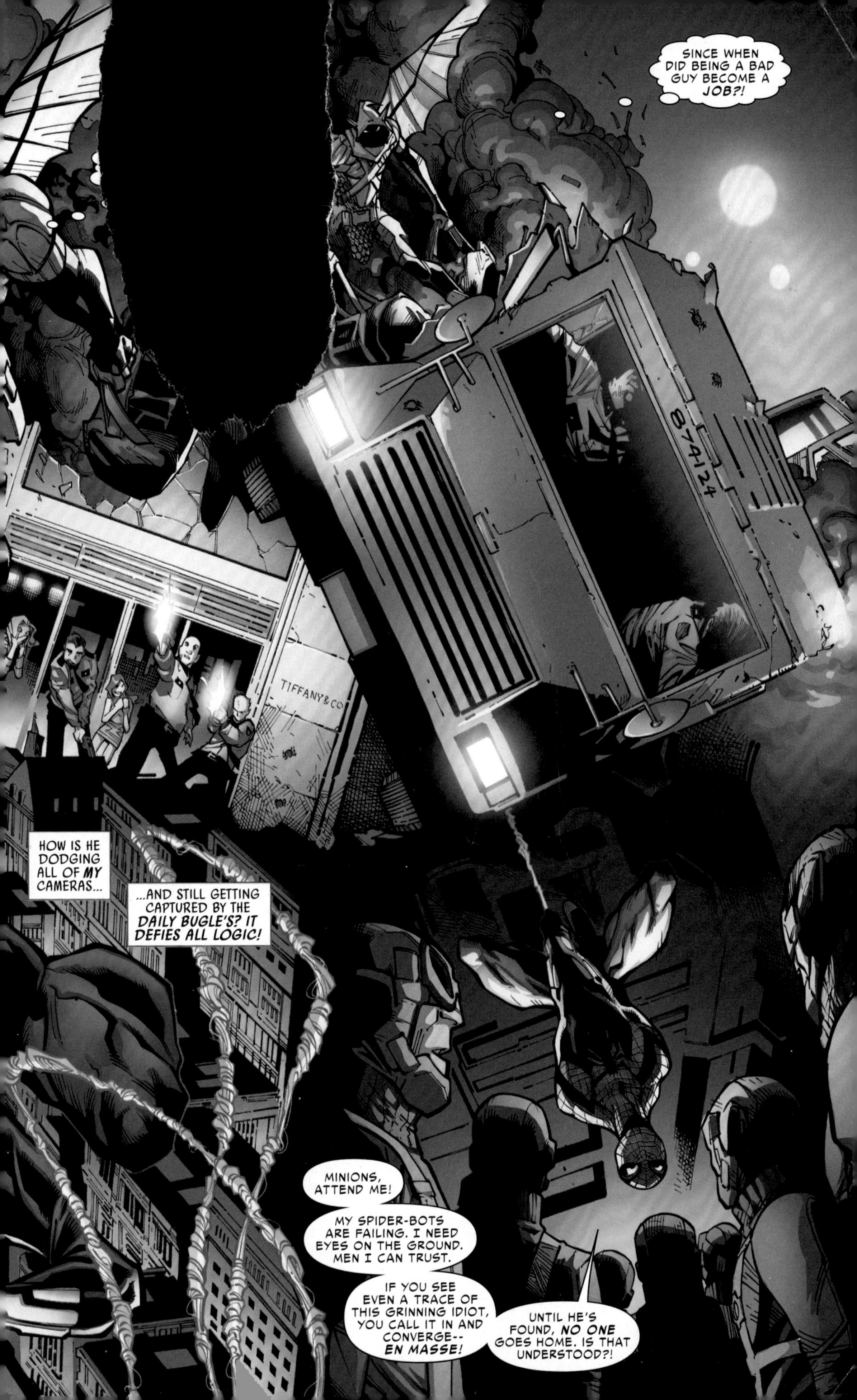
SINCE WHEN DID BEING A BAD GUY BECOME A JOB?!
874124
TIFFANY & CO.
HOW IS HE DODGING ALL OF MY CAMERAS...
...AND STILL GETTING CAPTURED BY THE DAILY BUGLE'S? IT DEFIES ALL LOGIC!
MINIONS, ATTEND ME!
MY SPIDER-BOTS ARE FAILING. I NEED EYES ON THE GROUND. MEN I CAN TRUST.
IF YOU SEE EVEN A TRACE OF THIS GRINNING IDIOT, YOU CALL IT IN AND CONVERGE-- EN MASSE!
UNTIL HE'S FOUND, NO ONE GOES HOME. IS THAT UNDERSTOOD?!

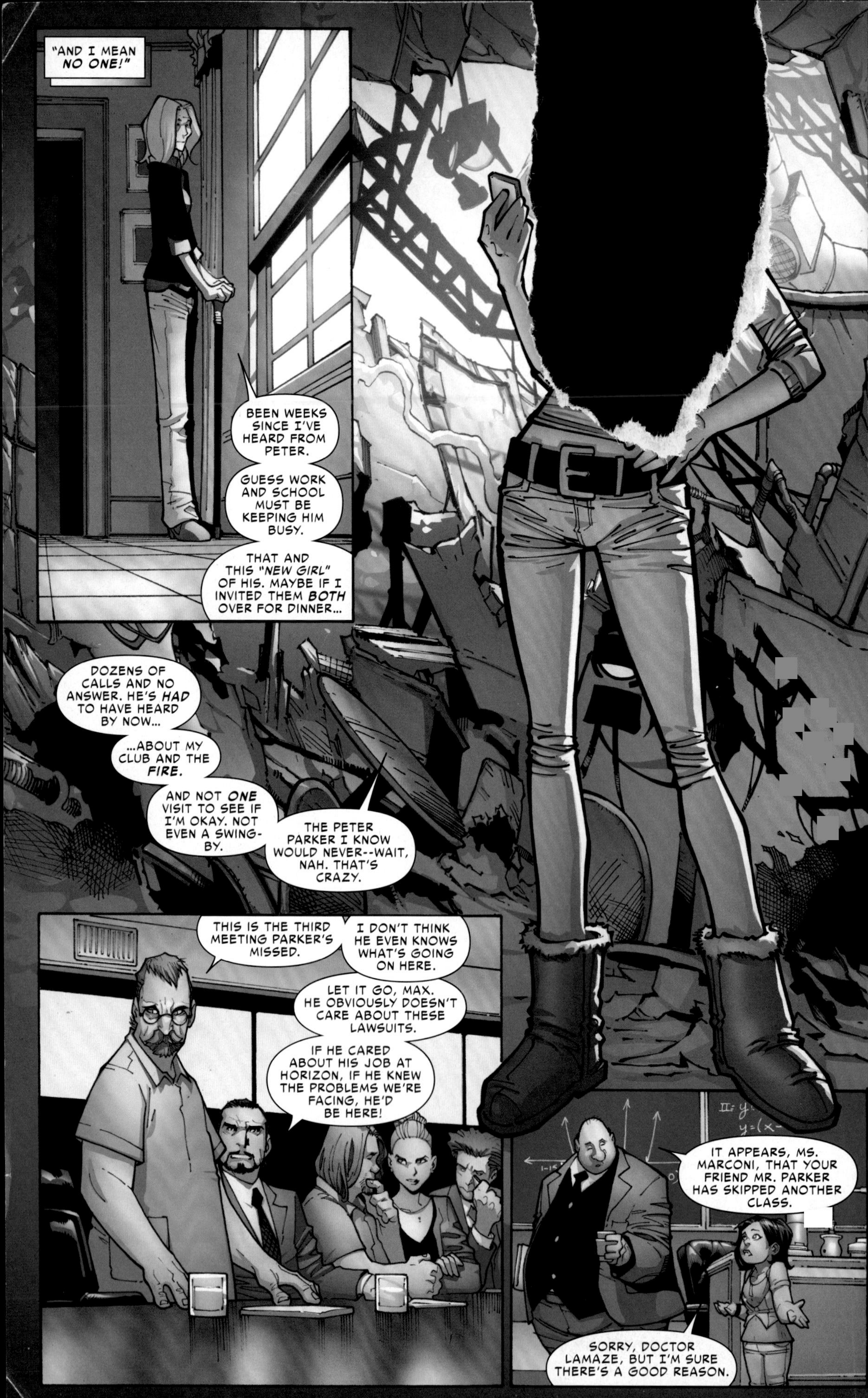
"AND I MEAN NO ONE!"
BEEN WEEKS SINCE I'VE HEARD FROM PETER.
GUESS WORK AND SCHOOL MUST BE KEEPING HIM BUSY.
THAT AND THIS "NEW GIRL" OF HIS. MAYBE IF I INVITED THEM BOTH OVER FOR DINNER...
DOZENS OF CALLS AND NO ANSWER. HE'S HAD TO HAVE HEARD BY NOW...
...ABOUT MY CLUB AND THE FIRE.
AND NOT ONE VISIT TO SEE IF I'M OKAY. NOT EVEN A SWING-BY.
THE PETER PARKER I KNOW WOULD NEVER--WAIT, NAH. THAT'S CRAZY.
THIS IS THE THIRD MEETING PARKER'S MISSED.
I DON'T THINK HE EVEN KNOWS WHAT'S GOING ON HERE.
LET IT GO, MAX. HE OBVIOUSLY DOESN'T CARE ABOUT THESE LAWSUITS.
IF HE CARED ABOUT HIS JOB AT HORIZON, IF HE KNEW THE PROBLEMS WE'RE FACING, HE'D BE HERE!
IT APPEARS, MS. MARCONI, THAT YOUR FRIEND MR. PARKER HAS SKIPPED ANOTHER CLASS.
SORRY, DOCTOR LAMAZE, BUT I'M SURE THERE'S A GOOD REASON.

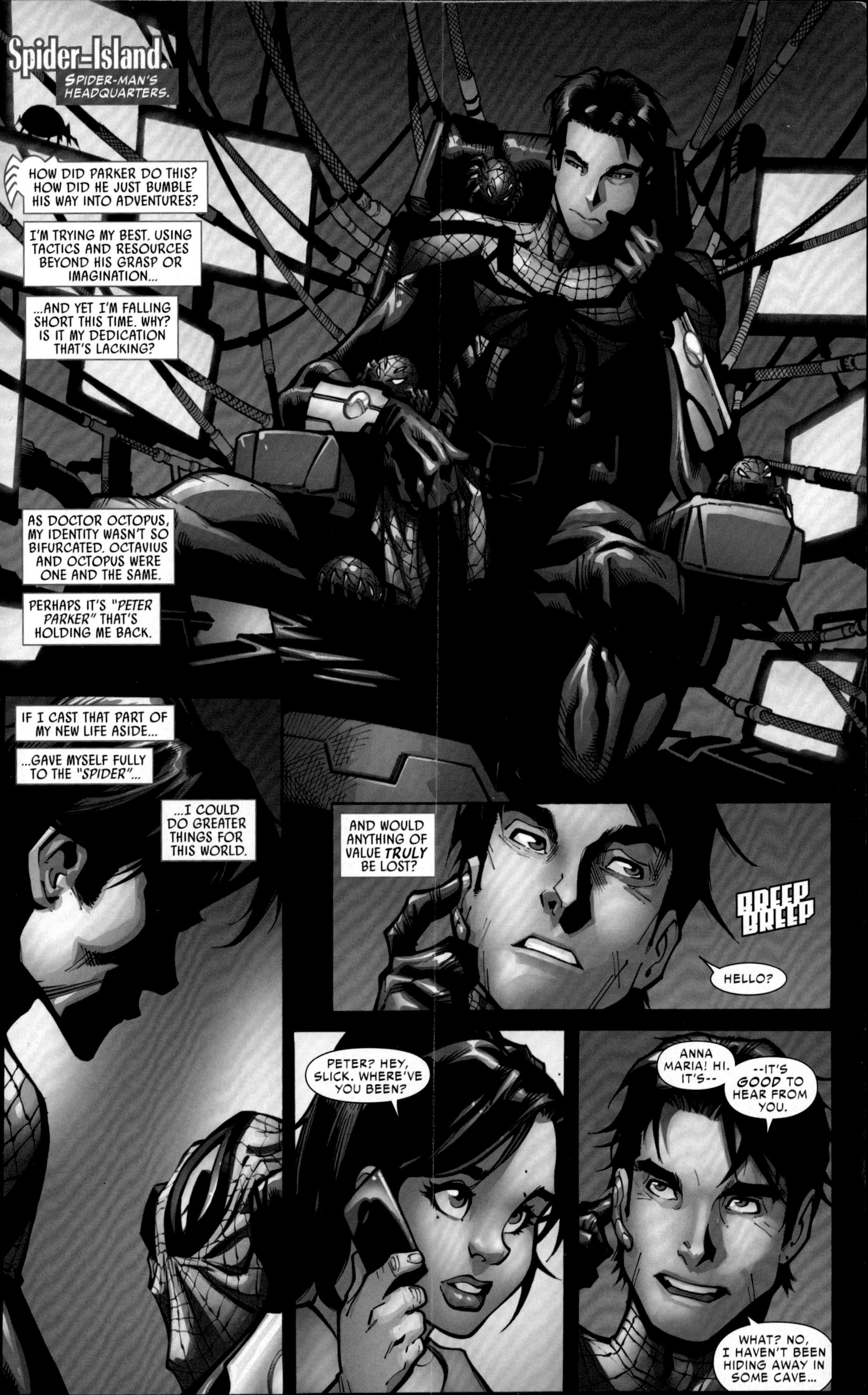
Spider-Island.
SPIDER-MAN'S HEADQUARTERS.
HOW DID PARKER DO THIS? HOW DID HE JUST BUMBLE HIS WAY INTO ADVENTURES?
I'M TRYING MY BEST. USING TACTICS AND RESOURCES BEYOND HIS GRASP OR IMAGINATION...
...AND YET I'M FALLING SHORT THIS TIME. WHY? IS IT MY DEDICATION THAT'S LACKING?
AS DOCTOR OCTOPUS, MY IDENTITY WASN'T SO BIFURCATED. OCTAVIUS AND OCTOPUS WERE ONE AND THE SAME.
PERHAPS IT'S "PETER PARKER" THAT'S HOLDING ME BACK.
IF I CAST THAT PART OF MY NEW LIFE ASIDE...
...GAVE MYSELF FULLY TO THE "SPIDER"...
...I COULD DO GREATER THINGS FOR THIS WORLD.
AND WOULD ANYTHING OF VALUE TRULY BE LOST?
BREEP BREEP
HELLO?
PETER? HEY, SLICK. WHERE'VE YOU BEEN?
ANNA MARIA! HI. IT'S--
--IT'S GOOD TO HEAR FROM YOU.
WHAT? NO, I HAVEN'T BEEN HIDING AWAY IN SOME CAVE...

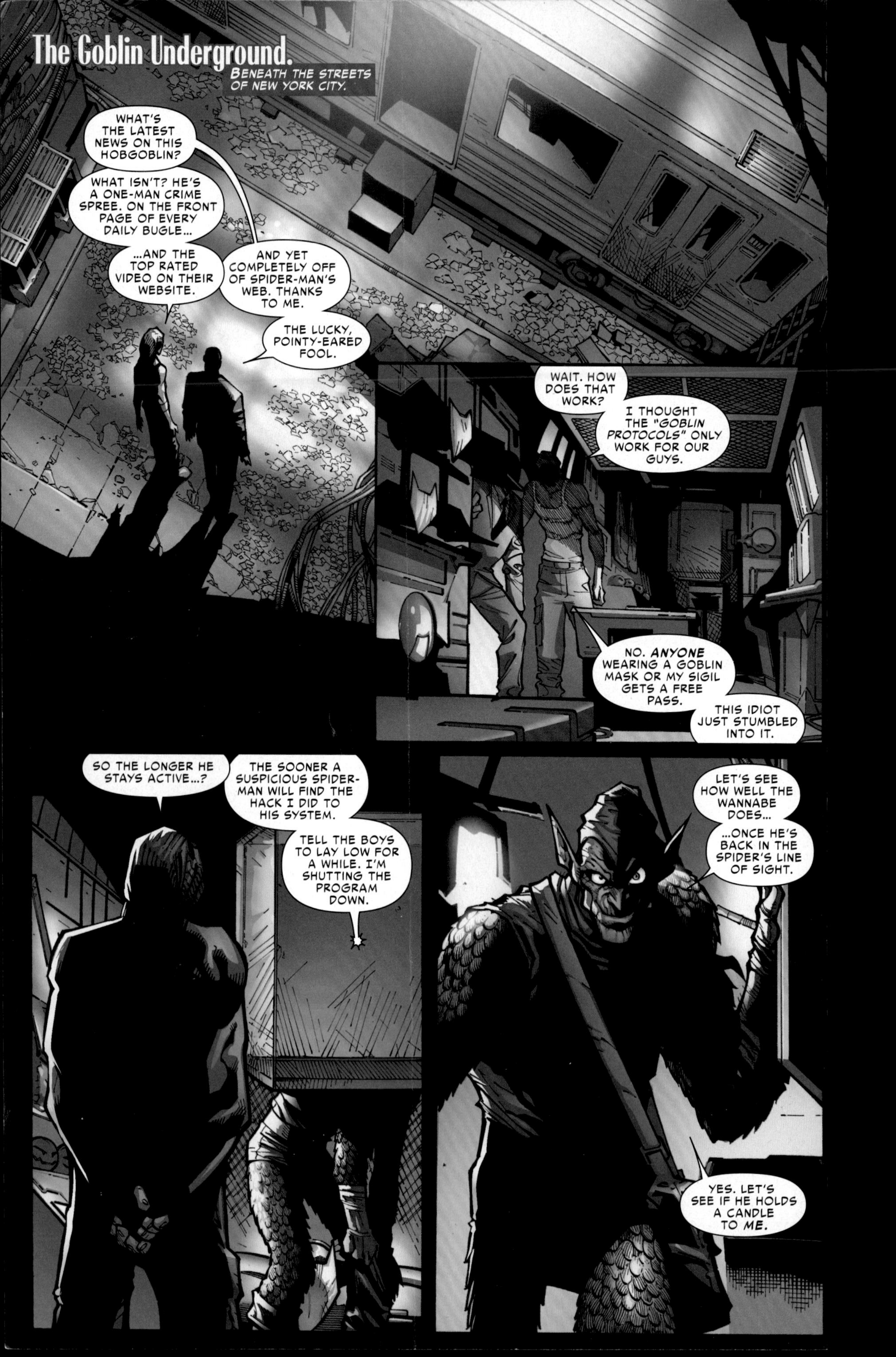
The Goblin Underground.
BENEATH THE STREETS OF NEW YORK CITY.
WHAT'S THE LATEST NEWS ON THIS HOBGOBLIN?
WHAT ISN'T? HE'S A ONE-MAN CRIME SPREE. ON THE FRONT PAGE OF EVERY DAILY BUGLE...
...AND THE TOP RATED VIDEO ON THEIR WEBSITE.
AND YET COMPLETELY OFF OF SPIDER-MAN'S WEB. THANKS TO ME.
THE LUCKY, POINTY-EARED FOOL.
WAIT. HOW DOES THAT WORK?
I THOUGHT THE "GOBLIN PROTOCOLS" ONLY WORK FOR OUR GUYS.
NO. ANYONE WEARING A GOBLIN MASK OR MY SIGIL GETS A FREE PASS.
THIS IDIOT JUST STUMBLED INTO IT.
SO THE LONGER HE STAYS ACTIVE...?
THE SOONER A SUSPICIOUS SPIDER-MAN WILL FIND THE HACK I DID TO HIS SYSTEM.
TELL THE BOYS TO LAY LOW FOR A WHILE. I'M SHUTTING THE PROGRAM DOWN.
LET'S SEE HOW WELL THE WANNABE DOES...
...ONCE HE'S BACK IN THE SPIDER'S LINE OF SIGHT.
YES. LET'S SEE IF HE HOLDS A CANDLE TO ME.

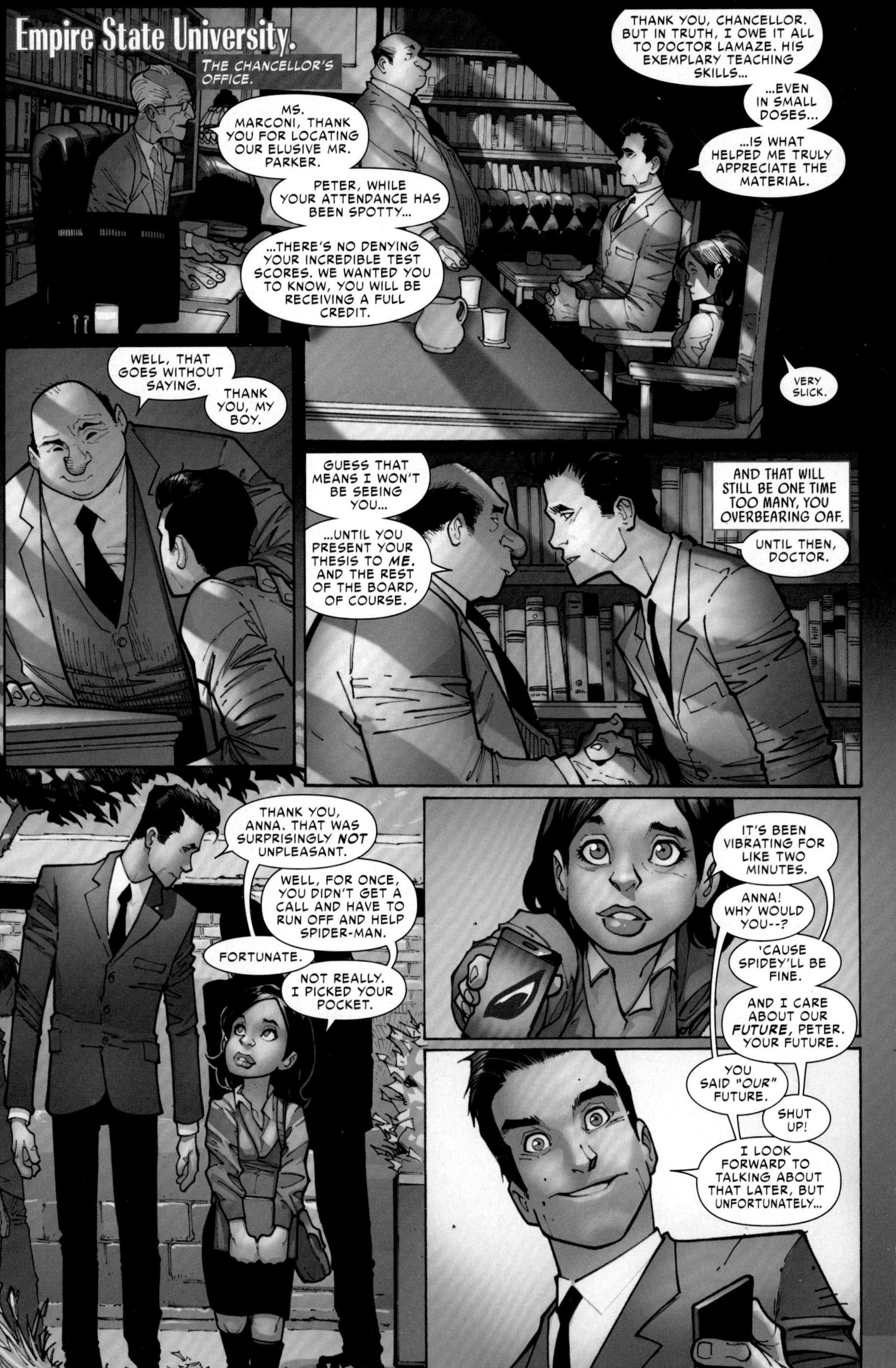

Empire State University.
THE CHANCELLOR'S OFFICE.
MS. MARCONI, THANK YOU FOR LOCATING OUR ELUSIVE MR. PARKER.
PETER, WHILE YOUR ATTENDANCE HAS BEEN SPOTTY...
...THERE'S NO DENYING YOUR INCREDIBLE TEST SCORES. WE WANTED YOU TO KNOW, YOU WILL BE RECEIVING A FULL CREDIT.
THANK YOU, CHANCELLOR. BUT IN TRUTH, I OWE IT ALL TO DOCTOR LAMAZE. HIS EXEMPLARY TEACHING SKILLS...
...EVEN IN SMALL DOSES...
...IS WHAT HELPED ME TRULY APPRECIATE THE MATERIAL.
VERY SLICK.
WELL, THAT GOES WITHOUT SAYING.
THANK YOU, MY BOY.
GUESS THAT MEANS I WON'T BE SEEING YOU...
...UNTIL YOU PRESENT YOUR THESIS TO ME. AND THE REST OF THE BOARD, OF COURSE.
AND THAT WILL STILL BE ONE TIME TOO MANY, YOU OVERBEARING OAF.
UNTIL THEN, DOCTOR.
THANK YOU, ANNA. THAT WAS SURPRISINGLY NOT UNPLEASANT.
WELL, FOR ONCE, YOU DIDN'T GET A CALL AND HAVE TO RUN OFF AND HELP SPIDER-MAN.
FORTUNATE.
NOT REALLY. I PICKED YOUR POCKET.
IT'S BEEN VIBRATING FOR LIKE TWO MINUTES.
ANNA! WHY WOULD YOU--?
'CAUSE SPIDEY'LL BE FINE.
AND I CARE ABOUT OUR FUTURE, PETER. YOUR FUTURE.
YOU SAID "OUR" FUTURE.
SHUT UP!
I LOOK FORWARD TO TALKING ABOUT THAT LATER, BUT UNFORTUNATELY...

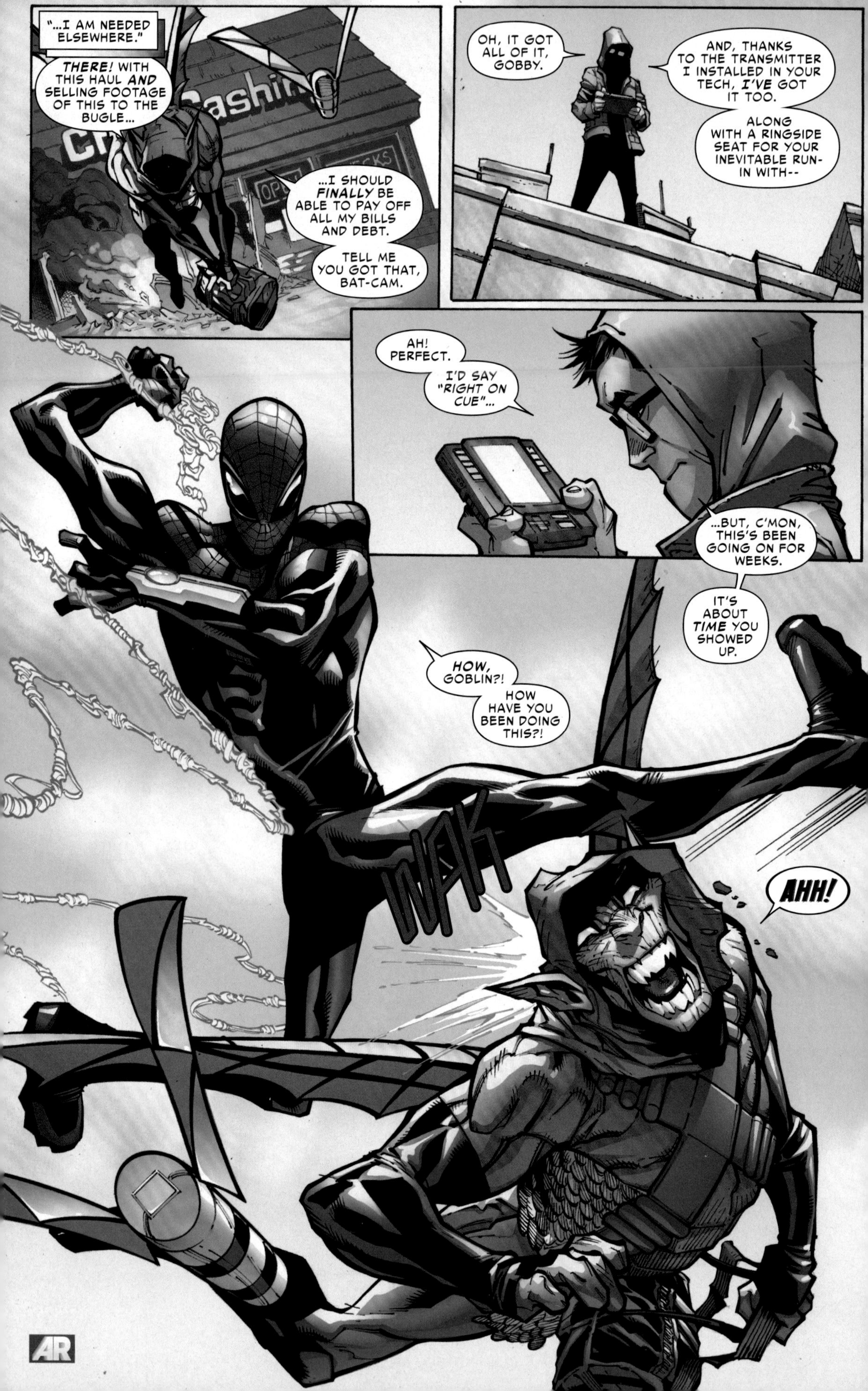
"...I AM NEEDED ELSEWHERE."
THERE! WITH THIS HAUL AND SELLING FOOTAGE OF THIS TO THE BUGLE...
...I SHOULD FINALLY BE ABLE TO PAY OFF ALL MY BILLS AND DEBT.
TELL ME YOU GOT THAT, BAT-CAM.
OH, IT GOT ALL OF IT, GOBBY.
AND, THANKS TO THE TRANSMITTER I INSTALLED IN YOUR TECH, I'VE GOT IT TOO.
ALONG WITH A RINGSIDE SEAT FOR YOUR INEVITABLE RUN-IN WITH--
AH! PERFECT.
I'D SAY "RIGHT ON CUE"...
...BUT, C'MON, THIS'S BEEN GOING ON FOR WEEKS.
IT'S ABOUT TIME YOU SHOWED UP.
HOW, GOBLIN?!
HOW HAVE YOU BEEN DOING THIS?!
WAK
AHH!

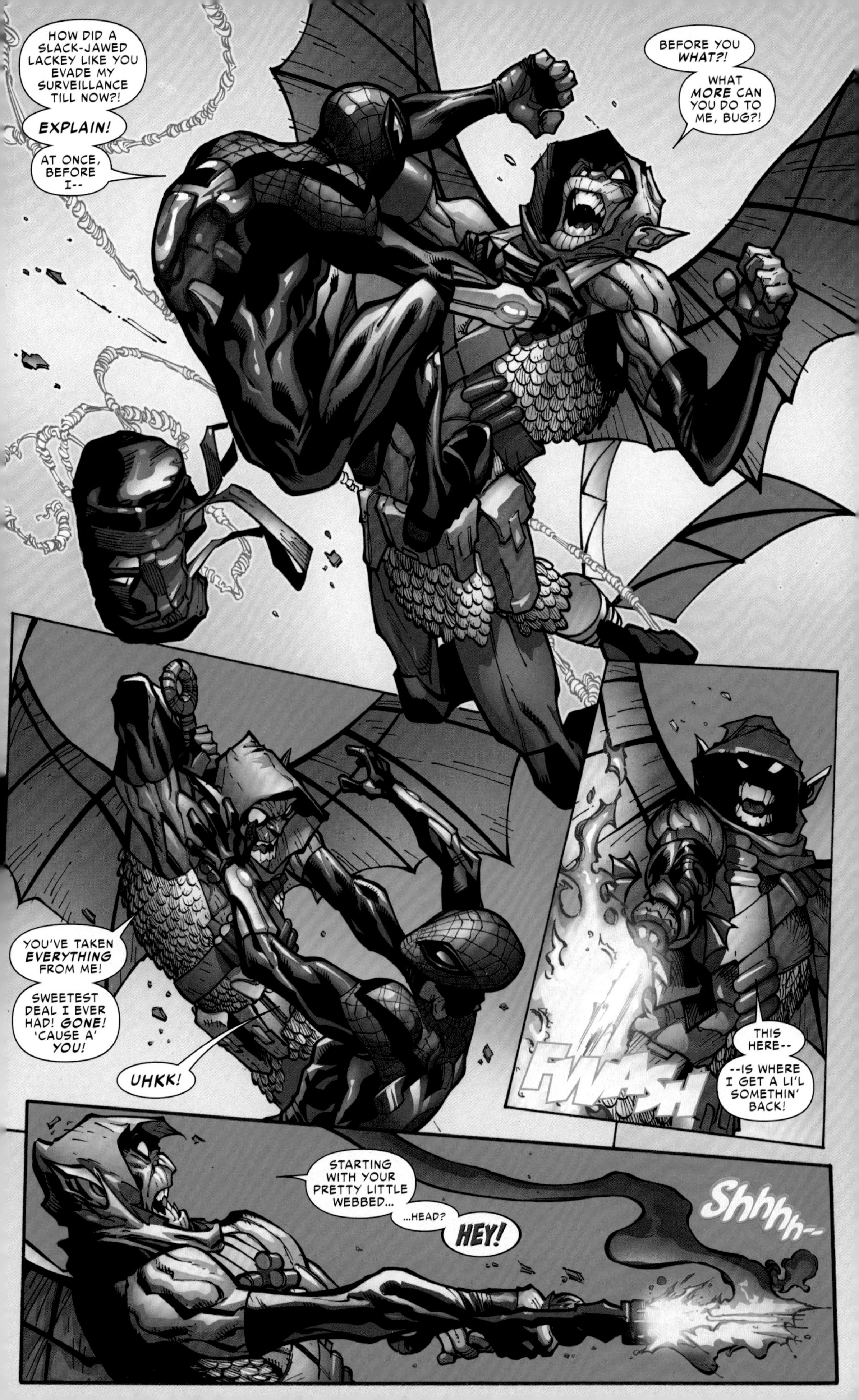
HOW DID A SLACK-JAWED LACKEY LIKE YOU EVADE MY SURVEILLANCE TILL NOW?!
EXPLAIN!
AT ONCE, BEFORE I--
BEFORE YOU WHAT?!
WHAT MORE CAN YOU DO TO ME, BUG?!
YOU'VE TAKEN EVERYTHING FROM ME!
SWEETEST DEAL I EVER HAD! GONE! 'CAUSE A' YOU!
UHKK!
FWASH
THIS HERE--
--IS WHERE I GET A LI'L SOMETHIN' BACK!
STARTING WITH YOUR PRETTY LITTLE WEBBED...
...HEAD?
HEY!
Shhhh--

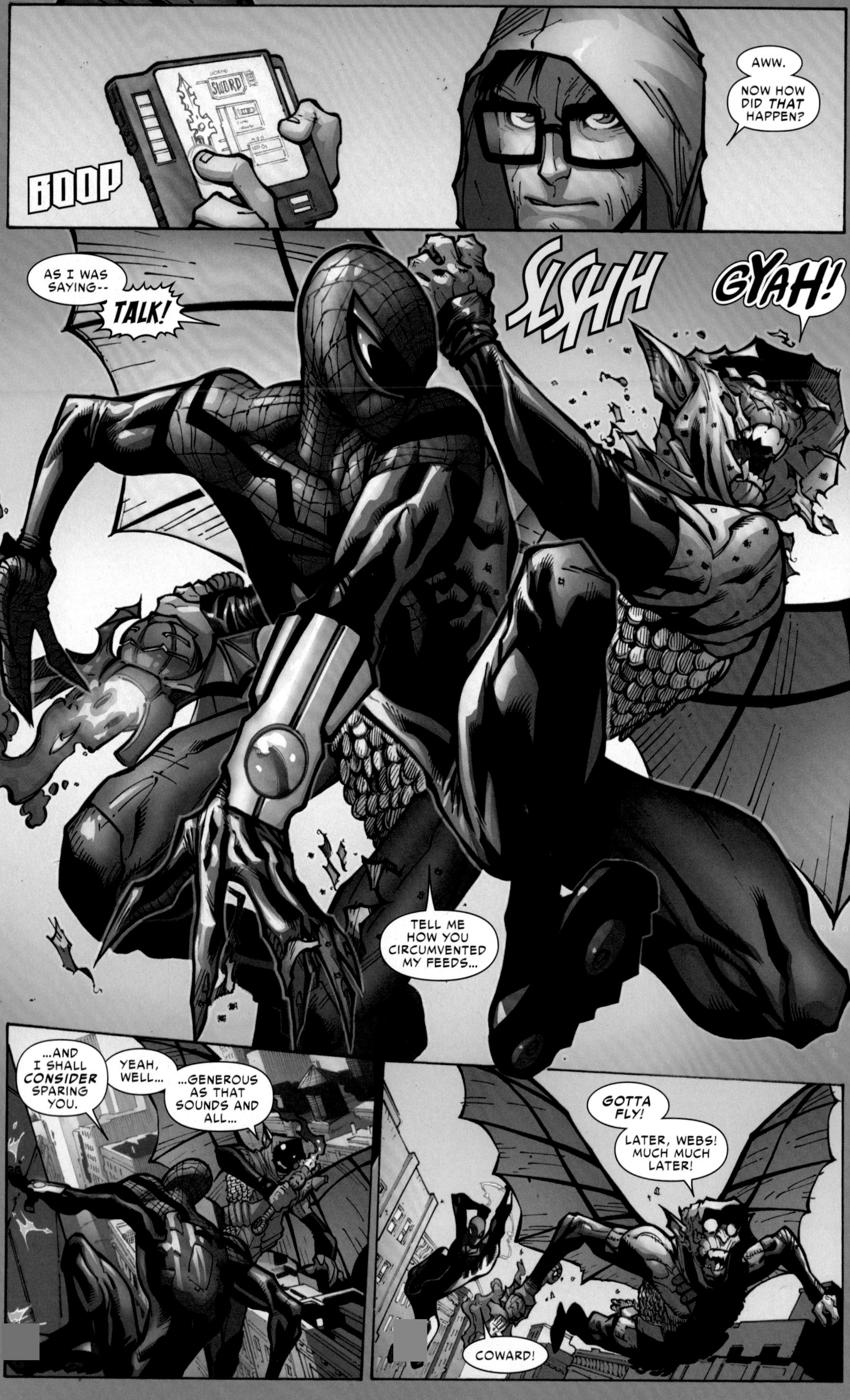
SWORD
BOOP
AWW.
NOW HOW DID THAT HAPPEN?
AS I WAS SAYING--
TALK!
GYAH!
TELL ME HOW YOU CIRCUMVENTED MY FEEDS...
...AND I SHALL CONSIDER SPARING YOU.
YEAH, WELL...
...GENEROUS AS THAT SOUNDS AND ALL...
GOTTA FLY!
LATER, WEBS! MUCH MUCH LATER!
COWARD!

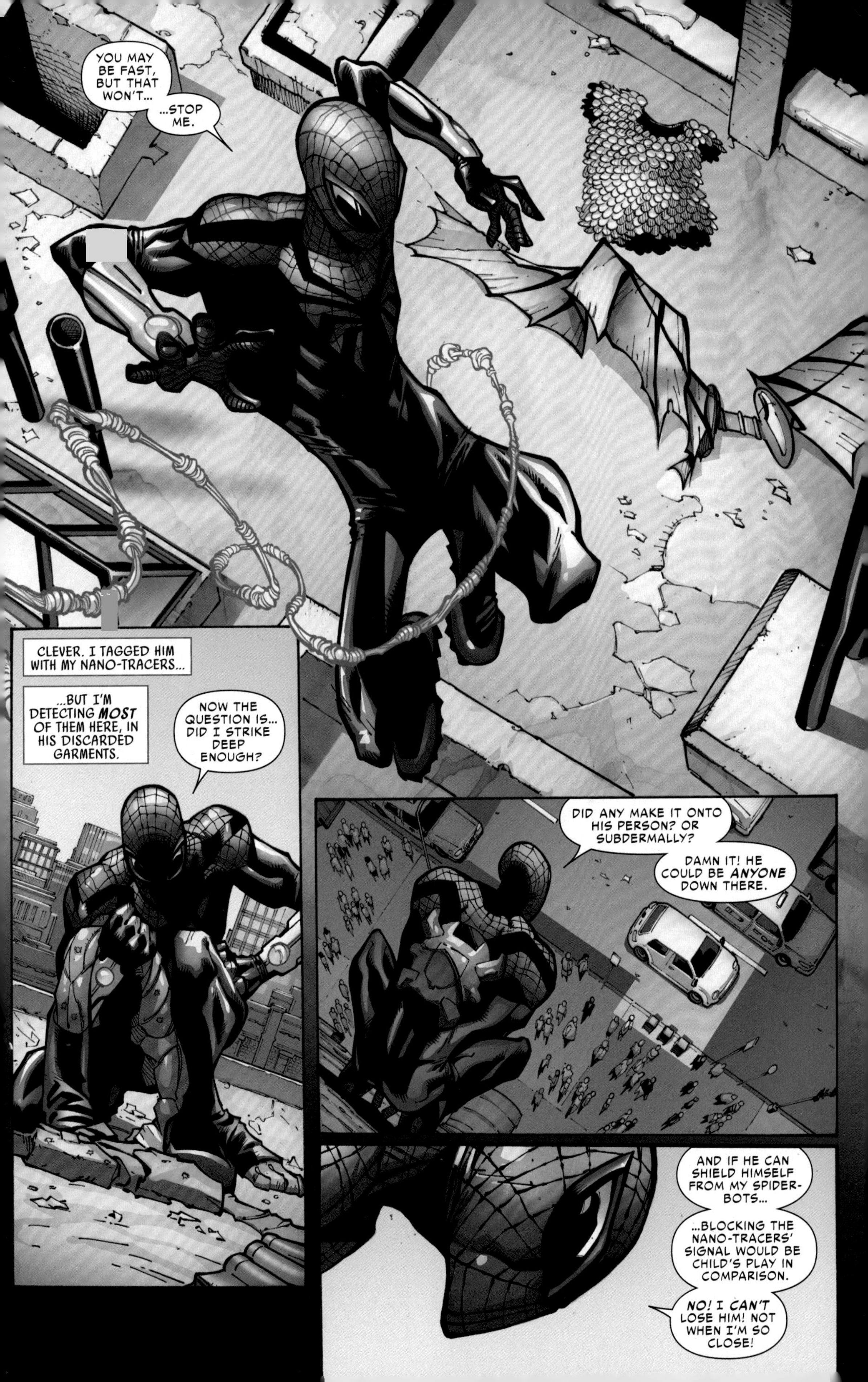
YOU MAY BE FAST, BUT THAT WON'T...
...STOP ME.
CLEVER. I TAGGED HIM WITH MY NANO-TRACERS...
...BUT I'M DETECTING MOST OF THEM HERE, IN HIS DISCARDED GARMENTS.
NOW THE QUESTION IS... DID I STRIKE DEEP ENOUGH?
DID ANY MAKE IT ONTO HIS PERSON? OR SUBDERMALLY?
DAMN IT! HE COULD BE ANYONE DOWN THERE.
AND IF HE CAN SHIELD HIMSELF FROM MY SPIDER-BOTS...
...BLOCKING THE NANO-TRACERS' SIGNAL WOULD BE CHILD'S PLAY IN COMPARISON.
NO! I CAN'T LOSE HIM! NOT WHEN I'M SO CLOSE!

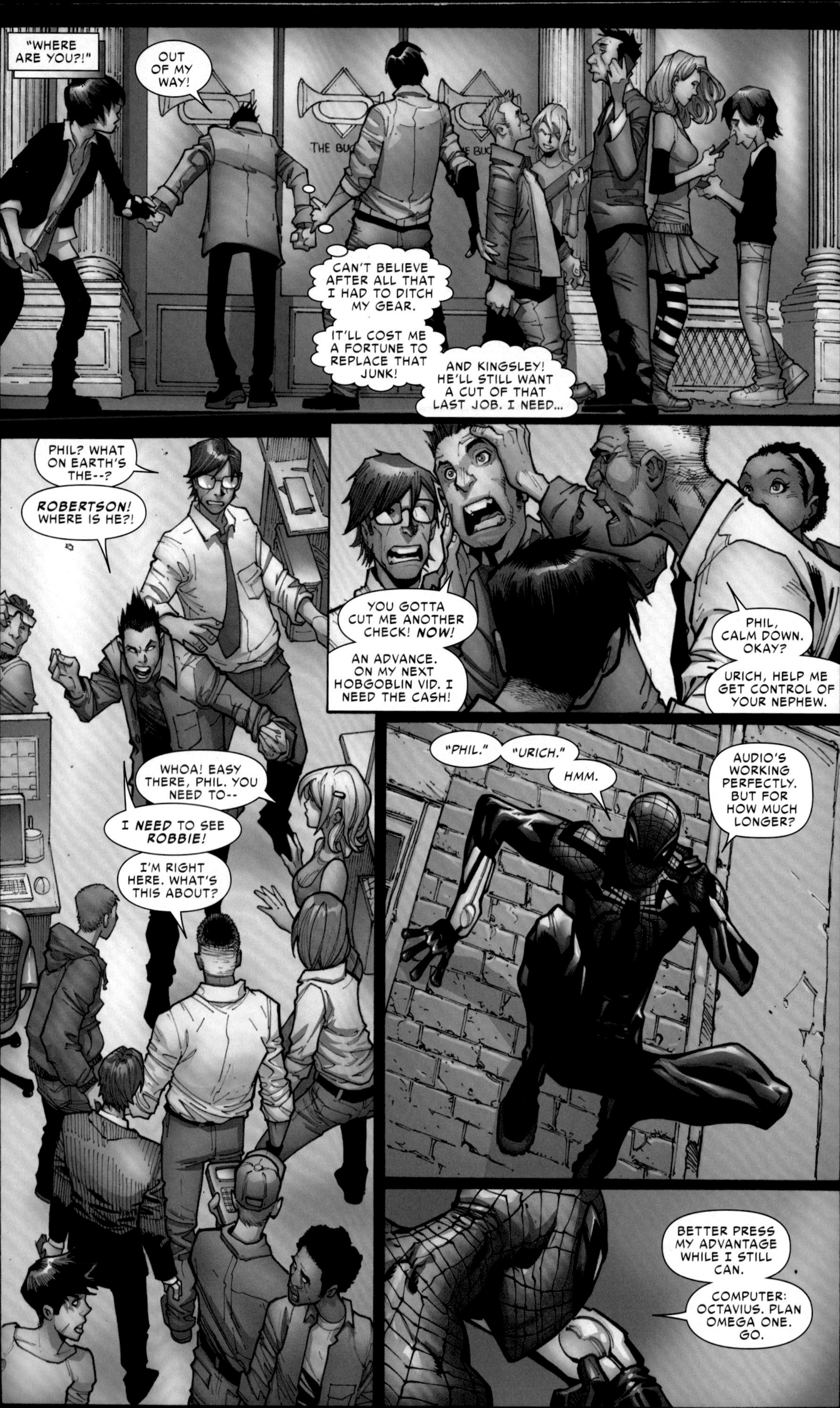
"WHERE ARE YOU?!"
OUT OF MY WAY!
CAN'T BELIEVE AFTER ALL THAT I HAD TO DITCH MY GEAR.
IT'LL COST ME A FORTUNE TO REPLACE THAT JUNK!
AND KINGSLEY! HE'LL STILL WANT A CUT OF THAT LAST JOB. I NEED...
PHIL? WHAT ON EARTH'S THE--?
ROBERTSON! WHERE IS HE?!
YOU GOTTA CUT ME ANOTHER CHECK! NOW!
AN ADVANCE. ON MY NEXT HOBGOBLIN VID. I NEED THE CASH!
PHIL, CALM DOWN. OKAY?
URICH, HELP ME GET CONTROL OF YOUR NEPHEW.
WHOA! EASY THERE, PHIL. YOU NEED TO--
I NEED TO SEE ROBBIE!
I'M RIGHT HERE. WHAT'S THIS ABOUT?
"PHIL."
"URICH."
HMM.
AUDIO'S WORKING PERFECTLY. BUT FOR HOW MUCH LONGER?
BETTER PRESS MY ADVANTAGE WHILE I STILL CAN.
COMPUTER: OCTAVIUS. PLAN OMEGA ONE. GO.

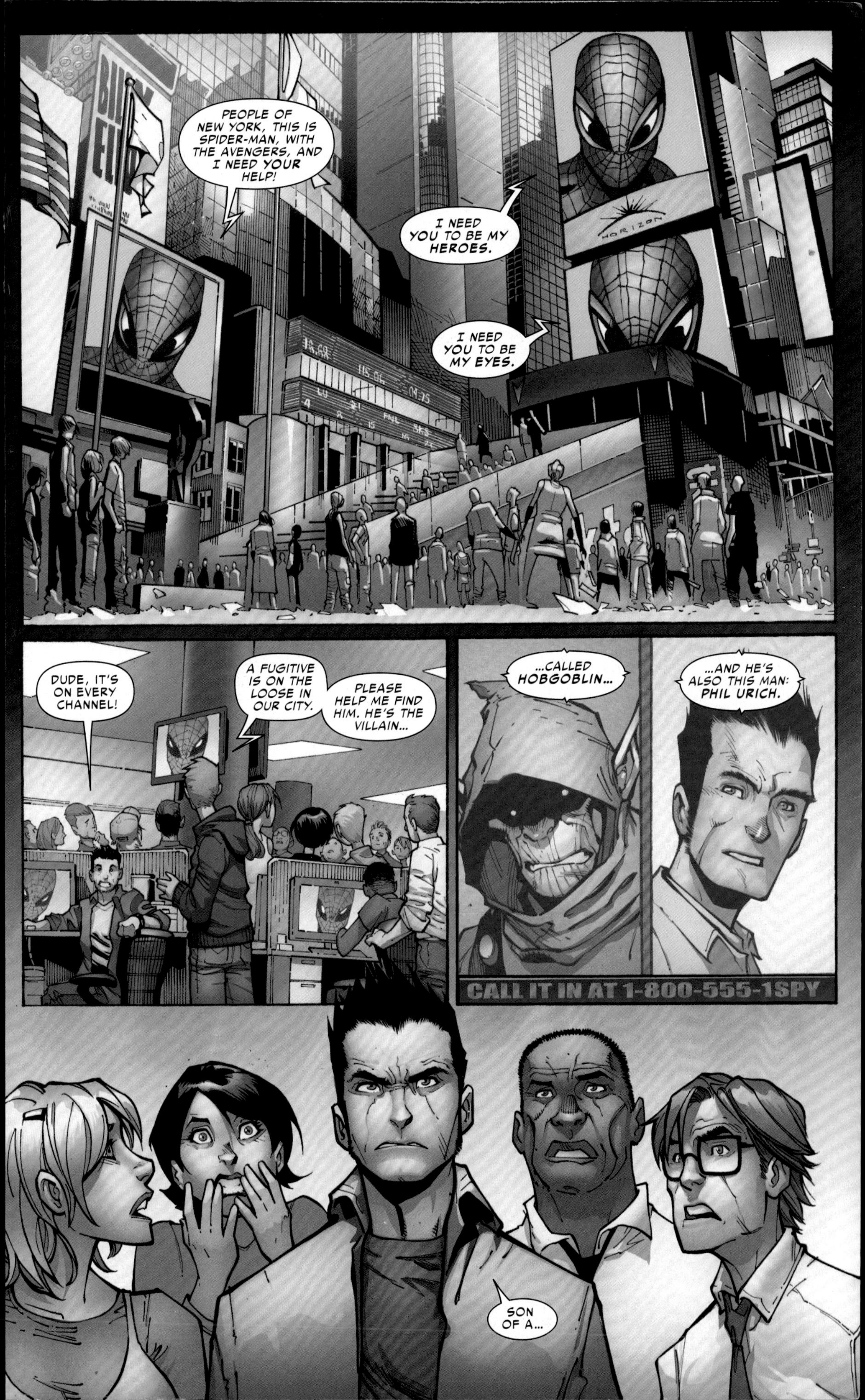
PEOPLE OF NEW YORK, THIS IS SPIDER-MAN, WITH THE AVENGERS, AND I NEED YOUR HELP!
I NEED YOU TO BE MY HEROES.
I NEED YOU TO BE MY EYES.
HORIZON
DUDE, IT'S ON EVERY CHANNEL!
A FUGITIVE IS ON THE LOOSE IN OUR CITY.
PLEASE HELP ME FIND HIM. HE'S THE VILLAIN...
...CALLED HOBGOBLIN...
...AND HE'S ALSO THIS MAN: PHIL URICH.
CALL IT IN AT 1-800-555-1SPY
SON OF A...

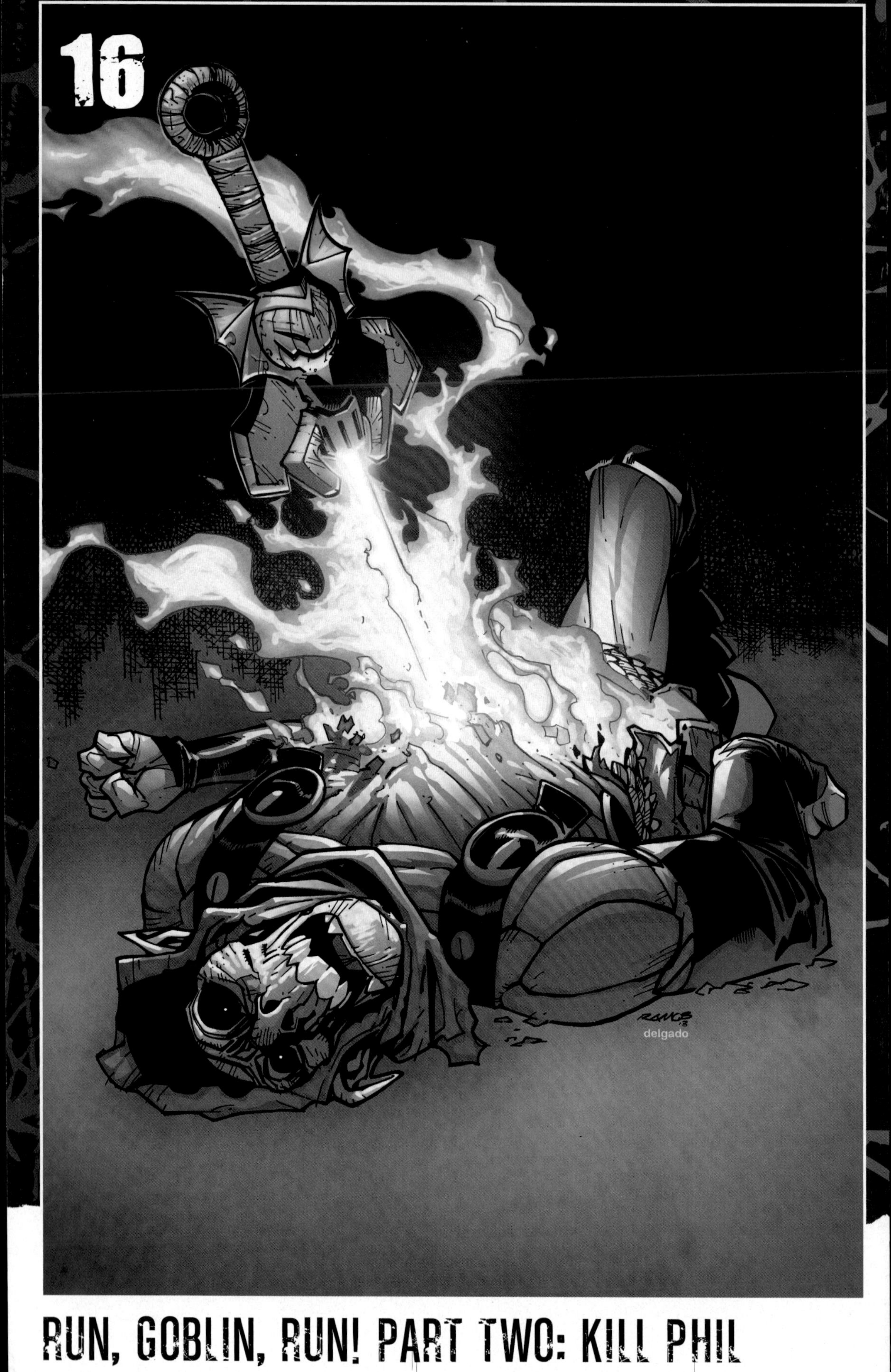
16
RAMOS '13
delgado

RUN, GOBLIN, RUN! PART TWO: KILL PHIL

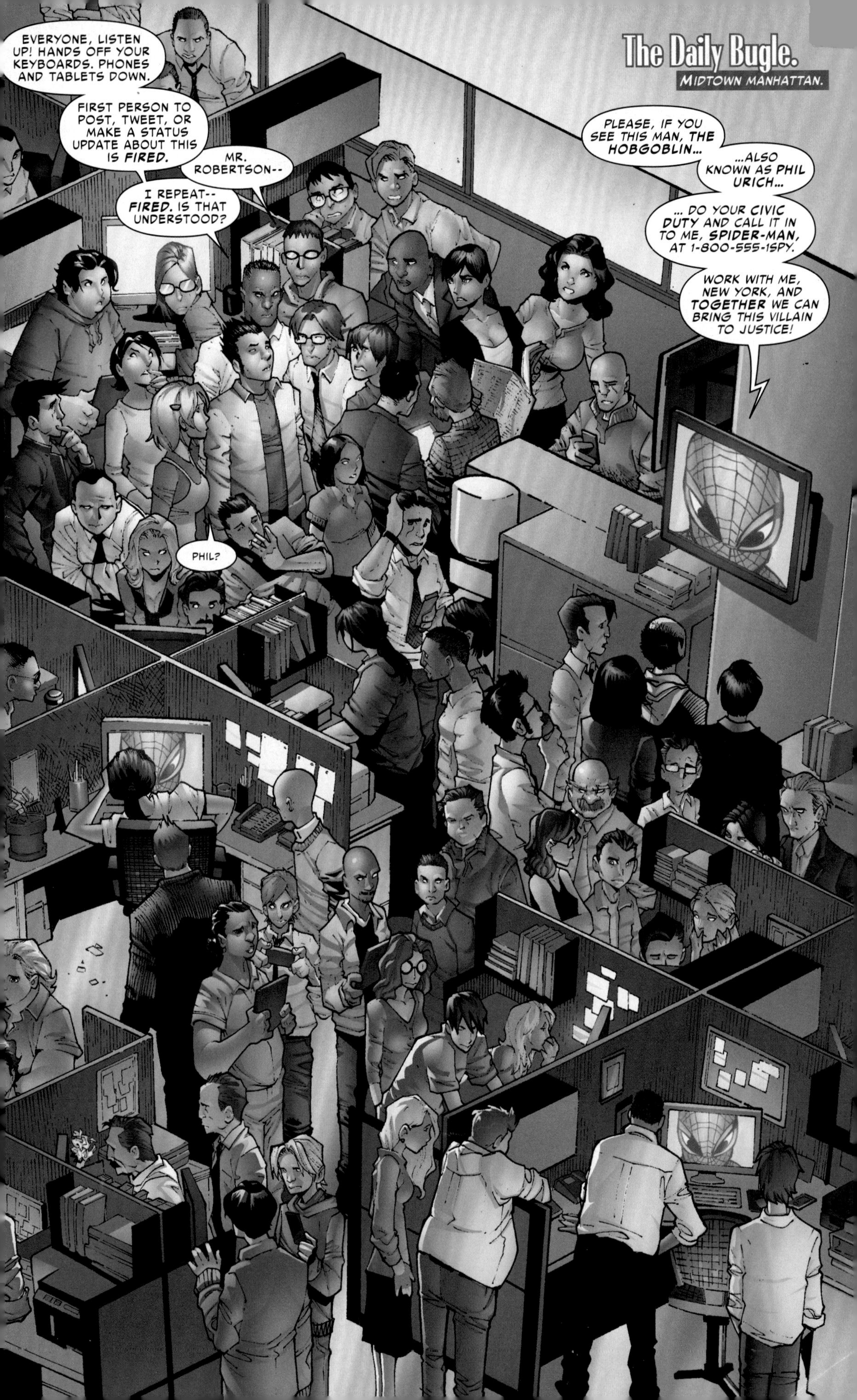
The Daily Bugle.
MIDTOWN MANHATTAN.
EVERYONE, LISTEN UP! HANDS OFF YOUR KEYBOARDS. PHONES AND TABLETS DOWN.
FIRST PERSON TO POST, TWEET, OR MAKE A STATUS UPDATE ABOUT THIS IS FIRED.
MR. ROBERTSON--
I REPEAT-- FIRED. IS THAT UNDERSTOOD?
PLEASE, IF YOU SEE THIS MAN, THE HOBGOBLIN...
...ALSO KNOWN AS PHIL URICH...
... DO YOUR CIVIC DUTY AND CALL IT IN TO ME, SPIDER-MAN, AT 1-800-555-1SPY.
WORK WITH ME, NEW YORK, AND TOGETHER WE CAN BRING THIS VILLAIN TO JUSTICE!
PHIL?

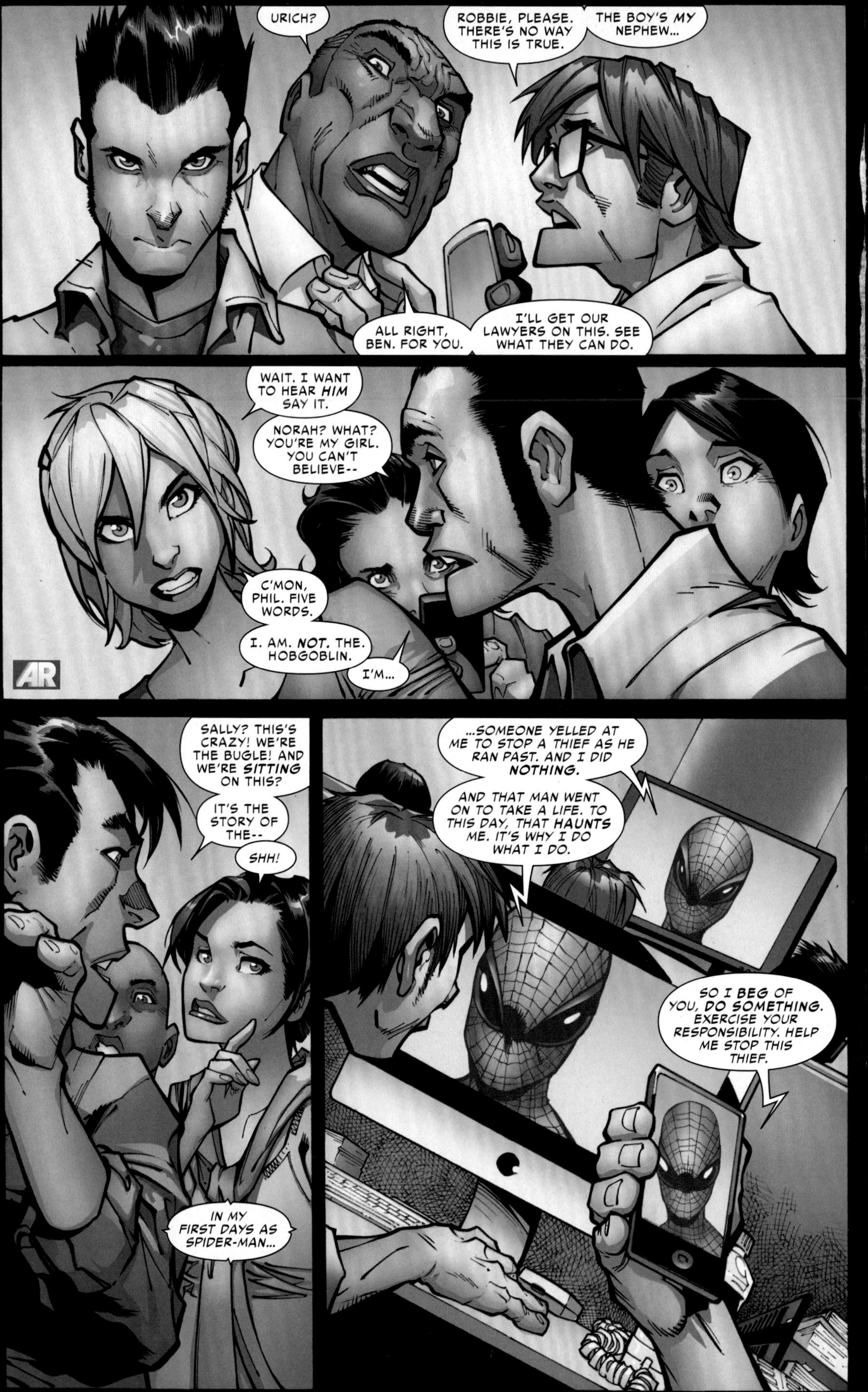
URICH?
ROBBIE, PLEASE. THERE'S NO WAY THIS IS TRUE.
THE BOY'S MY NEPHEW...
ALL RIGHT, BEN. FOR YOU.
I'LL GET OUR LAWYERS ON THIS. SEE WHAT THEY CAN DO.
WAIT. I WANT TO HEAR HIM SAY IT.
NORAH? WHAT? YOU'RE MY GIRL. YOU CAN'T BELIEVE--
C'MON, PHIL. FIVE WORDS.
I. AM. NOT. THE. HOBGOBLIN.
I'M...
SALLY? THIS'S CRAZY! WE'RE THE BUGLE! AND WE'RE SITTING ON THIS?
IT'S THE STORY OF THE--
SHH!
IN MY FIRST DAYS AS SPIDER-MAN...
...SOMEONE YELLED AT ME TO STOP A THIEF AS HE RAN PAST. AND I DID NOTHING.
AND THAT MAN WENT ON TO TAKE A LIFE. TO THIS DAY, THAT HAUNTS ME. IT'S WHY I DO WHAT I DO.
SO I BEG OF YOU, DO SOMETHING. EXERCISE YOUR RESPONSIBILITY. HELP ME STOP THIS THIEF.

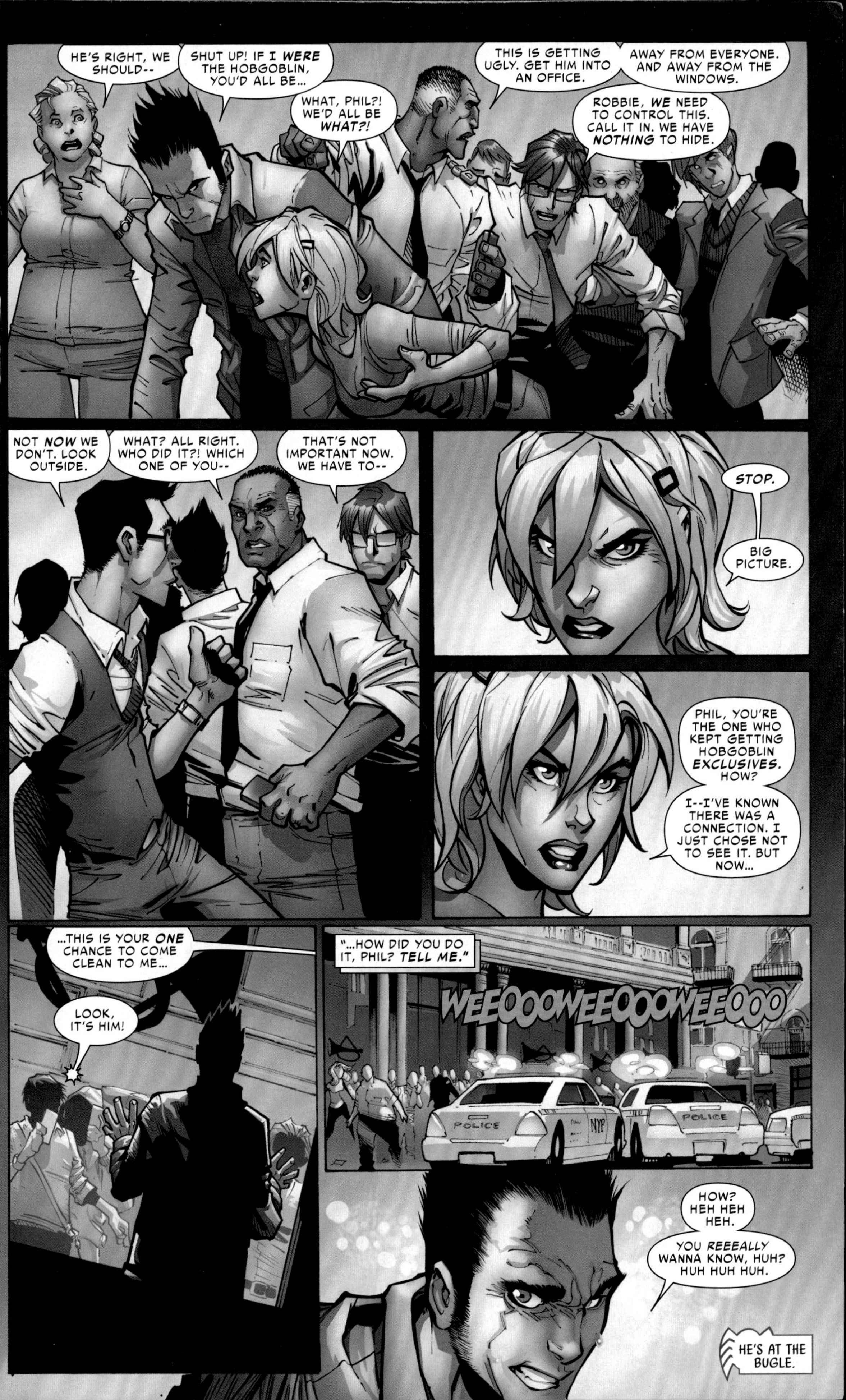
HE'S RIGHT, WE SHOULD--
SHUT UP! IF I WERE THE HOBGOBLIN, YOU'D ALL BE...
WHAT, PHIL?! WE'D ALL BE WHAT?!
THIS IS GETTING UGLY. GET HIM INTO AN OFFICE.
AWAY FROM EVERYONE. AND AWAY FROM THE WINDOWS.
ROBBIE, WE NEED TO CONTROL THIS. CALL IT IN. WE HAVE NOTHING TO HIDE.
NOT NOW WE DON'T. LOOK OUTSIDE.
WHAT? ALL RIGHT. WHO DID IT?! WHICH ONE OF YOU--
THAT'S NOT IMPORTANT NOW. WE HAVE TO--
STOP.
BIG PICTURE.
PHIL, YOU'RE THE ONE WHO KEPT GETTING HOBGOBLIN EXCLUSIVES. HOW?
I--I'VE KNOWN THERE WAS A CONNECTION. I JUST CHOSE NOT TO SEE IT. BUT NOW...
...THIS IS YOUR ONE CHANCE TO COME CLEAN TO ME...
LOOK, IT'S HIM!
"...HOW DID YOU DO IT, PHIL? TELL ME."
WEEOOOWEEOOOWEEOOO
POLICE
NYP
POLICE
HOW? HEH HEH HEH.
YOU REEEALLY WANNA KNOW, HUH? HUH HUH HUH.
HE'S AT THE BUGLE.

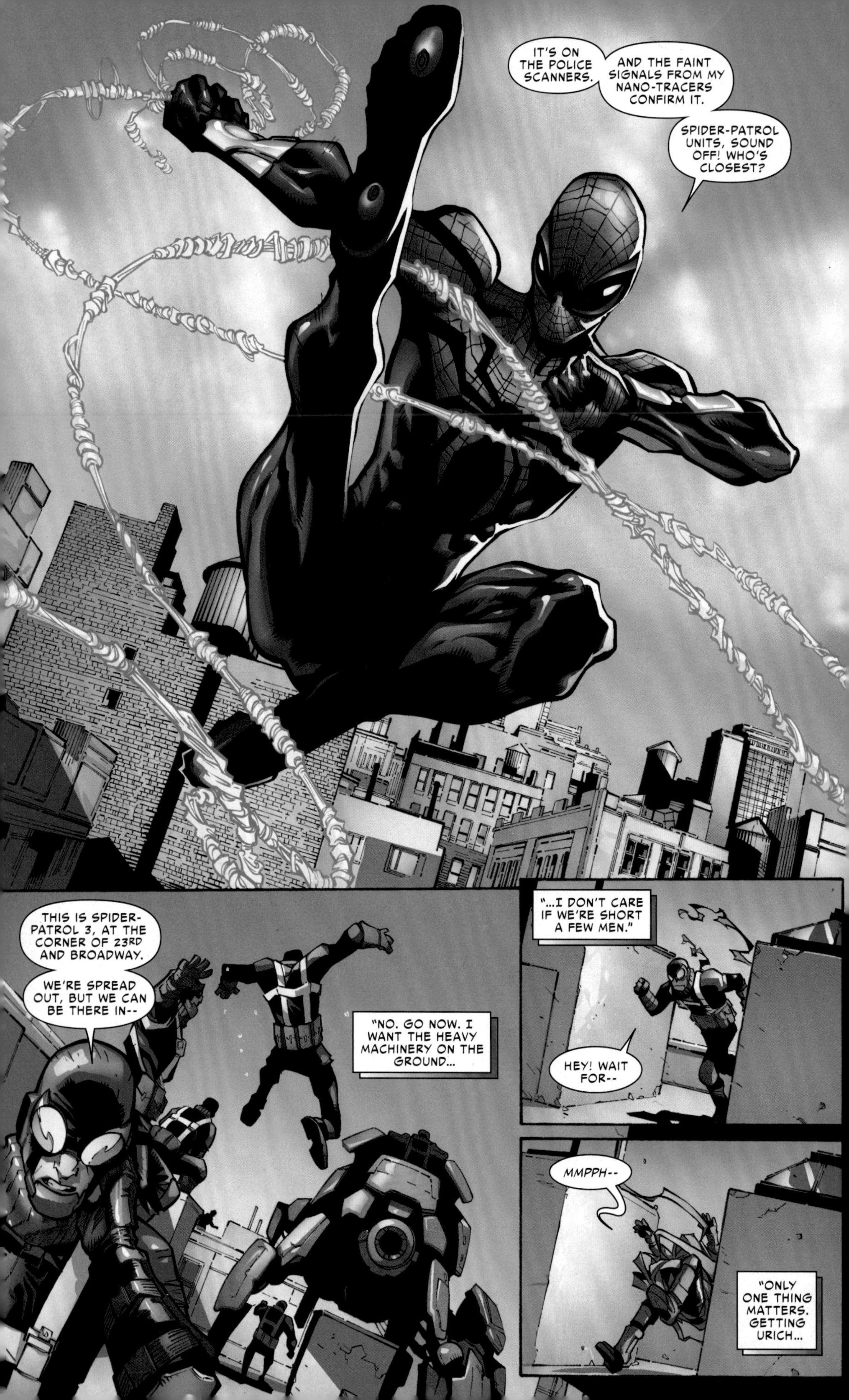

IT'S ON THE POLICE SCANNERS.
AND THE FAINT SIGNALS FROM MY NANO-TRACERS CONFIRM IT.
SPIDER-PATROL UNITS, SOUND OFF! WHO'S CLOSEST?
THIS IS SPIDER-PATROL 3, AT THE CORNER OF 23RD AND BROADWAY.
WE'RE SPREAD OUT, BUT WE CAN BE THERE IN--
"NO. GO NOW. I WANT THE HEAVY MACHINERY ON THE GROUND...
"...I DON'T CARE IF WE'RE SHORT A FEW MEN."
HEY! WAIT FOR--
MMPPH--
"ONLY ONE THING MATTERS. GETTING URICH...

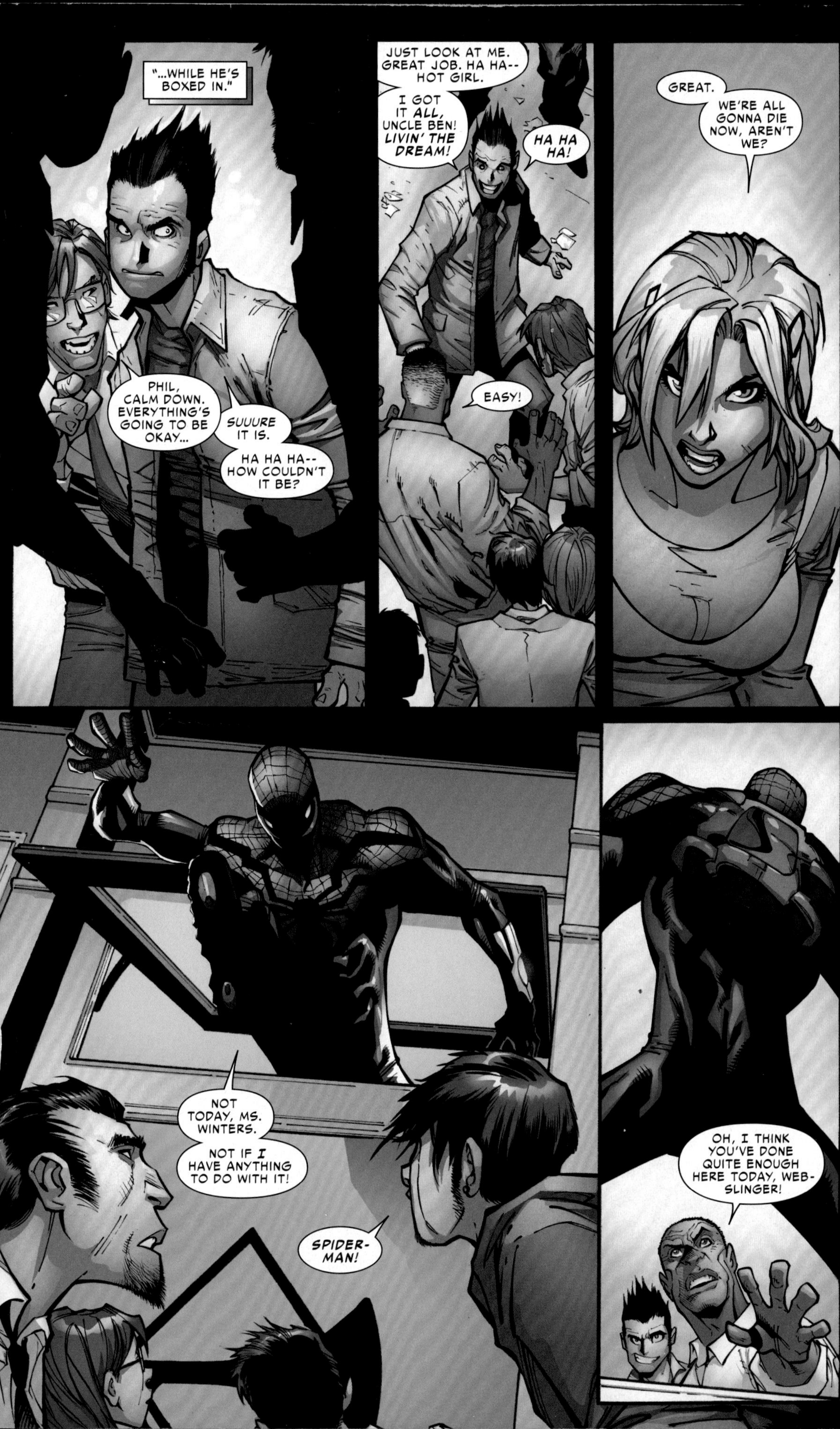

"...WHILE HE'S BOXED IN."
PHIL, CALM DOWN. EVERYTHING'S GOING TO BE OKAY...
SUUURE IT IS.
HA HA HA-- HOW COULDN'T IT BE?
JUST LOOK AT ME. GREAT JOB. HA HA-- HOT GIRL.
I GOT IT ALL, UNCLE BEN! LIVIN' THE DREAM!
HA HA HA!
EASY!
GREAT.
WE'RE ALL GONNA DIE NOW, AREN'T WE?
NOT TODAY, MS. WINTERS.
NOT IF I HAVE ANYTHING TO DO WITH IT!
SPIDER-MAN!
OH, I THINK YOU'VE DONE QUITE ENOUGH HERE TODAY, WEB-SLINGER!

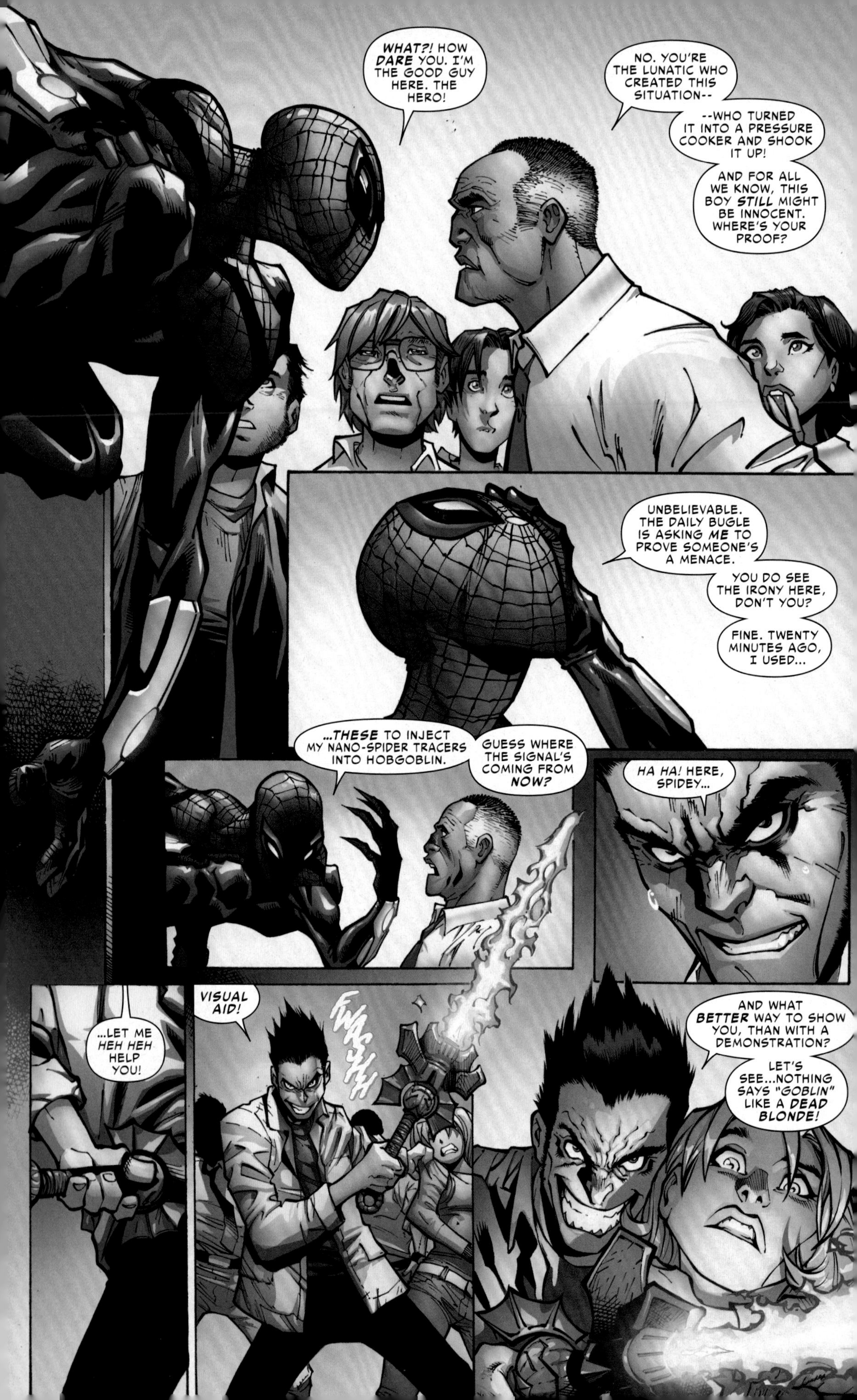
WHAT?! HOW DARE YOU. I'M THE GOOD GUY HERE. THE HERO!
NO. YOU'RE THE LUNATIC WHO CREATED THIS SITUATION--
--WHO TURNED IT INTO A PRESSURE COOKER AND SHOOK IT UP!
AND FOR ALL WE KNOW, THIS BOY STILL MIGHT BE INNOCENT. WHERE'S YOUR PROOF?
UNBELIEVABLE. THE DAILY BUGLE IS ASKING ME TO PROVE SOMEONE'S A MENACE.
YOU DO SEE THE IRONY HERE, DON'T YOU?
FINE. TWENTY MINUTES AGO, I USED...
...THESE TO INJECT MY NANO-SPIDER TRACERS INTO HOBGOBLIN.
GUESS WHERE THE SIGNAL'S COMING FROM NOW?
HA HA! HERE, SPIDEY...
...LET ME HEH HEH HELP YOU!
VISUAL AID!
FWASHH
AND WHAT BETTER WAY TO SHOW YOU, THAN WITH A DEMONSTRATION?
LET'S SEE...NOTHING SAYS "GOBLIN" LIKE A DEAD BLONDE!

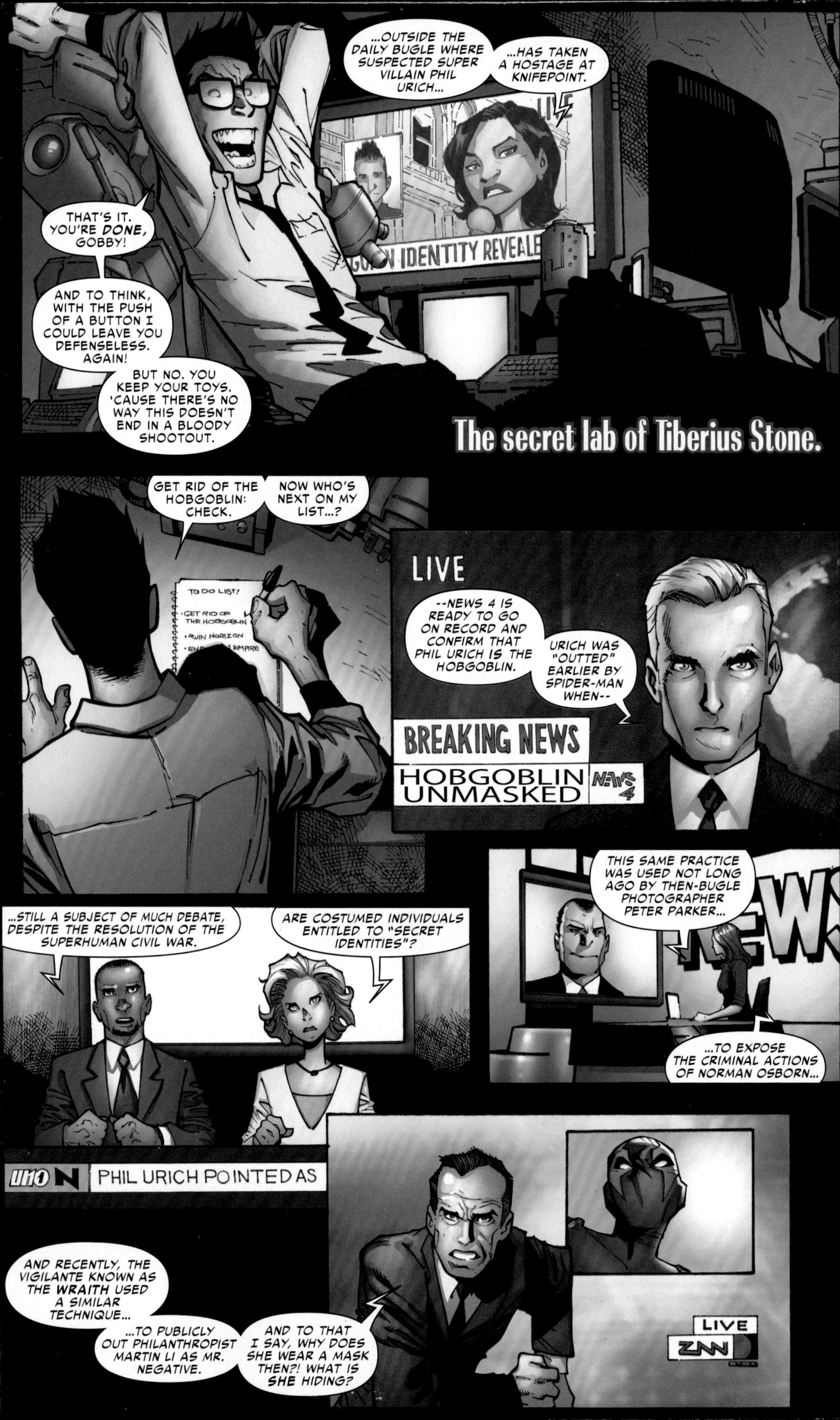
...OUTSIDE THE DAILY BUGLE WHERE SUSPECTED SUPER VILLAIN PHIL URICH...
...HAS TAKEN A HOSTAGE AT KNIFEPOINT.
LIVE
IDENTITY REVEALE
THAT'S IT. YOU'RE DONE, GOBBY!
AND TO THINK, WITH THE PUSH OF A BUTTON I COULD LEAVE YOU DEFENSELESS. AGAIN!
BUT NO. YOU KEEP YOUR TOYS. 'CAUSE THERE'S NO WAY THIS DOESN'T END IN A BLOODY SHOOTOUT.
The secret lab of Tiberius Stone.
GET RID OF THE HOBGOBLIN: CHECK.
NOW WHO'S NEXT ON MY LIST...?
TO DO LIST!
GET RID OF THE HOBGOBLIN
RUIN HORIZON
LIVE
--NEWS 4 IS READY TO GO ON RECORD AND CONFIRM THAT PHIL URICH IS THE HOBGOBLIN.
URICH WAS "OUTTED" EARLIER BY SPIDER-MAN WHEN--
BREAKING NEWS
HOBGOBLIN UNMASKED
NEWS 4
THIS SAME PRACTICE WAS USED NOT LONG AGO BY THEN-BUGLE PHOTOGRAPHER PETER PARKER...
...TO EXPOSE THE CRIMINAL ACTIONS OF NORMAN OSBORN...
...STILL A SUBJECT OF MUCH DEBATE, DESPITE THE RESOLUTION OF THE SUPERHUMAN CIVIL WAR.
ARE COSTUMED INDIVIDUALS ENTITLED TO "SECRET IDENTITIES"?
PHIL URICH POINTED AS
AND RECENTLY, THE VIGILANTE KNOWN AS THE WRAITH USED A SIMILAR TECHNIQUE...
...TO PUBLICLY OUT PHILANTHROPIST MARTIN LI AS MR. NEGATIVE.
AND TO THAT I SAY, WHY DOES SHE WEAR A MASK THEN?! WHAT IS SHE HIDING?
LIVE
ZNN

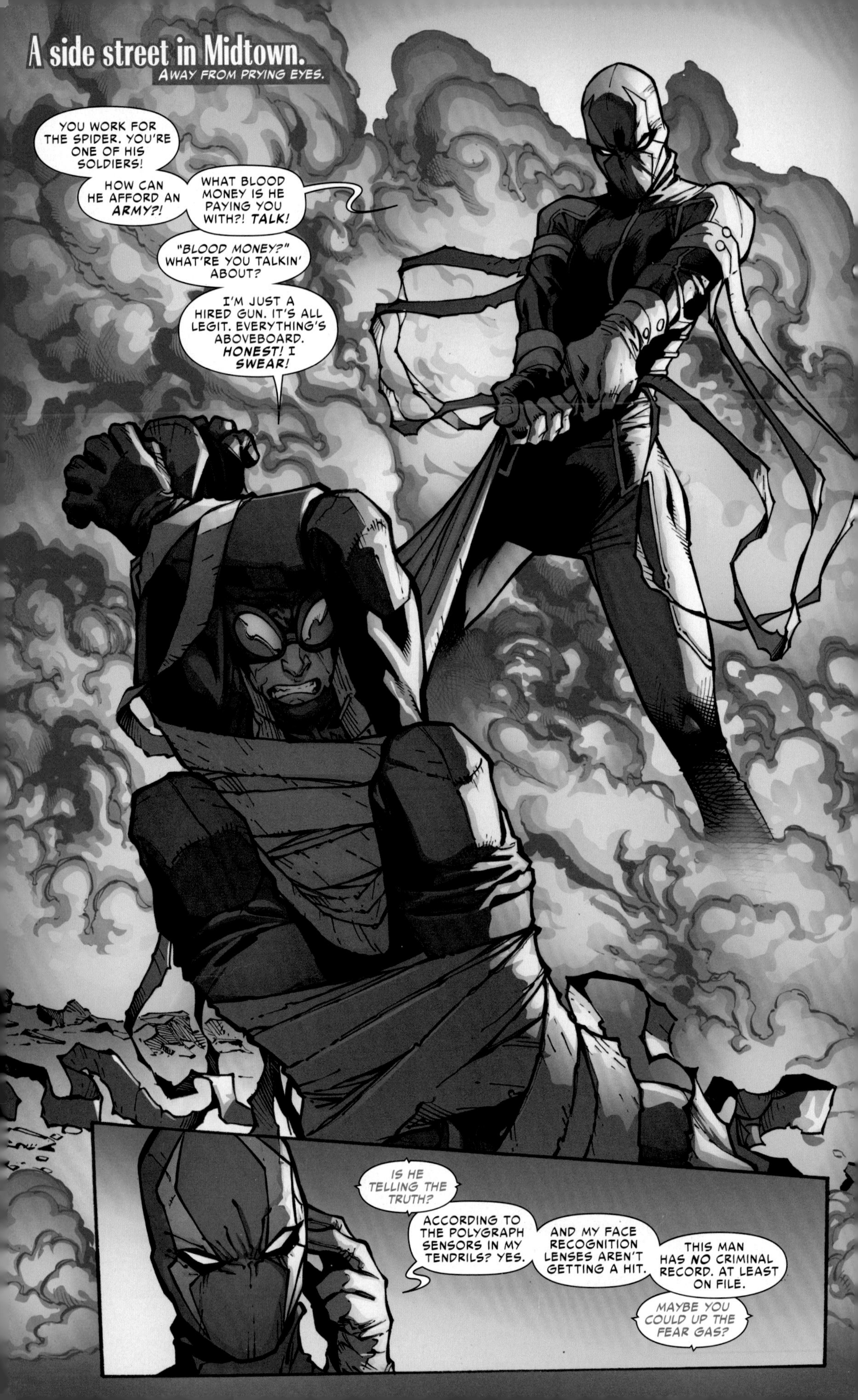
A side street in Midtown.
AWAY FROM PRYING EYES.
YOU WORK FOR THE SPIDER. YOU'RE ONE OF HIS SOLDIERS!
HOW CAN HE AFFORD AN ARMY?!
WHAT BLOOD MONEY IS HE PAYING YOU WITH?! TALK!
"BLOOD MONEY?" WHAT'RE YOU TALKIN' ABOUT?
I'M JUST A HIRED GUN. IT'S ALL LEGIT. EVERYTHING'S ABOVEBOARD. HONEST! I SWEAR!
IS HE TELLING THE TRUTH?
ACCORDING TO THE POLYGRAPH SENSORS IN MY TENDRILS? YES.
AND MY FACE RECOGNITION LENSES AREN'T GETTING A HIT.
THIS MAN HAS NO CRIMINAL RECORD. AT LEAST ON FILE.
MAYBE YOU COULD UP THE FEAR GAS?

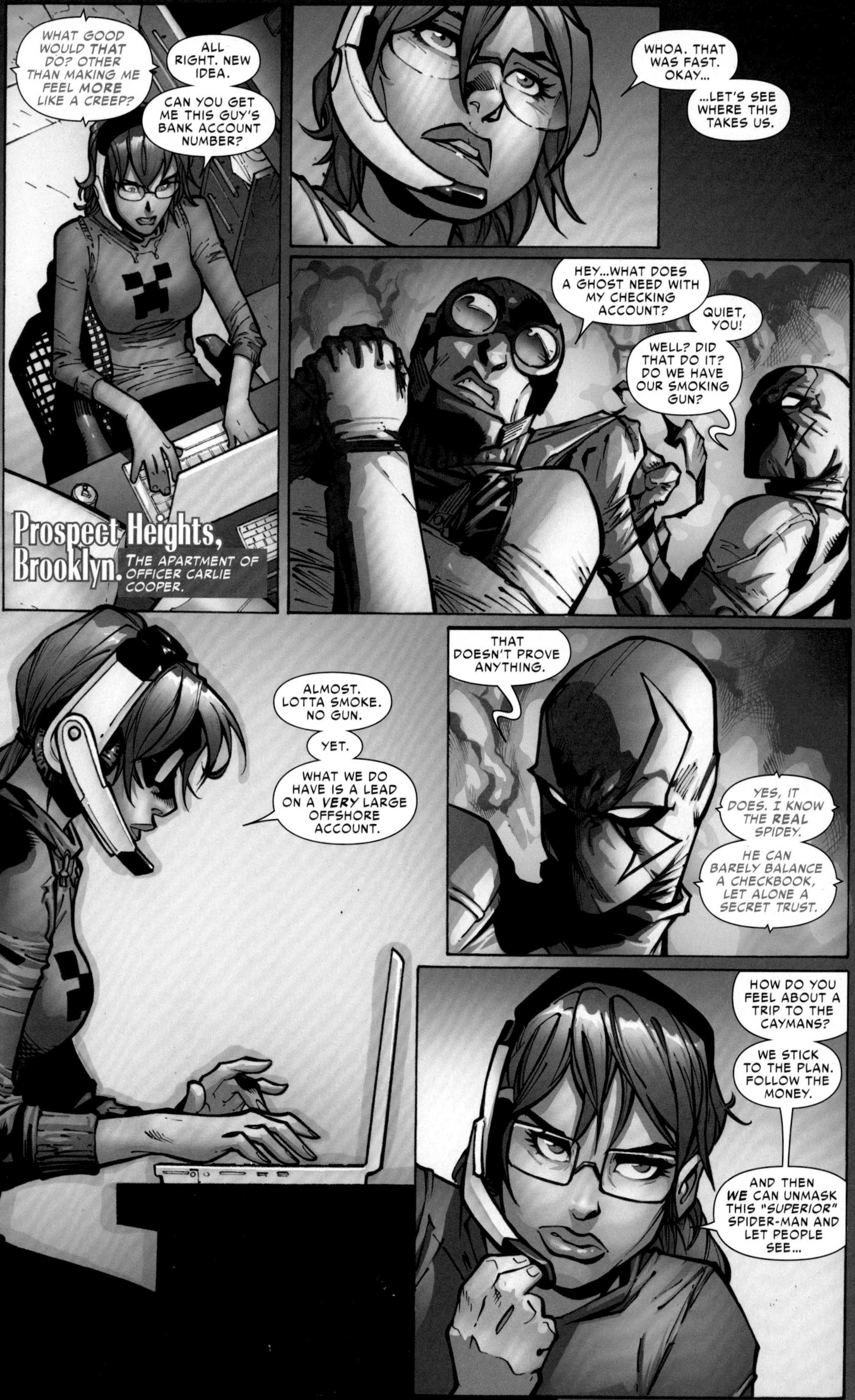
WHAT GOOD WOULD THAT DO? OTHER THAN MAKING ME FEEL MORE LIKE A CREEP?
ALL RIGHT. NEW IDEA.
CAN YOU GET ME THIS GUY'S BANK ACCOUNT NUMBER?
Prospect Heights, Brooklyn.
THE APARTMENT OF OFFICER CARLIE COOPER.
WHOA. THAT WAS FAST. OKAY...
...LET'S SEE WHERE THIS TAKES US.
HEY...WHAT DOES A GHOST NEED WITH MY CHECKING ACCOUNT?
QUIET, YOU!
WELL? DID THAT DO IT? DO WE HAVE OUR SMOKING GUN?
ALMOST. LOTTA SMOKE. NO GUN.
YET.
WHAT WE DO HAVE IS A LEAD ON A VERY LARGE OFFSHORE ACCOUNT.
THAT DOESN'T PROVE ANYTHING.
YES, IT DOES. I KNOW THE REAL SPIDEY.
HE CAN BARELY BALANCE A CHECKBOOK, LET ALONE A SECRET TRUST.
HOW DO YOU FEEL ABOUT A TRIP TO THE CAYMANS?
WE STICK TO THE PLAN. FOLLOW THE MONEY.
AND THEN WE CAN UNMASK THIS "SUPERIOR" SPIDER-MAN AND LET PEOPLE SEE...

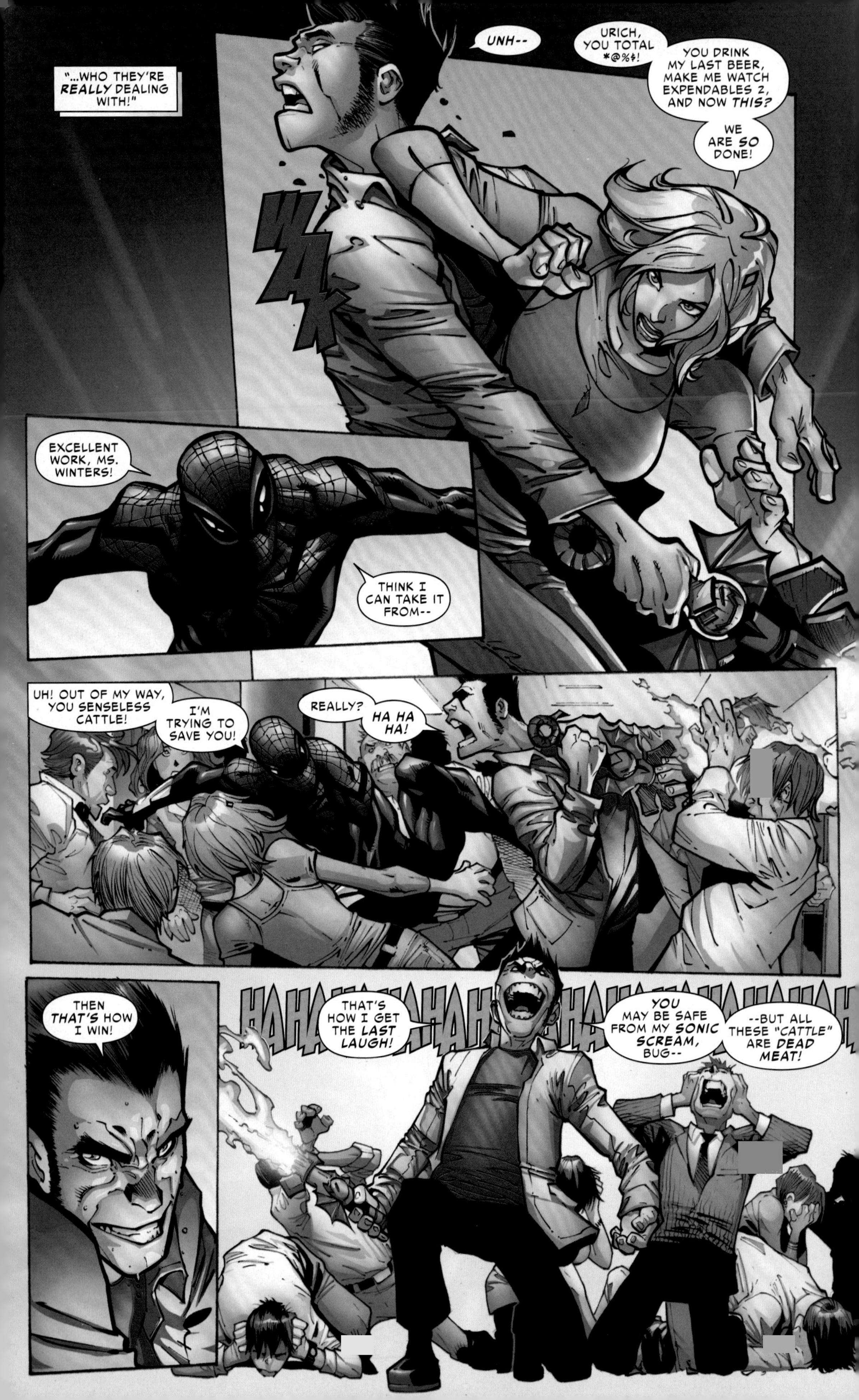
"...WHO THEY'RE REALLY DEALING WITH!"
UNH--
URICH, YOU TOTAL *@%$!
YOU DRINK MY LAST BEER, MAKE ME WATCH EXPENDABLES 2, AND NOW THIS?
WE ARE SO DONE!
WAK
EXCELLENT WORK, MS. WINTERS!
THINK I CAN TAKE IT FROM--
UH! OUT OF MY WAY, YOU SENSELESS CATTLE!
I'M TRYING TO SAVE YOU!
REALLY?
HA HA HA!
THEN THAT'S HOW I WIN!
THAT'S HOW I GET THE LAST LAUGH!
YOU MAY BE SAFE FROM MY SONIC SCREAM, BUG--
--BUT ALL THESE "CATTLE" ARE DEAD MEAT!

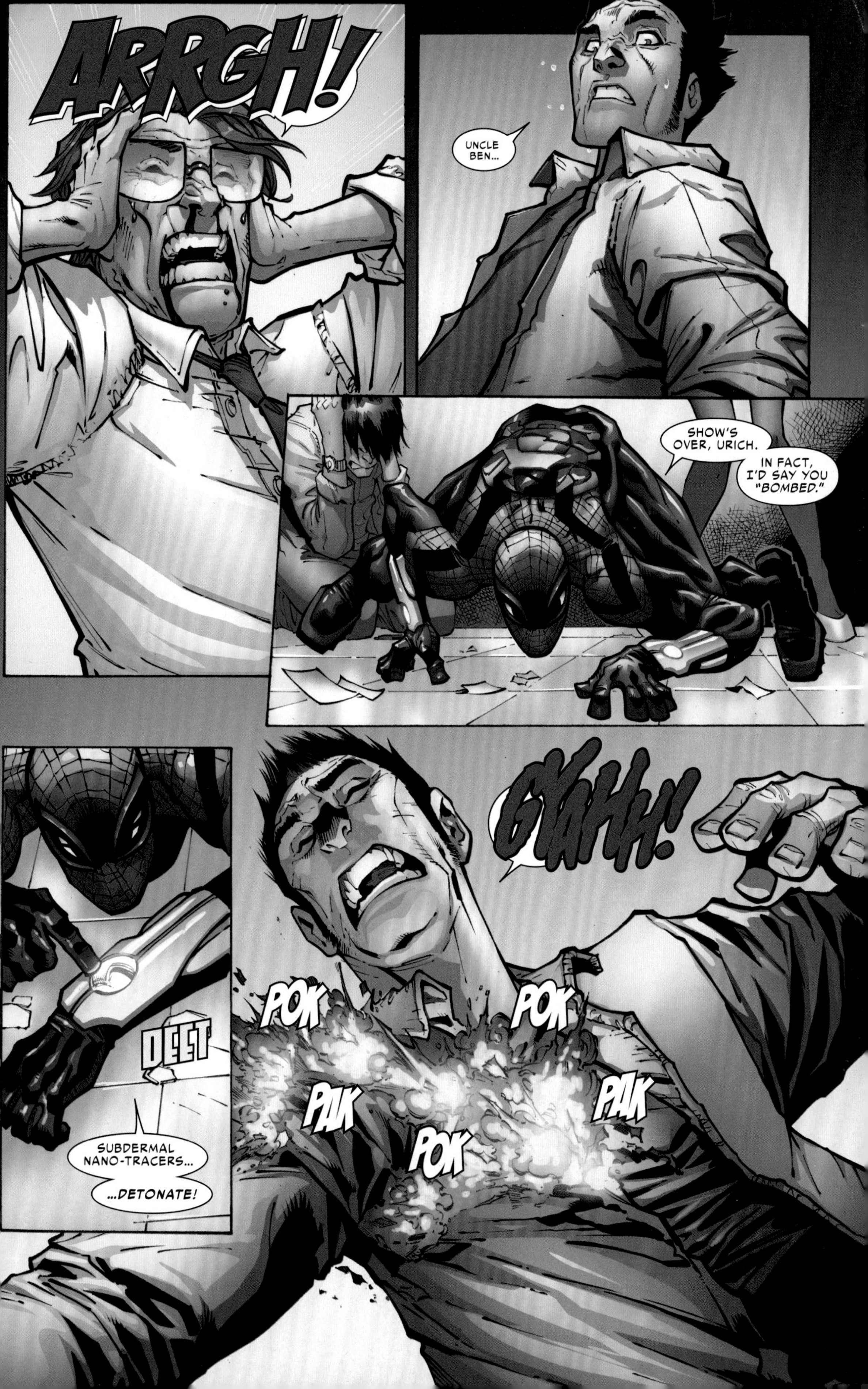
ARRGH!
UNCLE BEN...
SHOW'S OVER, URICH.
IN FACT, I'D SAY YOU "BOMBED."
DEET
SUBDERMAL NANO-TRACERS...
...DETONATE!
GYAHH!
POK
POK
PAK
PAK
POK

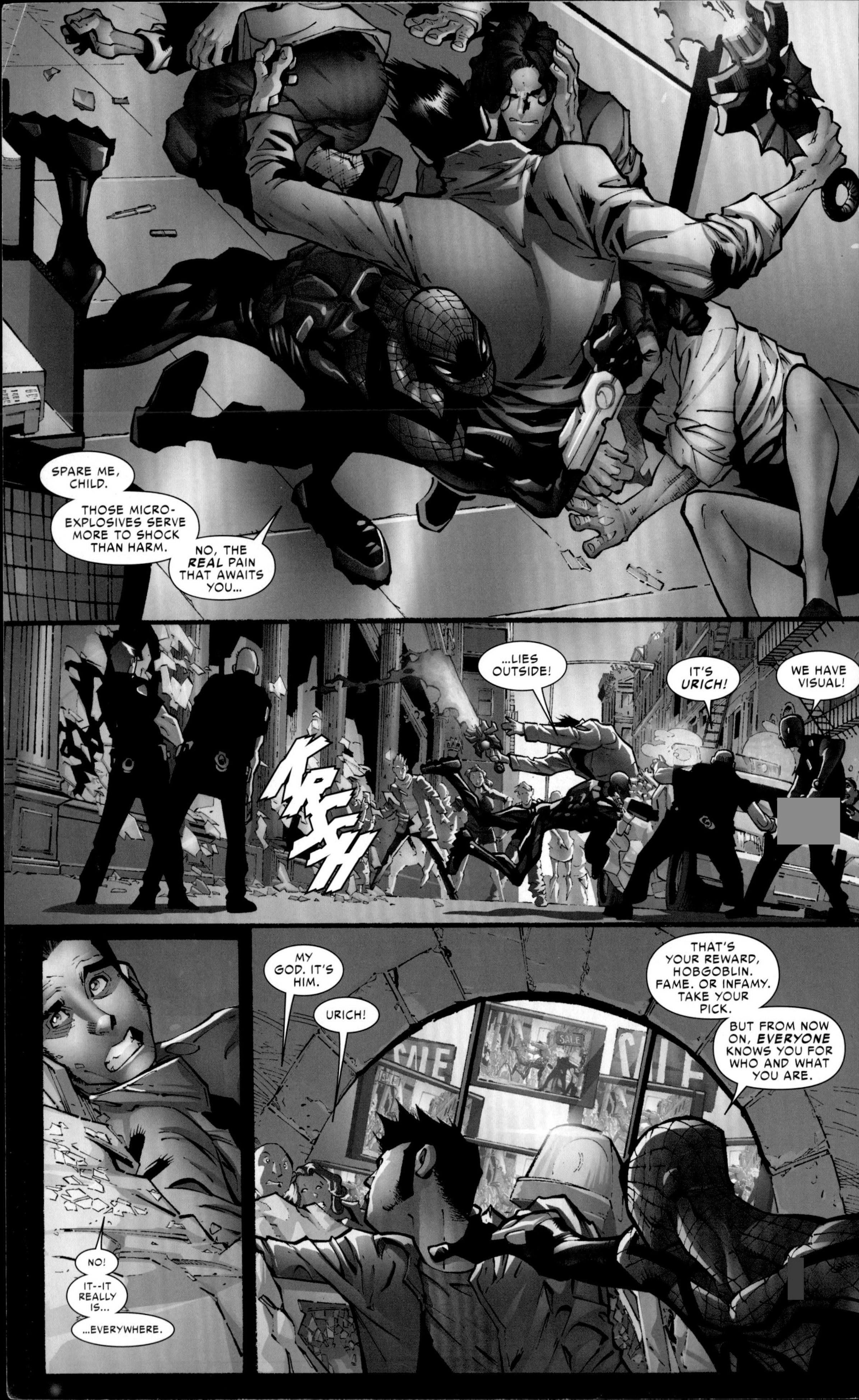
SPARE ME, CHILD.
THOSE MICRO-EXPLOSIVES SERVE MORE TO SHOCK THAN HARM.
NO, THE *REAL* PAIN THAT AWAITS YOU...
...LIES OUTSIDE!
IT'S *URICH!*
WE HAVE VISUAL!
KRSH
MY GOD. IT'S HIM.
URICH!
THAT'S YOUR REWARD, HOBGOBLIN. FAME. OR INFAMY. TAKE YOUR PICK.
BUT FROM NOW ON, *EVERYONE* KNOWS YOU FOR WHO AND WHAT YOU ARE.
NO!
IT--IT REALLY IS...
...EVERYWHERE.

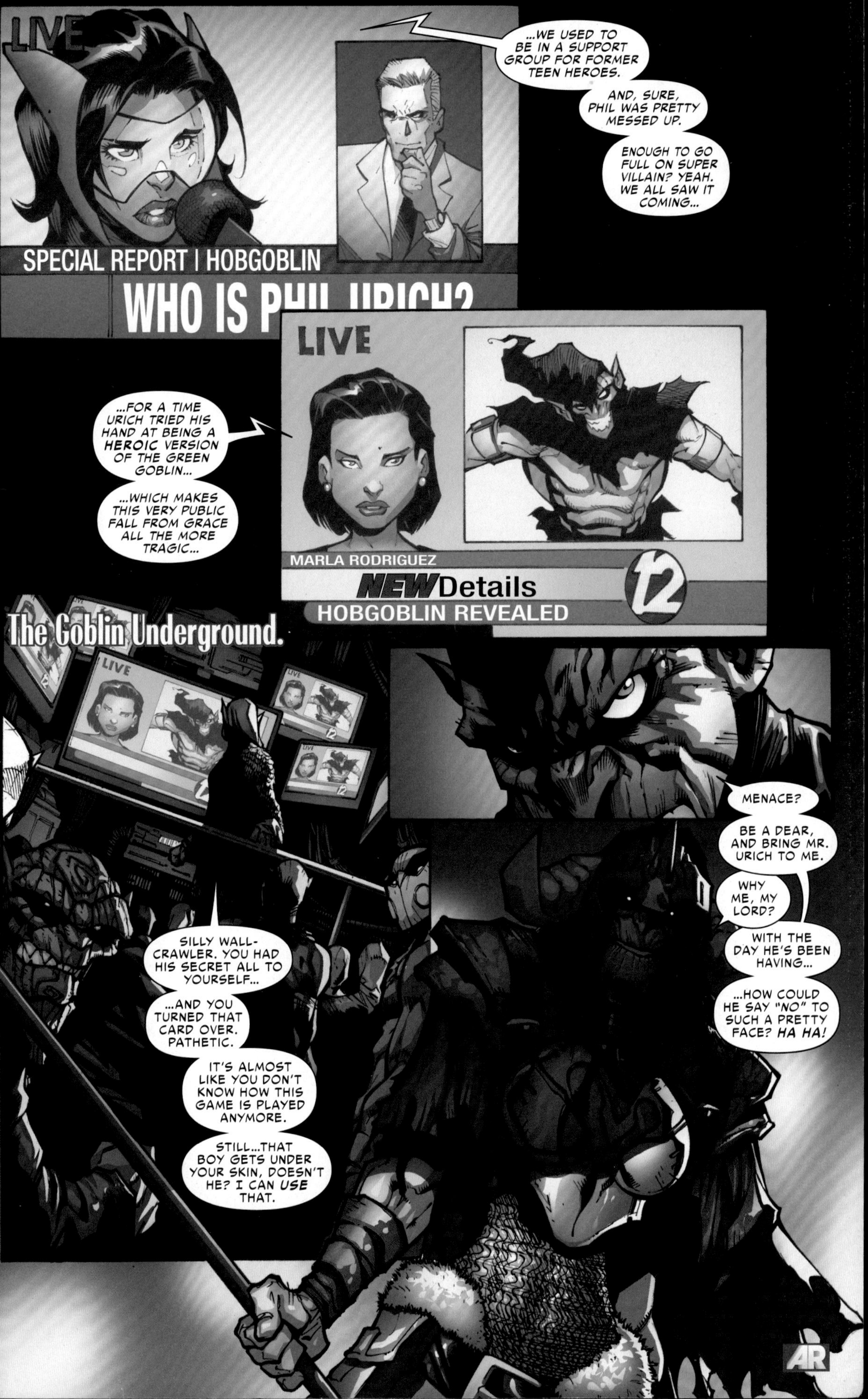
LIVE
...WE USED TO BE IN A SUPPORT GROUP FOR FORMER TEEN HEROES.
AND, SURE, PHIL WAS PRETTY MESSED UP.
ENOUGH TO GO FULL ON SUPER VILLAIN? YEAH. WE ALL SAW IT COMING...
SPECIAL REPORT | HOBGOBLIN
WHO IS PHIL URICH?
LIVE
...FOR A TIME URICH TRIED HIS HAND AT BEING A HEROIC VERSION OF THE GREEN GOBLIN...
...WHICH MAKES THIS VERY PUBLIC FALL FROM GRACE ALL THE MORE TRAGIC...
MARLA RODRIGUEZ
NEW Details
HOBGOBLIN REVEALED
12
The Goblin Underground.
MENACE?
BE A DEAR, AND BRING MR. URICH TO ME.
WHY ME, MY LORD?
WITH THE DAY HE'S BEEN HAVING...
...HOW COULD HE SAY "NO" TO SUCH A PRETTY FACE? HA HA!
SILLY WALL-CRAWLER. YOU HAD HIS SECRET ALL TO YOURSELF...
...AND YOU TURNED THAT CARD OVER. PATHETIC.
IT'S ALMOST LIKE YOU DON'T KNOW HOW THIS GAME IS PLAYED ANYMORE.
STILL...THAT BOY GETS UNDER YOUR SKIN, DOESN'T HE? I CAN USE THAT.
AR

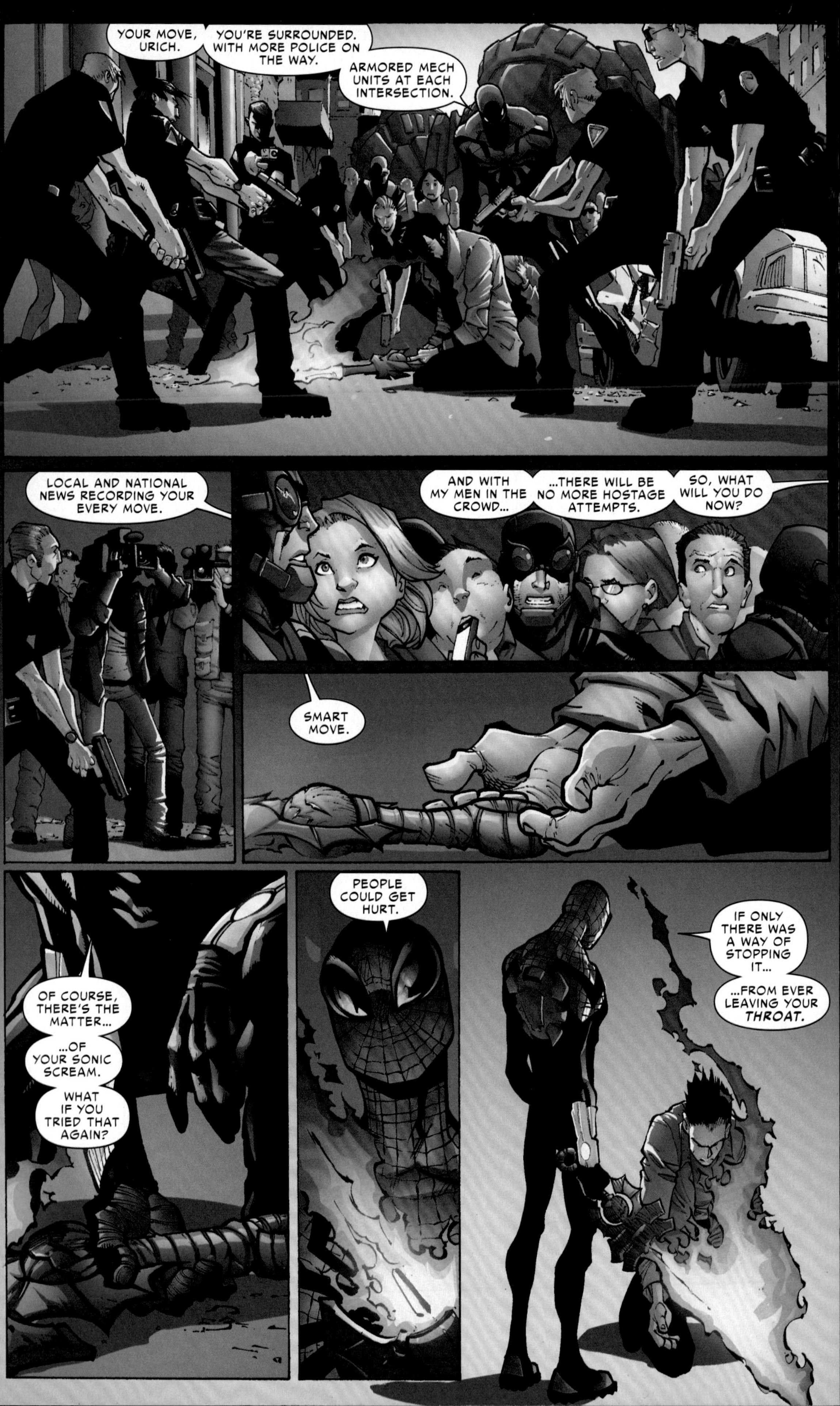
YOUR MOVE, URICH.
YOU'RE SURROUNDED. WITH MORE POLICE ON THE WAY.
ARMORED MECH UNITS AT EACH INTERSECTION.
LOCAL AND NATIONAL NEWS RECORDING YOUR EVERY MOVE.
AND WITH MY MEN IN THE CROWD...
...THERE WILL BE NO MORE HOSTAGE ATTEMPTS.
SO, WHAT WILL YOU DO NOW?
SMART MOVE.
OF COURSE, THERE'S THE MATTER...
...OF YOUR SONIC SCREAM.
WHAT IF YOU TRIED THAT AGAIN?
PEOPLE COULD GET HURT.
IF ONLY THERE WAS A WAY OF STOPPING IT...
...FROM EVER LEAVING YOUR THROAT.

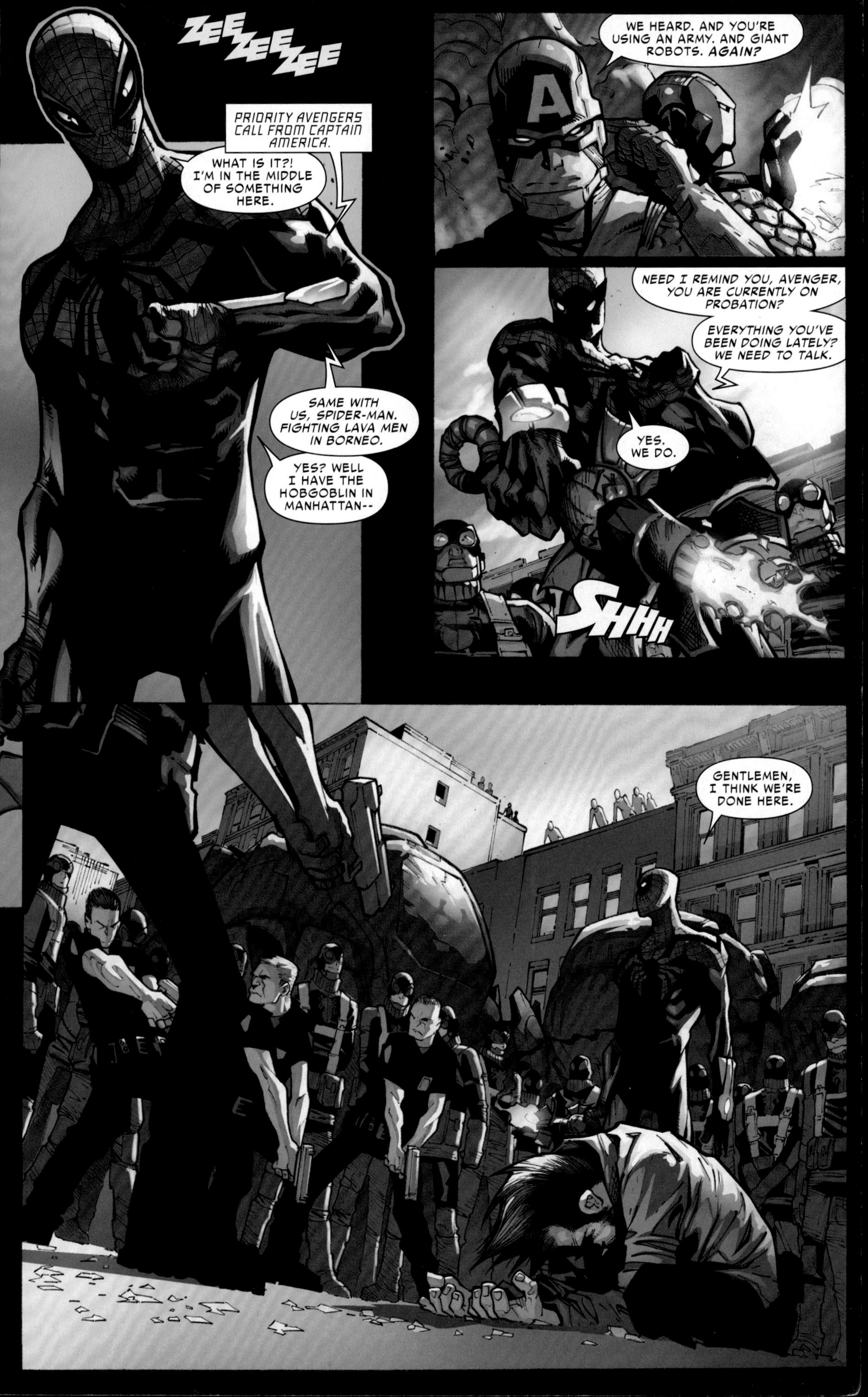
ZEE ZEE ZEE
PRIORITY AVENGERS CALL FROM CAPTAIN AMERICA.
WHAT IS IT?! I'M IN THE MIDDLE OF SOMETHING HERE.
SAME WITH US, SPIDER-MAN. FIGHTING LAVA MEN IN BORNEO.
YES? WELL I HAVE THE HOBGOBLIN IN MANHATTAN--
WE HEARD. AND YOU'RE USING AN ARMY. AND GIANT ROBOTS. AGAIN?
NEED I REMIND YOU, AVENGER, YOU ARE CURRENTLY ON PROBATION?
EVERYTHING YOU'VE BEEN DOING LATELY? WE NEED TO TALK.
YES. WE DO.
SHHH
GENTLEMEN, I THINK WE'RE DONE HERE.

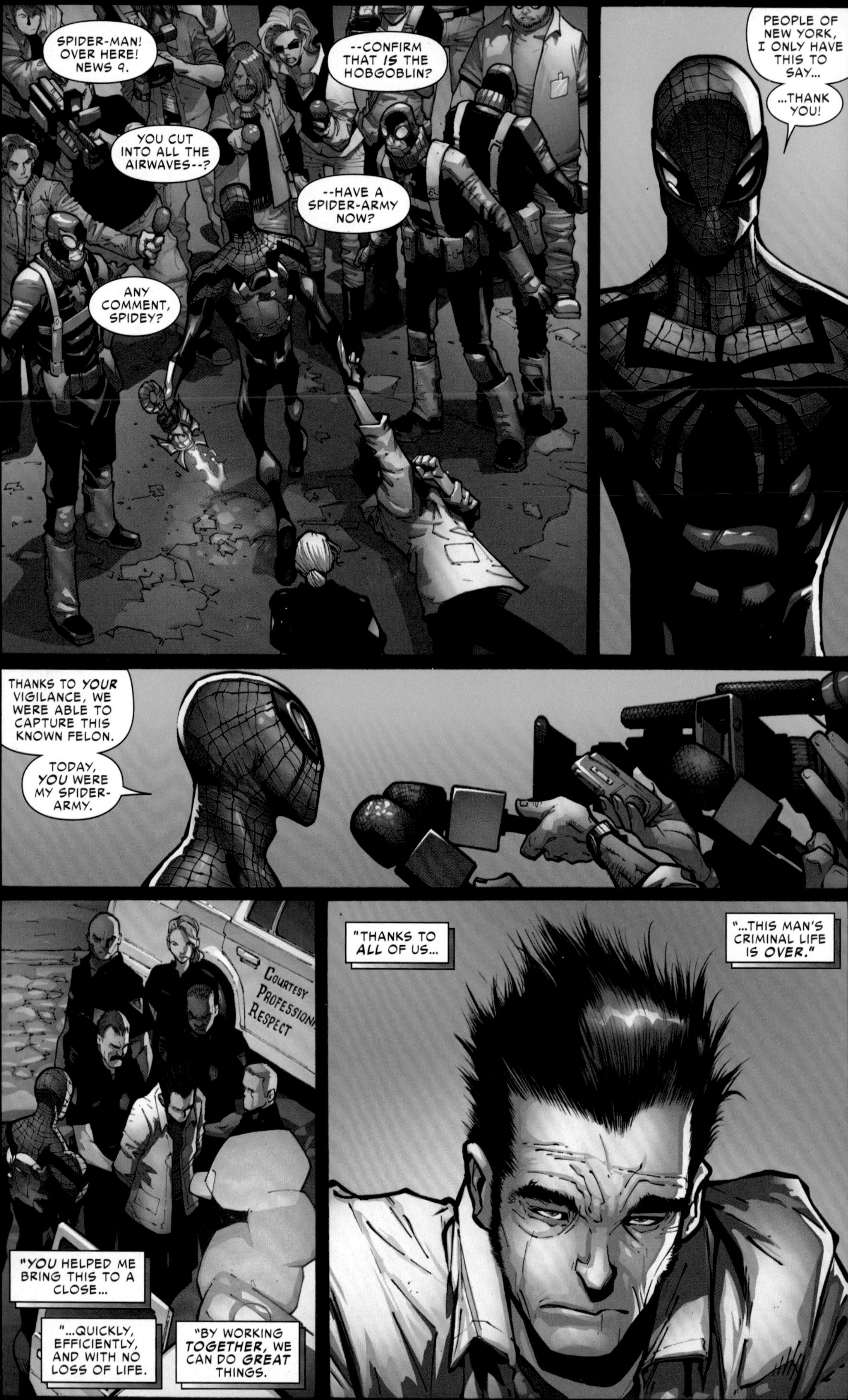
SPIDER-MAN! OVER HERE! NEWS 9.
--CONFIRM THAT IS THE HOBGOBLIN?
YOU CUT INTO ALL THE AIRWAVES--?
--HAVE A SPIDER-ARMY NOW?
ANY COMMENT, SPIDEY?
PEOPLE OF NEW YORK, I ONLY HAVE THIS TO SAY...
...THANK YOU!
THANKS TO YOUR VIGILANCE, WE WERE ABLE TO CAPTURE THIS KNOWN FELON.
TODAY, YOU WERE MY SPIDER-ARMY.
COURTESY PROFESSION RESPECT
"YOU HELPED ME BRING THIS TO A CLOSE...
"...QUICKLY, EFFICIENTLY, AND WITH NO LOSS OF LIFE.
"BY WORKING TOGETHER, WE CAN DO GREAT THINGS.
"THANKS TO ALL OF US...
"...THIS MAN'S CRIMINAL LIFE IS OVER."

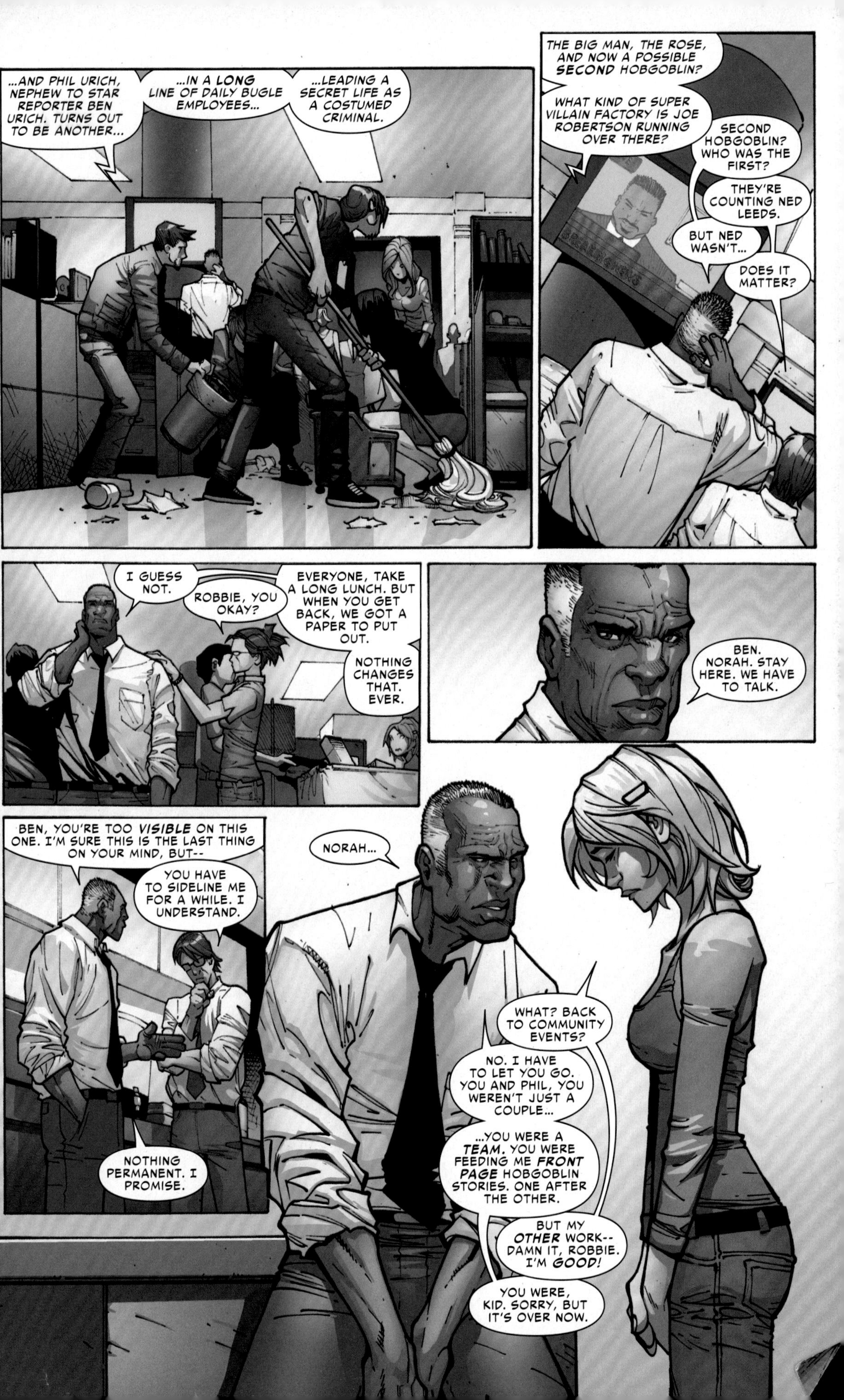

...AND PHIL URICH, NEPHEW TO STAR REPORTER BEN URICH. TURNS OUT TO BE ANOTHER...
...IN A LONG LINE OF DAILY BUGLE EMPLOYEES...
...LEADING A SECRET LIFE AS A COSTUMED CRIMINAL.
THE BIG MAN, THE ROSE, AND NOW A POSSIBLE SECOND HOBGOBLIN?
WHAT KIND OF SUPER VILLAIN FACTORY IS JOE ROBERTSON RUNNING OVER THERE?
SECOND HOBGOBLIN? WHO WAS THE FIRST?
THEY'RE COUNTING NED LEEDS.
BUT NED WASN'T...
DOES IT MATTER?
I GUESS NOT.
ROBBIE, YOU OKAY?
EVERYONE, TAKE A LONG LUNCH. BUT WHEN YOU GET BACK, WE GOT A PAPER TO PUT OUT.
NOTHING CHANGES THAT. EVER.
BEN. NORAH. STAY HERE. WE HAVE TO TALK.
BEN, YOU'RE TOO VISIBLE ON THIS ONE. I'M SURE THIS IS THE LAST THING ON YOUR MIND, BUT--
YOU HAVE TO SIDELINE ME FOR A WHILE. I UNDERSTAND.
NOTHING PERMANENT. I PROMISE.
NORAH...
WHAT? BACK TO COMMUNITY EVENTS?
NO. I HAVE TO LET YOU GO. YOU AND PHIL, YOU WEREN'T JUST A COUPLE...
...YOU WERE A TEAM. YOU WERE FEEDING ME FRONT PAGE HOBGOBLIN STORIES. ONE AFTER THE OTHER.
BUT MY OTHER WORK-- DAMN IT, ROBBIE. I'M GOOD!
YOU WERE, KID. SORRY, BUT IT'S OVER NOW.

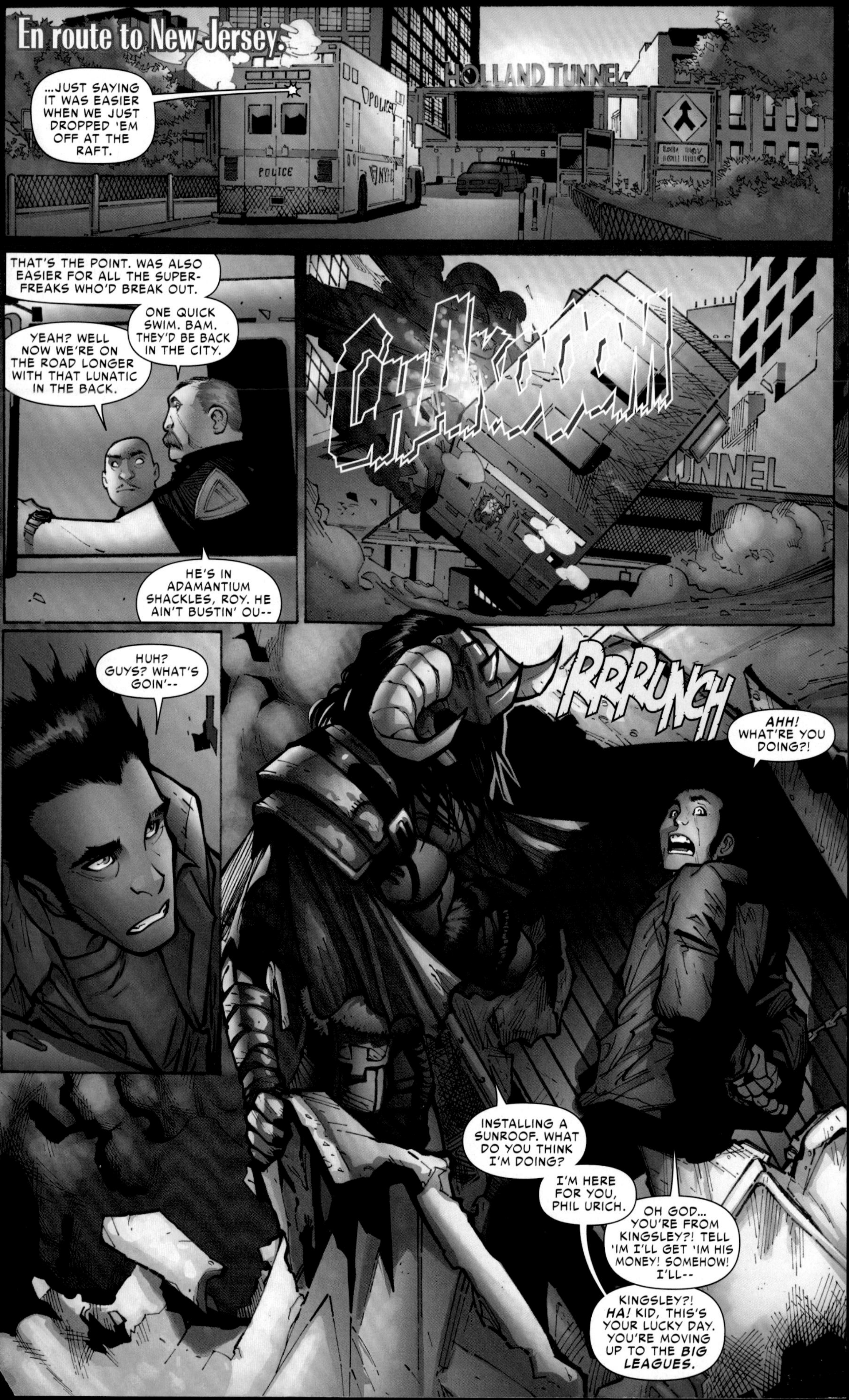

En route to New Jersey.
HOLLAND TUNNEL
POLICE
...JUST SAYING IT WAS EASIER WHEN WE JUST DROPPED 'EM OFF AT THE RAFT.
THAT'S THE POINT. WAS ALSO EASIER FOR ALL THE SUPER-FREAKS WHO'D BREAK OUT.
ONE QUICK SWIM. BAM. THEY'D BE BACK IN THE CITY.
YEAH? WELL NOW WE'RE ON THE ROAD LONGER WITH THAT LUNATIC IN THE BACK.
HE'S IN ADAMANTIUM SHACKLES, ROY. HE AIN'T BUSTIN' OU--
TUNNEL
HUH? GUYS? WHAT'S GOIN'--
RRRUNCH
AHH! WHAT'RE YOU DOING?!
INSTALLING A SUNROOF. WHAT DO YOU THINK I'M DOING?
I'M HERE FOR YOU, PHIL URICH.
OH GOD... YOU'RE FROM KINGSLEY?! TELL 'IM I'LL GET 'IM HIS MONEY! SOMEHOW! I'LL--
KINGSLEY?! HA! KID, THIS'S YOUR LUCKY DAY. YOU'RE MOVING UP TO THE BIG LEAGUES.

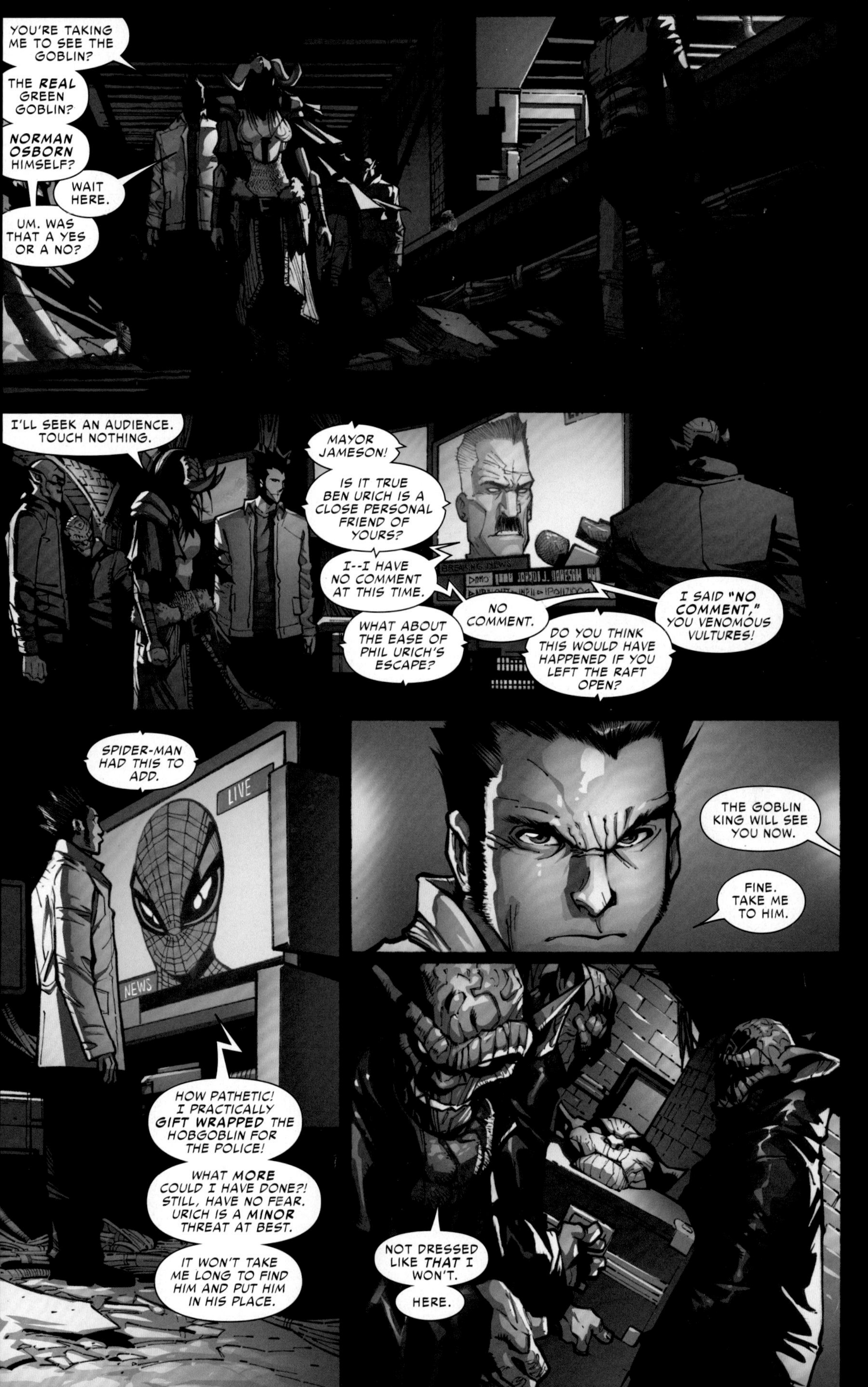

YOU'RE TAKING ME TO SEE THE GOBLIN?
THE REAL GREEN GOBLIN?
NORMAN OSBORN HIMSELF?
WAIT HERE.
UM. WAS THAT A YES OR A NO?
I'LL SEEK AN AUDIENCE. TOUCH NOTHING.
MAYOR JAMESON!
IS IT TRUE BEN URICH IS A CLOSE PERSONAL FRIEND OF YOURS?
I--I HAVE NO COMMENT AT THIS TIME.
WHAT ABOUT THE EASE OF PHIL URICH'S ESCAPE?
NO COMMENT.
DO YOU THINK THIS WOULD HAVE HAPPENED IF YOU LEFT THE RAFT OPEN?
I SAID "NO COMMENT," YOU VENOMOUS VULTURES!
SPIDER-MAN HAD THIS TO ADD.
LIVE
NEWS
HOW PATHETIC! I PRACTICALLY GIFT WRAPPED THE HOBGOBLIN FOR THE POLICE!
WHAT MORE COULD I HAVE DONE?! STILL, HAVE NO FEAR. URICH IS A MINOR THREAT AT BEST.
IT WON'T TAKE ME LONG TO FIND HIM AND PUT HIM IN HIS PLACE.
THE GOBLIN KING WILL SEE YOU NOW.
FINE. TAKE ME TO HIM.
NOT DRESSED LIKE THAT I WON'T.
HERE.

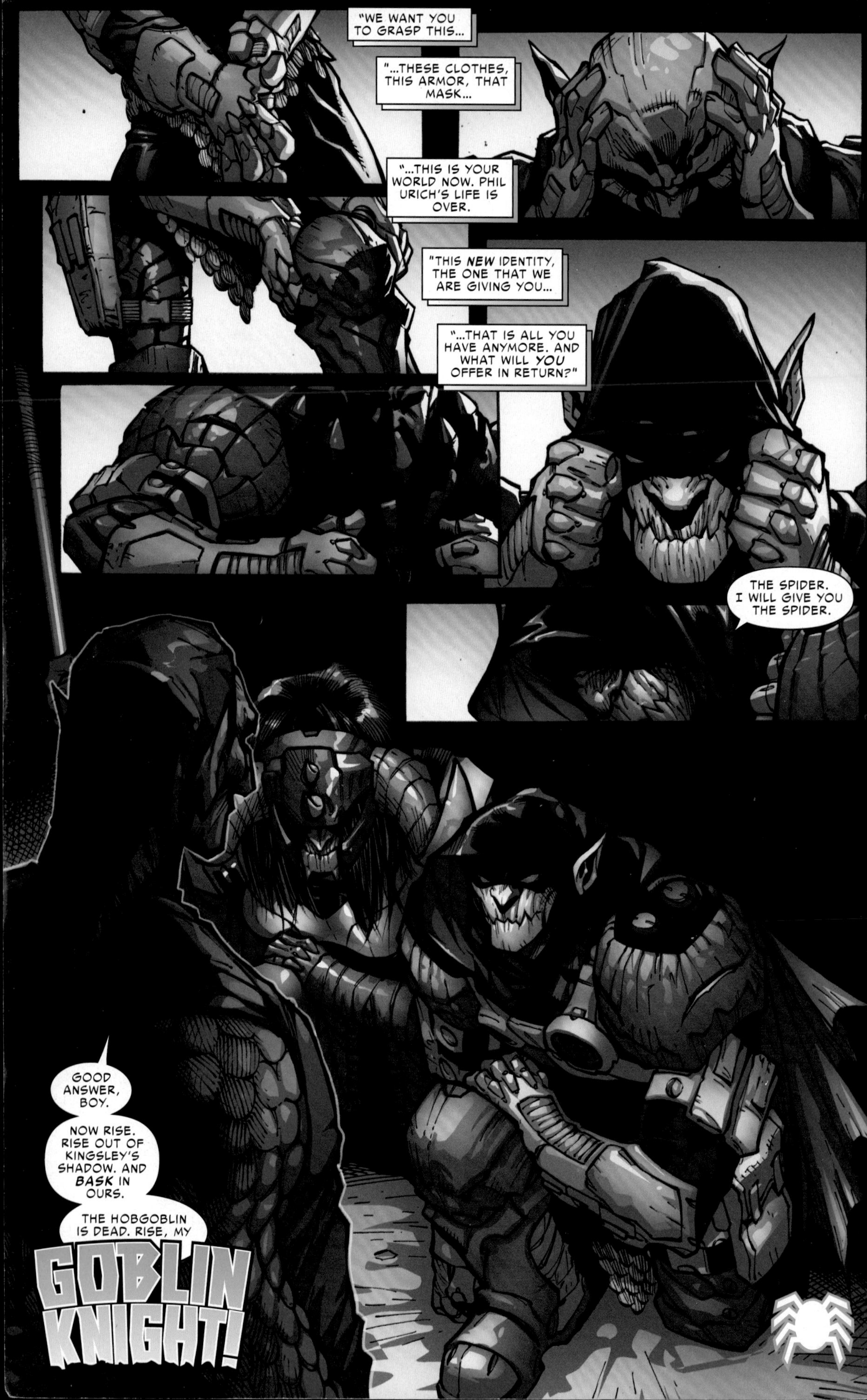
"WE WANT YOU TO GRASP THIS...
"...THESE CLOTHES, THIS ARMOR, THAT MASK...
"...THIS IS YOUR WORLD NOW. PHIL URICH'S LIFE IS OVER.
"THIS *NEW* IDENTITY, THE ONE THAT WE ARE GIVING YOU...
"...THAT IS ALL YOU HAVE ANYMORE. AND WHAT WILL *YOU* OFFER IN RETURN?"
THE SPIDER. I WILL GIVE YOU THE SPIDER.
GOOD ANSWER, BOY.
NOW RISE. RISE OUT OF KINGSLEY'S SHADOW. AND *BASK* IN OURS.
THE HOBGOBLIN IS DEAD. RISE, MY
GOBLIN KNIGHT!

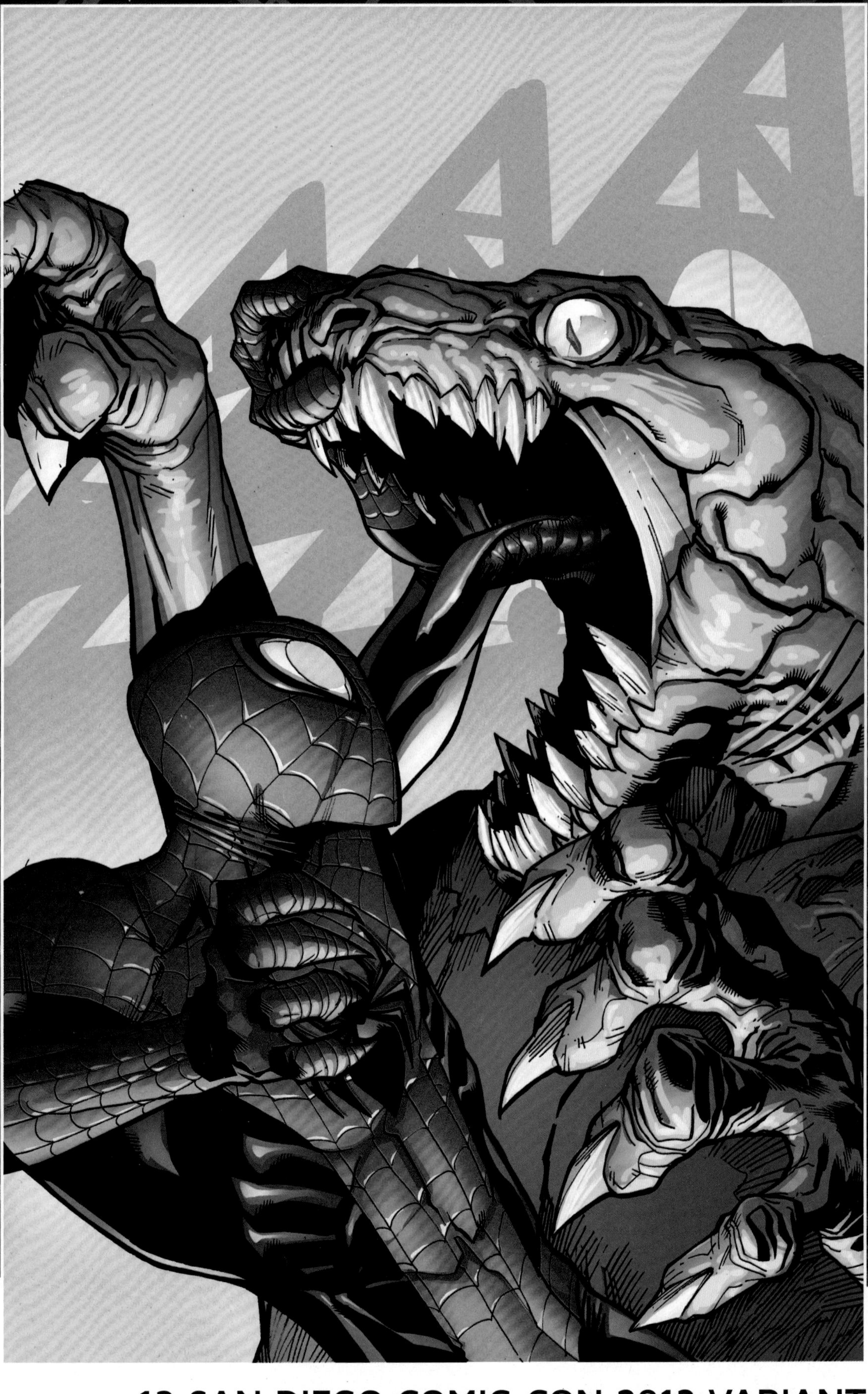

#13 SAN DIEGO COMIC-CON 2013 VARIANT
BY HUMBERTO RAMOS & EDGAR DELGADO

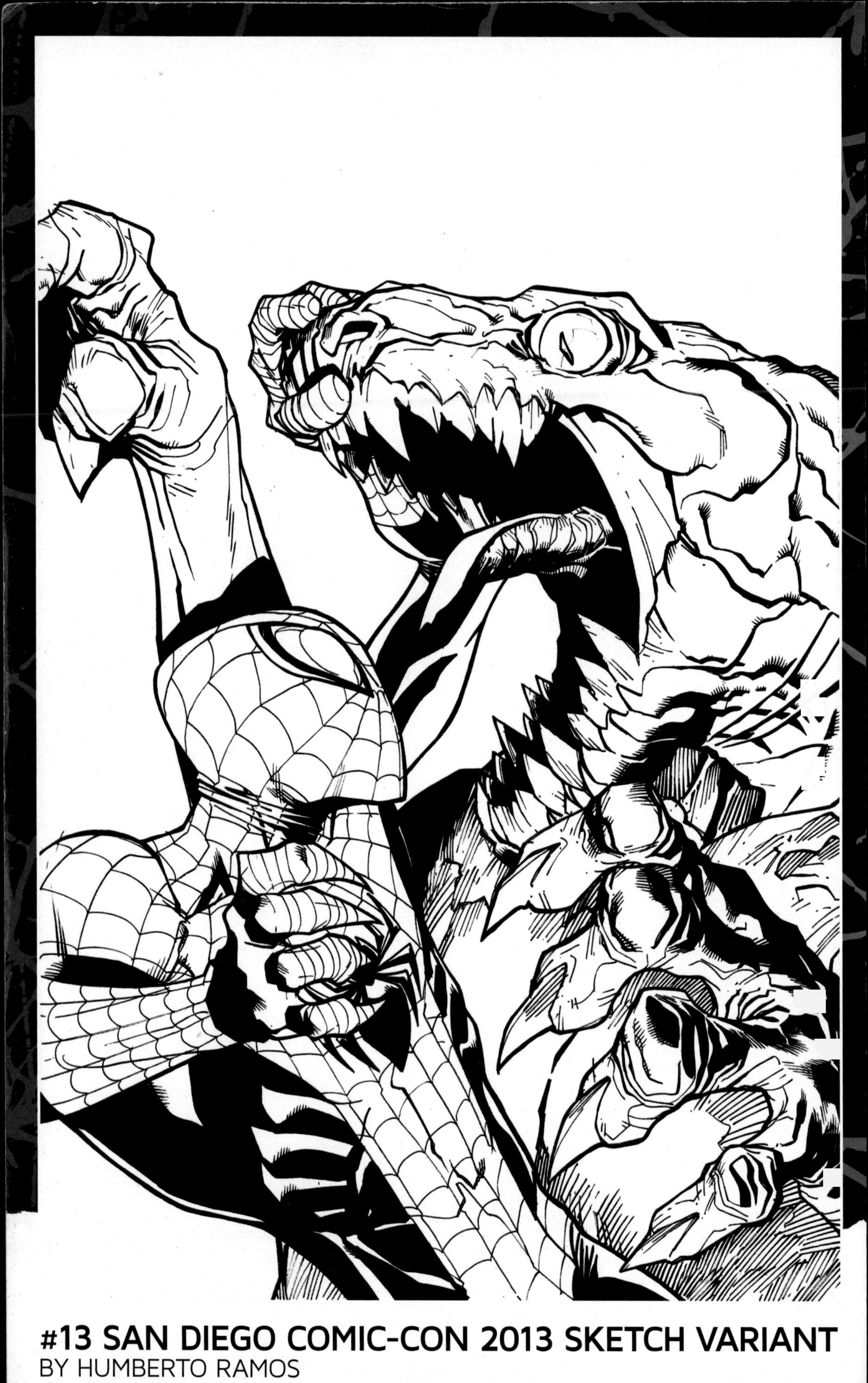

#13 SAN DIEGO COMIC-CON 2013 SKETCH VARIANT
BY HUMBERTO RAMOS

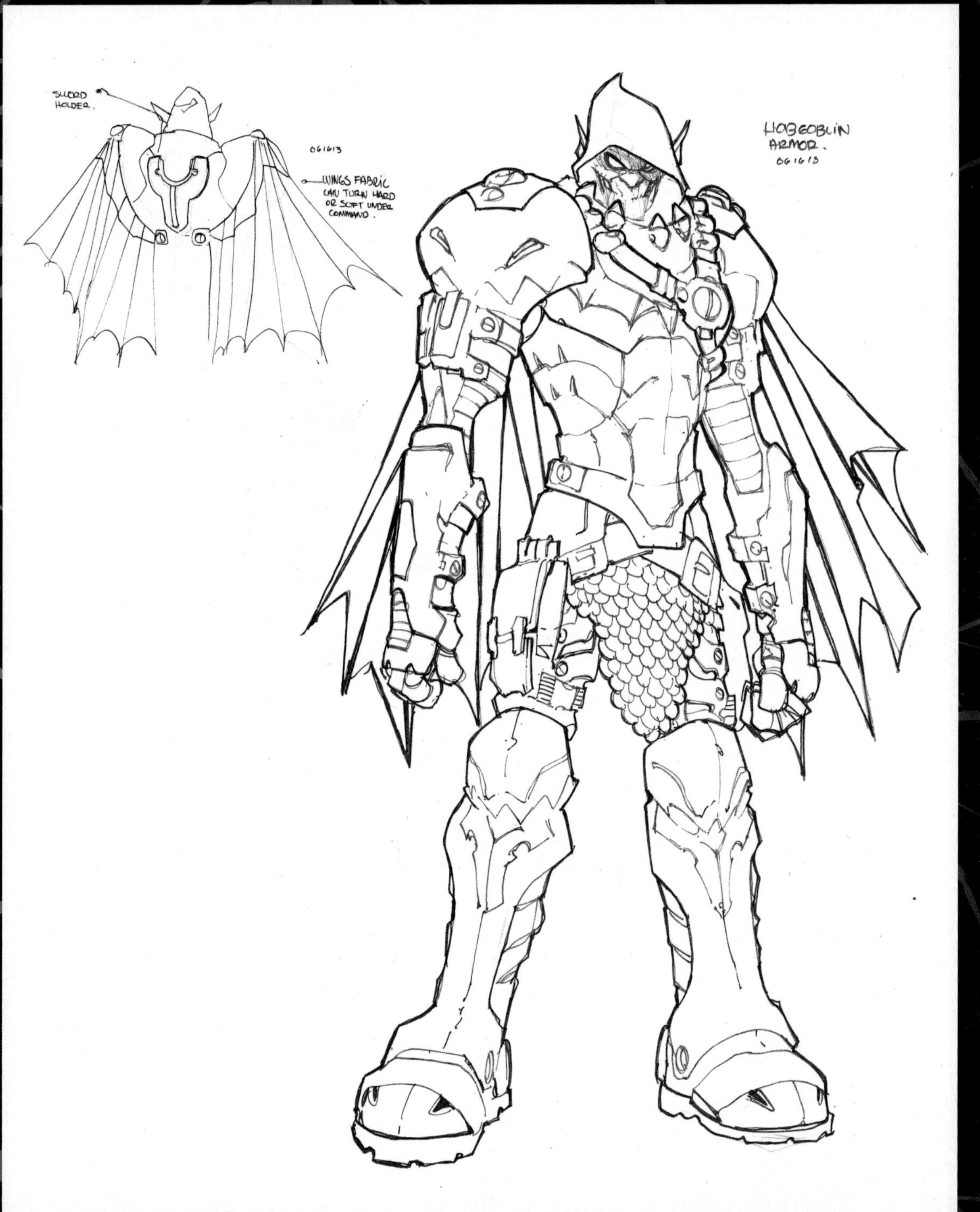
SWORD HOLDER.
061613
WINGS FABRIC CAN TURN HARD OR SOFT UNDER COMMAND.
HOBGOBLIN ARMOR.
061613

HOBGOBLIN ARMOR DESIGN
BY HUMBERTO RAMOS

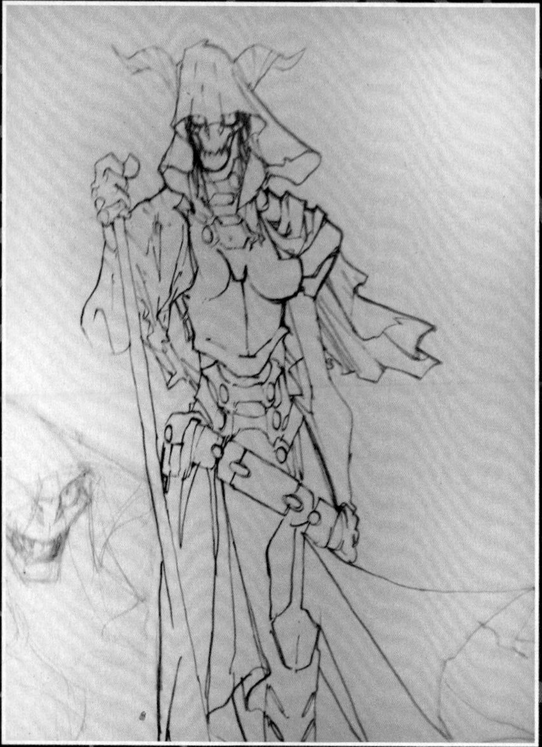
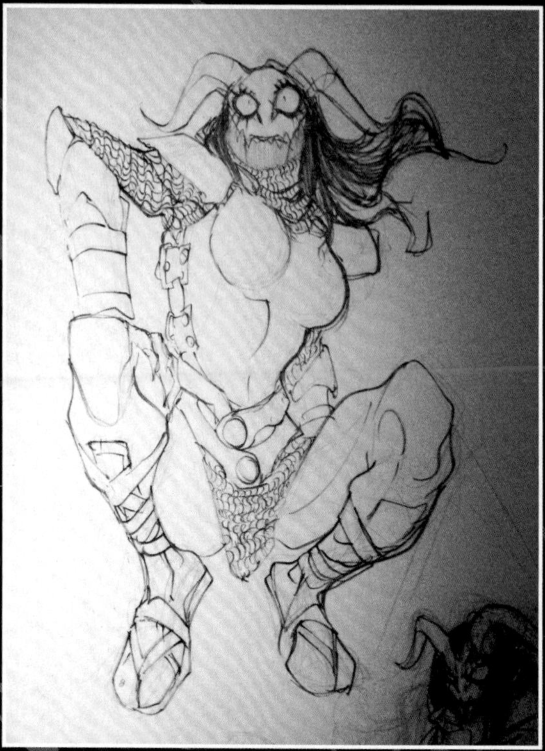
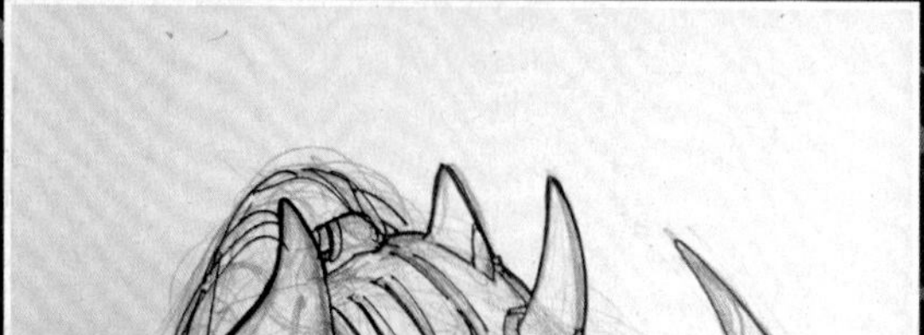
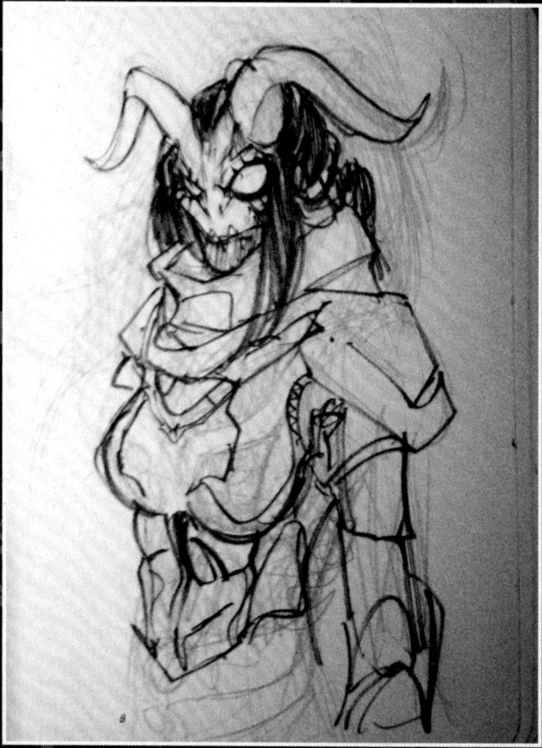

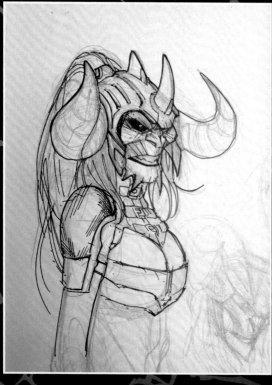

MENACE DESIGNS
BY HUMBERTO RAMOS

"A FRESH START!" – *The Comics Beat*

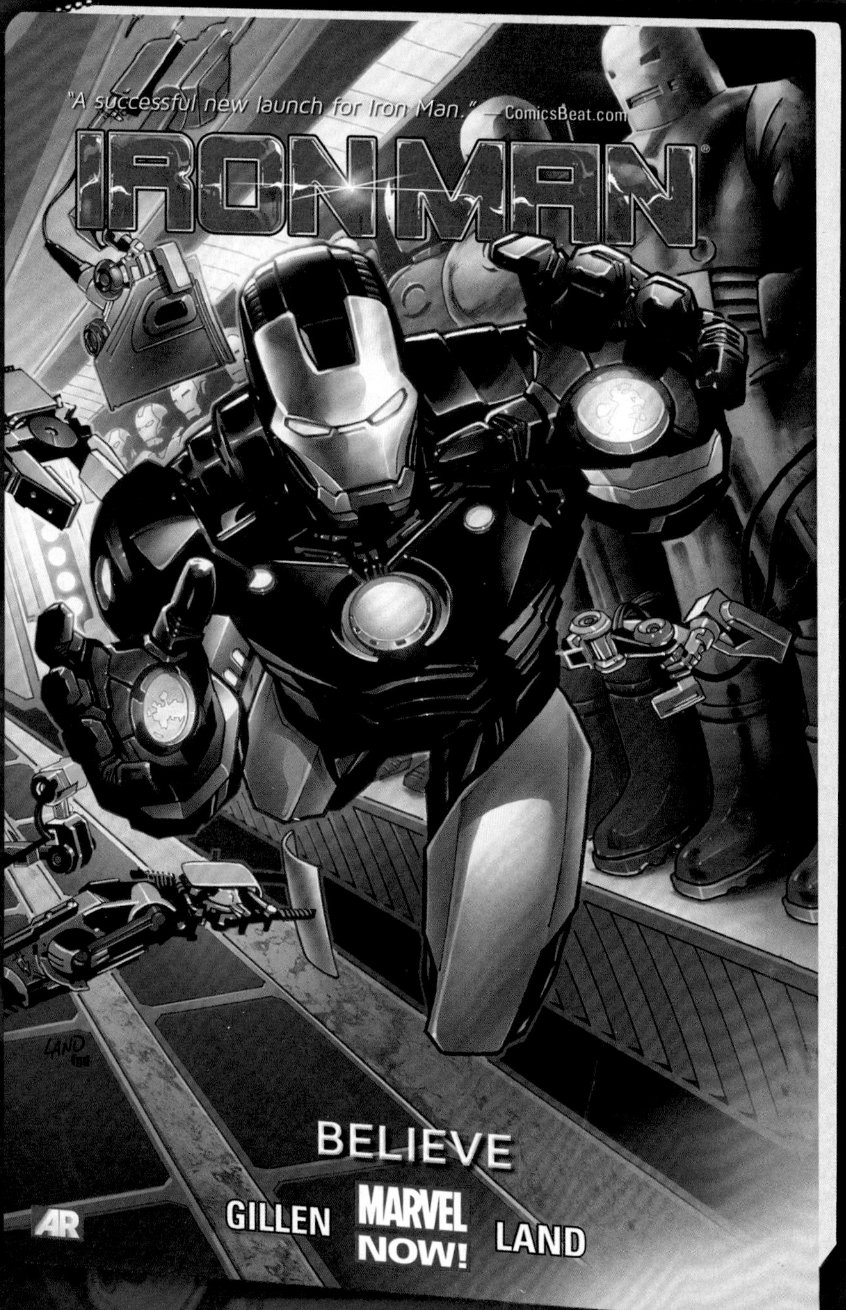
"A successful new launch for Iron Man." —ComicsBeat.com
IRON MAN
BELIEVE
GILLEN
MARVEL NOW!
LAND

IRON MAN VOL. 1: BELIEVE

978-0-7851-6844-7 • NOV130718

"A SUCCESSFUL NEW LAUNCH FOR IRON MAN."
– *The Comics Beat*

MARVEL NOW!

MARVEL AR AUGMENTED REALITY

MARVEL AUGMENTED REALITY (AR) ENHANCES AND CHANGES THE WAY YOU EXPERIENCE COMICS!

TO ACCESS THE FREE MARVEL AR CONTENT IN THIS BOOK*:

1. Locate the AR logo within the comic.
2. Go to Marvel.com/AR in your web browser.
3. Search by series title to find the corresponding AR.
4. Enjoy Marvel AR!

*All AR content that appears in this book has been archived and will be available only at Marvel.com/AR – no longer in the Marvel AR App. Content subject to change and availability.

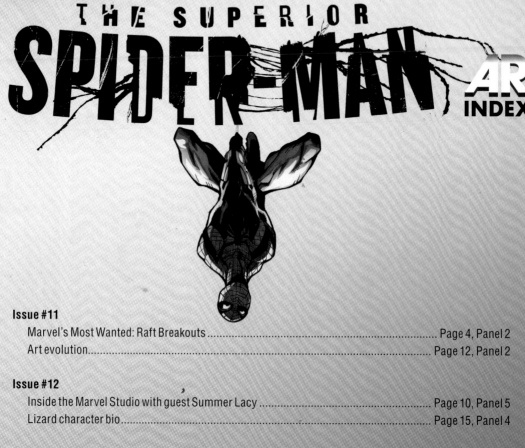

THE SUPERIOR SPIDER-MAN

AR INDEX